The Arab-Israeli
Confrontation
of June 1967

The Arab-Israeli Confrontation of June 1967:

An Arab Perspective

EDITED BY IBRAHIM ABU-LUGHOD

WITH A FOREWORD BY MALCOLM H. KERR

NORTHWESTERN UNIVERSITY PRESS

EVANSTON

1970

Ibrahim Abu-Lughod is Professor of Political Science
and Associate Director of the Program of African
Studies at Northwestern University. He is the
author of *Arab Rediscovery of Europe* and co-author
of *Patterns of African Development*.

Contents

Foreword

We hear much today about the pitfalls of being culture-bound. Our perceptions of the world are distorted not only by the incompleteness of our information but also by the way in which our established habits of thought and taste and our inherited forms of moral preference tend to mold our consciousness of events into familiar patterns. The truly cultivated man is marked by empathy—by his recognition that the thought and understanding of men of other cultures may differ sharply from his own, that what seems natural to him may appear grotesque to others, and that each pattern without the complement of the others is parochial.

American perceptions of the Arab-Israeli conflict present a prime example of such parochialism. Our understanding of what the conflict is about tends to be cut according to a comfortably familiar pattern of attitudes and sympathies ingrained in the American experience. This pattern sustains almost complete identification with the people of Israel and reduces the Arabs to little more than caricatures. Israel is seen as a "Western" state populated by technologically minded, energetic, democratic, pioneering frontiersmen who are transforming a wilderness and providing a home for the persecuted; the Arabs are seen as exasperatingly inscrutable, unreliable, inept, backward, authoritarian, and emotional. Israel is our staunch friend; the Arabs throw stones at American embassies.

More particularly, the Israelis are Jews. This single fact is probably enough to be decisive by itself for it invests sympathy with Israel with all the sanctity of rejection of mass extermination and disavowal of country-club bigotry. American liberals, it seems, cannot find fault with a collective Jewish cause because of the implication of anti-Semitism. In consequence, in the Middle East conflict the critical faculties of otherwise sensitive Americans have been anesthetized. Support for Israel is an automatic liberal cause, and Israeli actions that would draw strong condemnation if undertaken by another country are defended by liberals with the same arguments that apologists for colonialism and racial inequality have invoked elsewhere.

The nine essays in this volume, written by Arab scholars living in the United States and Britain, provide a badly needed antidote to the one-sided and selective attention given in this country to the Middle East conflict. The imbalance must surely be rectified if Americans are to form independent judgments. This volume alone is hardly enough for that purpose, but it is a step in the right direction.

Many readers will be surprised to learn to what extent these intelligent, moderate, well-informed Arabs reject basic propositions that have become axiomatic among Americans. Various of these authors maintain, for example, that Israel's policy has been to avoid rather than promote a peaceful settlement; that the Arab states' intervention in Palestine was legally and morally justified; that the religious attachment of Jews to the Wailing Wall is of recent, politically inspired origin; that Israel planned to wage the 1967 war weeks before President Nasser sought the evacuation of United Nations forces from Sinai; and that the purpose of Nasser's diplomacy in the May crisis was not to move toward war but toward a full peace settlement with Israel.

While some will no doubt dismiss such arguments as absurd propaganda, more thoughtful readers will want to follow the authors' train of evidence and logic closely enough to consider whether their conclusions are plausible. They will find that the evidence available on these and other aspects of the Palestine conflict can reasonably be interpreted in ways very different from those familiar to them. Whether or not they are persuaded by all that they read, they will find the arguments intelligent, careful, sober, and responsible, in the tradition of serious scholarship. This is a great deal more than can be said of much of the literature circulating in America about the Middle East. We must ask ourselves whether those of us who have a perspective of Middle Eastern events different from that of these authors suffer any less than they from cultural bias. If not, then perhaps the views we have so easily adopted ought to be re-examined.

Professor of Political Science　　　　　　　　MALCOLM H. KERR
University of California at Los Angeles

Preface

Although more than two years have elapsed since the Arabs and Israelis faced each other on the battlefield in June, 1967, not a single scholarly, objective, and detached investigation of the factors that have led to that confrontation has appeared in the English language. Arabs, Israelis, and noninvolved third parties have contributed differentially to an understanding of some of these factors through innumerable publications, but as the reader will observe from the bibliography appended to this volume—which lists those sources that specifically deal with the 1967 June War—the preponderant majority of the works published in English, or for that matter in any European language, have come from Israeli or Israeli-inspired sources. This is of course neither accidental nor unexpected. The Jewish involvement in the Israeli experiment has placed highly trained manpower at the service of various Israeli objectives, not the least of which is the dissemination of information calculated to enhance Israel's international interests and gain sympathy and support. Israel has considerable support among other groups as well, which in turn have contributed to the dissemination of information equally favorable to Israel and Israel's perspective.

In part as the result of such publications but perhaps more importantly as the result of the sustained efforts of the mass media, the cultured layman and the concerned citizen alike may have arrived at a certain set of conclusions with reference to the causes of the eruption of conflict in June which reflect a particular view of its historical perspective and its ultimate objectives. These conclusions have, in the opinion of some, an apparent validity, yet most scholars recognize that the bases of international conflict are neither simple nor as clear as protagonists in the conflict wish people to believe. This simplification of issues has applied not only to the eruption of hostilities in June, 1967, but to the totality of the Palestine conflict which constitutes the essence of the continuing tension between Arabs and Zionists.

The series of essays contained in this volume has one major objective: to present an alternative perspective which should be considered in any full assessment of the origins or subsequent development of the June, 1967, conflict. The essays are not intended to provide a comprehensive review or discussion of the totality of the Palestine conflict and its international ramifications, but they do answer specific questions that are of direct relevance to the eruption and immediate aftermath of war in the Middle East in June, 1967, and they provide an interpretation of events surrounding that conflict which must be taken into account by scholars and students of international relations.

There is no doubt but that the true and full origins of that war will ultimately become common knowledge. Scholars cannot help but increasingly direct their intellectual efforts to a conflict which has already demonstrated its potential for the disturbance of world peace. They may assess the origins and immediate causes differently from those individuals who are sympathetic to Israel or to the Palestinians or to the Arabs. Whatever their assessment may turn out to be, scholars would of necessity have to examine all available data in order to insure that the assessment is based upon unimpeachable and verifiable evidence. The intended users of this volume are those scholars and students who may wish to ascertain the causes and origins of the Arab-Israeli confrontation of June, 1967.

Several characteristics of the contributors to the volume and of their essays may be of interest to the reader. First, with one exception, all are Americans of Arab ancestry or origin. Second, each of the contributors is a scholar whose previous intellectual contributions, again with one exception, have revolved around questions and issues unrelated to the Palestine conflict. Finally, the authors—applying the same rules of evidence employed in all scientific endeavors—come to conclusions that contrast with those hitherto accepted in current Western literature.

"The Arab Portrayed," the essay which introduces this volume, powerfully and poetically probes the cultural values that surround and underlie an appreciation of the immediate issues and consequences of the Arab-Israeli confrontation of June, 1967. Its author, Dr. Edward

Preface

Said, an American humanist of Palestinian ancestry, is Associate Professor of English and Comparative Literature at Columbia University. His essay highlights the cultural distortions which lie at the base of much of the existing literature on the subject.

The annexation of the city of Jerusalem and the persistent attempt by the Israeli government to disfigure its cultural uniqueness may turn out to be the single most significant and potentially explosive consequence of the June, 1967, confrontation. Knowingly or otherwise, the Israelis may have generated forces for further conflict between themselves and other communities which transcend the territorial confines of the immediate region. Jerusalem's place in the hearts and minds of Christians is well known; its place in the hearts and minds of Muslims is known only to the Believers and to a handful of scholars who have grasped the Islamic significance of that place. Professor A. L. Tibawi of the Institute of Education at the University of London is one of the most distinguished scholars of the Palestinian community. As an officer of education throughout the period of the mandate in Palestine, he was concerned with the educational advancement of the Palestinian community. Subsequent to the uprooting of the Palestinian community, Professor Tibawi has had a distinguished and fruitful career as a scholar, author, and lecturer, primarily at the University of London and occasionally at Harvard University. His many contributions include *Arab Education in Mandatory Palestine; British Interests in Palestine, 1800–1901; American Interests in Syria, 1800–1901;* and *A History of Syria.* Professor Tibawi's essay "Jerusalem: Its Place in Islam and Arab History" is his most recent contribution to a more profound knowledge of the history of the region.

With some minor exceptions—such as the sober essay "The Arab-Israeli War: How It Began," in *Foreign Affairs* (January, 1968) written by Charles Yost on the sequence of events that led to the outbreak of the June hostilities—most published material has verged on the "potboiler" variety. No amount of generous examination of the literature would lead any but the most committed investigator to an enlightened understanding of the fundamental and immediate issues that contributed to the outbreak of war. Two essays in this volume offer an alternative approach to the study of some of the issues which should be considered in assessing the forces that were no longer controllable on June 5, 1967. Dr. Hisham Sharabi, Professor of Government at Georgetown University, is a scholar of Palestinian origin whose previous contributions to the study of Arab culture and politics include *Government and Politics of the Middle East in the Twentieth Century* and *Nationalism and Revolution in the Arab World*. In his interpretative and analytical essay "Prelude to War: The Crisis of May–June, 1967," Professor Sharabi details the steps that made war inevitable. This is followed by an essay on "Israel's Arab Policy" by the editor of this volume. Ibrahim Abu-Lughod is of Palestinian origin and is Professor of Political Science at Northwestern University.

On a formalistic level, the conflict of June, 1967, was related to disputed legal rights and obligations on the part of states presumably adhering to the rule of law. Many sources suggest that the conflict was in part precipitated by the declaration closing the Gulf of Aqaba to Israeli shipping. Freedom of navigation and the unilateral diversion of the waters of the Jordan River by Israel are fundamentally legal questions and are susceptible to legal solutions. As more than one observer has noted, despite the United Arab Republic's acceptance of the compulsory jurisdiction of the International Court of Justice, not a single attempt was made to deal with the basic as well as the derivative legal issues through any established legal machinery. Dr. Cherif Bassiouni, of Egyptian origin, is Associate Professor of Law at De Paul University's College of Law. His contributions are well known to legal scholars. In "Some Legal Aspects of the Arab-Israeli Conflict" Professor Bassiouni examines the legal questions that may have been used by the protagonists as pretexts for renewal of conflict in June, 1967.

The June War was brought to a temporary halt in part as a result of intervention by the United Nations. United Nations intervention meant, in addition, that an attempt would be made to utilize the existing machinery of the organization to resolve the basic conflict to the satisfaction of both protagonists. While such a resolution is as remote today as it ever was, the discussions and debates in the Security Council and General Assembly subsequent to the cease-fire order revealed important configurations and conceptions of the role of the United Nations. Dr. Samir Anabtawi, of Palestinian origin, has long been a student of the United Nations; his contributions have appeared in many scholarly journals, including *International Organization*. He is Associate Professor of Political Science at Vanderbilt University. In his essay "The United Nations and the Middle East Conflict of June, 1967," he highlights significant aspects of the debates and steps undertaken by the United Nations in its effort to resolve the conflict.

Israel's military ascendancy was more than matched by a skilled capacity to disguise that ascendancy in a world-wide campaign for sympathy and support. Nowhere was the success of that strategy more evident than in the overwhelming support Israel received from the mass media, especially in the United States and Western Europe. Dr. Michael Suleiman, also of Palestinian origin, whose contributions include *Political Parties in Lebanon* and numerous essays on the communication gap between the Arabs and the West, is Associate Professor of Political Science at Kansas State University. His essay "Mass Media and the June Conflict" examines the various ways in which the protagonists were portrayed. His essay presents additional empirical support for the thesis presented earlier by Dr. Said.

Undoubtedly the policy commitments of the United States government affect the portrayal of the protagonists in a conflict situation. Had United States policy been more understanding, perhaps a truly judicious examination of the issues would have been possible in May and June of 1967. Dr. Kamel Abu-Jaber, of Jordanian origin, is Associate Professor of Government at Smith College; his previous contributions include *The Arab Ba'th Socialist Party*. His essay "American Policy toward the June Conflict" confines itself to the examination of the official manifestations and implementations of that policy.

The thrust of these essays indicates quite clearly that Israel's case was accorded a measure of sympathy and support in Western mass media as well as on a more formal and official level. At this point in time, no one can be certain of the degree to which the American public felt involved with the protagonists and the issues. Two things are unmistakable however: on the one hand, there was considerable public support for Israel; on the other hand, certain segments of the American community managed to make their voices of dissent heard throughout the United States and the world. These groups denounced in strong terms the racist policies of Israel and its aggressive designs in the Middle East. Since the eruption of the conflict, the Black community and the New Left have taken a position diametrically opposed to that of the government and the mass media. Mr. Abdeen Jabara, an American attorney-at-law of Lebanese ancestry, has been a student of the Palestine conflict and is the author of *The Armistice in International Law*. More recently he has been concerned with the growth and development of radical political movements in the United States. His essay "The American Left and the June Conflict" analyzes the underlying basis of support for the Arab community by significant elements within the broad spectrum of American politics.

The authors whose essays are included in this volume have felt a special responsibility to their readers which has impelled them to devote their scientific energies to the investigation of the particular topic to which they were assigned. Each is responsible for all statements of fact and interpretation in his essay. Yet it is obvious that there is a collective thrust to the essays as a whole. All authors are critical of existing "knowledge" on the subject, and each has endeavored to provide within his area of investigation an important corrective to that "knowledge." We do not in any way claim that we have succeeded in presenting the whole truth, but we hope that our careful and disciplined presentations will merit consideration by scholars regardless of their previous orientation.

The editor wishes to acknowledge his debt to a number of individuals who have rendered assistance at various stages in the preparation of this volume of essays. Mr. Tahseen Basheer has been consistently generous with his advice, and Mrs. Runda Fattal, Miss Patricia Revey, and Mr. M. al-Okdah were helpful at the stage when these essays were originally prepared for the *Arab World*. Mrs. Ann Paden's editorial skills also contributed considerably to what merits this volume possesses. Finally, I am particularly grateful to Professor Malcolm Kerr for his comments introducing this volume to the reader.

IBRAHIM ABU-LUGHOD

The Arab Portrayed

H ere are two examples of how the Arab is often represented or, more correctly, misrepresented. What is disheartening in both representations is how readily he seems to accommodate the transformations and reductions into which he is continually being forced by vulgar pressures.

The costume for Princeton's tenth-reunion class in 1967 had been planned before the June War. The motif was to have been Arab—robe, headgear, and sandals. Immediately after the war, and before the reunion, when it became clear that the motif was an embarrassment a change in the program was legislated: wearing the Arab costume as originally planned, the class were to walk in procession with their hands above their heads in a gesture of abject defeat. Surprisingly, there was no serious complaint made about the really vile taste at work as there might have been if any other national or racial group had been similarly insulted. The logic, not so much of events in the war but of events in the American consciousness of the Arab, permitted this tasteless demotion of a people into a stupid and offensive caricature.

The second example is to be found in the average film in which an Arab appears. He comes on as an over-sexed degenerate capable—it is true—of cleverly devious intrigues, but essentially sadistic, treacherous, and low. For example, the Arab leader is often seen snarling at the captured American hero and a blonde girl, "My men are going to kill you, but—they like to amuse themselves beforehand." He leers suggestively as he speaks.

The American imagination has always turned westward. The romantic impulse has been generously capable of attention lavished upon

1

the Pacific, as in Melville's novels and tales of the Pacific. And this has been the direction toward which the frontier has moved—even if, as in the case of Vietnam, the adventure was incorrigibly misguided, or, as in the case of the Indian wars, cruelly dedicated. I have in mind the American capacity—an imaginative one—for taking in the exotic and the strange, since interest in the European, as we find it embodied in Henry James' international theme, is rather more a recovery of the subtly *different-but-similar* than of a genuinely *rival* culture. America has not, as have England and France, had a T. E. Lawrence, a Doughty, a Blunt, a Jacques Berque, a Maspero—shapers of a sympathetic eastward movement of the imagination. The vision of such men has complicated and enriched, I believe, their national modes of perceiving the Arab, and it has enlivened all dealings with the Arab on the part of England and of France. That this has been the case in countries whose historic interest in the East has also been patently colonial is far less ironic than the almost unthinkable contradiction between the Princeton reunion costume and march and the existence at Princeton of one of America's oldest and most distinguished departments of Near Eastern studies. In the case of the British and the French colonialist, dealings with the Arab were balanced, if not finally moderated or redeemed, by enthusiasts like Doughty and Blunt, who deeply acknowledged the presence of the Arab in the European consciousness. What is strikingly apparent here is how little human space is occupied by the Arab in the American mind.

During and after the June War few things could have been more depressing than the way in which the Arabs were portrayed. Press pictures of the Arabs were almost always of large numbers of people, mobs of hysterical, anonymous men, whereas photographs of the Israelis were almost always of stalwart individuals, the light of simple heroism shining from their eyes. Before the war Renata Adler wrote a "Letter from Israel," published after the war in *The New Yorker,* in which heroism, sentimentality, earthy practicality, and life near the apocalypse were celebrated in about equal parts. This piece, together with advertisements solemnly exhorting America to rally to Israel in her hour of need, were published at a time when it ought to have been clear, if only because the war had been handily won, that Israel was beyond danger. Still, these and other offenses to reality were very much the order of the day. The symbolism repeated the simple pattern of a Cooper novel—was not the June War the conflict between the white

European bravely facing the amoral wilderness in the person of savage natives bent on destruction? As an intelligible unit in the mind, the Arab has been reduced to pure antagonism to Israel. The sheer mass of his numbers—against which, it seems, any injustice counts for very little—has been abstracted into unitary order, the better to deal with the uncomfortable moral demands his history and actuality might make. Indeed, one can speculate on the connection between, on the one hand, a kind of cybernetic process that converts the gigantic tragedy of the Final Solution into voluble but proxy support for Israel, which works as a symbol of compensation for the tragedy, and, on the other hand, the process that essentializes the Arab presence on all sides of Israel into pure opposition to rightful compensation for a people that suffered outrageously in World War II. Two tragedies thus lose their density: one becomes a sop for the bewildered conscience of guilty Western supporters of Israel, the other disappears in exertions on behalf of the former. The history of the Jews and Arabs in its full detail is thus telescoped into a convenient formula of opposition which, with its every use in descriptions of the Near Eastern situation, reinforces the poverty of the formula as well as its hold on the mind.

All sorts of contradictions stem from this formula. For instance, although Israel illegally occupies a vast amount of territory, Arabs who resist the occupation are "terrorists" rather than "resistance fighters" or even "guerrillas." In the demands for direct negotiations reported constantly in the American press, Israel seems justified in requiring of the Arabs a radical examination of their past and present, yet this would appear to place no moral burden on Israel to account for the fact that its existence is dependent upon the displacement of an entire people, the Palestinian Arabs. Thus any argument from the Arabs is suppressed and converted into what is now a mindless cliché of the sullen Arab who will not "face reality." Liberal sentiment, always quick to champion liberation causes, will continue to bypass the Arabs so long as there remains a conflict between Arab and Israeli claims for attention. Interestingly enough, the Arabs can become acceptable as objects of admiration in the context of Third World struggles against colonialism, but only if Israel is not involved. This was clearly the case with Pontecorvo's film *The Battle of Algiers*. To most Arabs the Algerian struggle against French paratroopers and *colons* depicted in the film is easily translatable into the Arab-Israeli conflict—the analogies are too obvious to miss. But in the United States these implica-

3

tions are ignored, and what is appreciated is an easy revolt of natives against foreign domination. Similarly, while it is expected that liberal sentiment will interest itself seriously in the plight of North Vietnam—as, for instance, in Mary McCarthy's first-rate set of articles for the *New York Review of Books*—it has occurred to no one to dramatize, or even to report, the dilemmas, problems, and agonies of the thousands of Arabs now subject to Israeli rule. The *Times Literary Supplement* of September 26, 1968, put the problem admirably:

> Part of the Arab case against the West is that they cannot get through. The communications are blocked, or so it seems to them. They see themselves in the same situation as any other non-European people subjected to European colonization and the force of European arms, but their situation is not recognized. The liberal and left-wing sympathies which are so freely engaged for Africans and Vietnamese today as once upon a time they were for the Irish or the various Balkan nationalities have never been available for the Palestine Arabs. Their Zionist opponents seem to control all the lines to liberal world opinion. . . . There will have to be some penetration of world opinion by the Arab, that is the Palestine Arab, point of view.

In the mind's syntax, then, the Arab, if thought of singly, is a creature without dimension. His history is obscure, for it is written neither in terms of institutions the American can recognize nor in a language he can read. Where his story has actually informed the history of the West, as in Spain for example, the Arab has been assimilated by the consciousness, in this case into a figure of the Spaniard. This cuts off the Arab at a point where European traits begin to weaken. (The work of Américo Castro is an exception to this attenuation.) What is most telling about Western consciousness of the Arab is how few ordinary categories of human existence seem applicable to him. Suffering and injustice, it seems, can never be his lot. I recall that during the summer of 1967 when I. F. Stone, a lone courageous voice, remarked on the irony of fate that made the Arabs suffer at the hands of a people which had itself suffered egregiously, there came a barrage of complaints (in *Commentary* especially) registering outrage at the "obscenity" of speaking of Arab suffering in the same breath as that of the Jews. In the Near East, then, suffering has been monopolized, for it is a European import. Furthermore, suffering does not grow locally except, as in June, 1967, in its hybrid variety. Arab lives and property taken, lost, or destroyed, Arab villages bull-dozed out of existence, Arab resistance of any sort mercilessly liqui-dated—all these do not count for very much, even though they have gone, and are still going, into the making of Israel. When, in the introduction to his remarkable June, 1967, issue of *Les Temps Mod-ernes* on the Arab-Israeli conflict, Jean-Paul Sartre noted that two bodies of live history sat next to each other in the Near East, each inert to the other except as a pure antagonist, he was formulating a complex truth of a sort unacceptable to the American consciousness of the problem.

If the Arab occupies space in the mind at all, it is of negative value. He is seen as the disrupter of Israel's continuing existence, or, in a larger view, a surmountable obstacle to Israel's creation in 1948. This has been, of course, part of the Zionist attitude toward the Arab, especially in the years before 1948 when Israel was being promulgated ideologically. Palestine was imagined as an empty desert waiting to burst into bloom, its inhabitants imagined as inconsequential nomads possessing no stable claim to the land and therefore no cultural permanence. At worst, the Arab is conceived as a shadow that dogs the Jew. In that shadow (because Arab and Jew are Semites) can be placed whatever traditional latent mistrust Americans might feel to-ward the Jew. The Jew of pre-Nazi Europe has split in two: what we now have is a Jewish hero, constructed out of a revived cult of the adventurer-pioneer, and his creeping, mysteriously fearsome shadow, the Arab. Thus isolated from his past, the Arab is chained to a destiny that fixes and dooms him to a series of spastic reactions, which are periodically chastised by what Barbara Tuchman imperiously calls "Israel's terrible swift sword."

At the very least, then, the Arab must be admitted to one's consciousness as a human quality with which one must come to terms. I do not want to be hortatory about this, but I do want to connect this need with what is going to have to take place in the West generally and in the American political imagination in particular. The change is already taking place among the youth, which has forced itself, impelled by the pressures of actuality, to venture into political complexities hitherto ignored or unnoticed by previous generations. The McCarthy campaign in 1968 had the effect of stimulating just that sort of ex-posure and excursion, though it was only a first step.

A superb way of watching an individual mind allowing itself full exposure to a political situation is to read I. F. Stone over the years. His efforts at rich vision culminate in his essay in the *New York Review of Books* of August 3, 1967, an essay which originated as a review of the June, 1967, *Les Temps Modernes*. Stone's personal background includes notable reporting of voyages made by Jewish refugees from Europe to Palestine before 1948, and though his commitments as a Jew are never compromised, his integrity has always enabled him to *see* the Arabs. Hence one has his view in August, 1967, of the Arab-Israeli conflict as a tragedy, and, more important, his assessment of Nasser in the July, 1967, *Ramparts* as a truly estimable, as opposed to a simply hateful, leader of the Arabs.

Stone, in short, is the only major political commentator in America to have grasped and sustained in his work most of the intricacies of the Arab-Israeli imbroglio. These intricacies are not so much a matter of recording every pull and push in the struggle—this is the pretense of Theodore Draper's *Israel and World Politics,* which is premised on the legitimacy of Israel's domination and mastery of the Near East—but more a record of the enduring presence of the Arab in the Near East. It is precisely this latter sort of reckoning that characterizes, for instance, a set of three articles entitled "Israel and the Palestinians" by Jacques Lefort, which appeared in *Le Monde* in August, 1967, or the reports from occupied Gaza by Michael Adams, which were published throughout the last half of 1967 in the *Manchester Guardian Weekly,* or Isaac Deutscher's view of the conflagration in the July-August, 1967, *New Left Review*. Lefort's particular accuracy derives from two fundamental truths: first, that there is such a thing as an authentic Palestinian Arab culture now, as before, in danger of total extermination by Israel, and second, that—and I quote from Lefort—"in practice, one finds in Israel, however, the banal attitudes that exist in colonial societies, going from latent racism to a paternalism with regard to 'the good Arab,' which is supported by a knowledge of 'the Arab psychology.' " What is extremely important here is how the official Israeli view of the Arab as a kind of troublesome non-person feeds the common and accepted view of the Arab that is currently held in America. It would not be accurate to neglect, in this connection, the converse or the commonly held view of America by the Arabs. Thus one simplification and reduction generates a supporting set, and this

6

mutual reinforcement abets further misapprehension, disaster, and suffering.

The contrast between Lefort's work and, to take a recent example, Joel Carmichael's *The Shaping of the Arabs: A Study in Ethnic Identity* is striking indeed. For this book, admittedly a popular work that draws on secondhand sources, rides the demotic view of the Arab to a logical conclusion—one supported by events, at least as Carmichael sees them through an ungenerous squint. Because they are a dislodged, un-centered people *now,* the Arabs, according to Carmichael, have always been that. They have no identity as such, no ideology—"It is incon-testable that the Arab national movement has demonstrated a singular vacuum of ideas; the phrase 'Arab nationalist ideology' implies little beyond itself" (p. 386). And they have no life that any decent middle-class Westerner would deign to call life—ghetto life "is a natural condition, perhaps, of the Middle East as a whole" (p. 281).

Lefort's major effort, however, is to argue for the continued exis-tence of the Palestinian Arab: this is an identity with its own civiliza-tion, history, and social organization. Threatened as he is with total extinction, and by a kind of retrospective fiat denying his history, the Palestinian rarely features in recent American accounts of the Near East. Martha Gellhorn's articles on the Palestine refugees (first in the *Manchester Guardian,* then in the *Nation*) portrays them as a people incapable of telling the truth, nurtured on a kind of vacant hatred of Israel, and doomed to an aimless existence. These are refugees, she seems to be saying, and in some way they have deserved it because they think and talk and act like refugees; take away their hatred of Israel (which alone has made them refugees) and they will no longer be refugees. This is like the scientist in *Gulliver's Travels* who argues that since a sunbeam went into the making of a cucumber, it must be possible somehow to extract sunbeams out of cucumbers. Take away the refugee's hatred and ignorance—not, of course, the cause of his hatred, or whatever it was that made him a refugee—and he will be a refugee no longer, just a better-adjusted Arab.

Another type of polemic turns up in the July, 1967, *Ramparts* in an article by Michael Walzer and Martin Peretz, both of Harvard, entitled "Israel Is Not Vietnam." Once again there are instructive contrasts to be made, this time with Deutscher's interview in the *New Left Review* of July–August, 1967, and with Maxime Rodinson's "Israel, fait colonial?" in the June, 1967, *Les Temps Modernes.* What is clearly the

7

case with Israel—that it is based on Western ideology militantly claiming for itself the status of an exclusively indigenous (because of "timeless" attachments to Palestine) presence in the Near East—is obscured in a rush of furious casuistry. Peretz's and Walzer's main point is that, unlike America's presence in Vietnam, Israel's presence in the Arab world is neither colonial nor oppressive: it merely is, by force of historical legitimacy and necessary strength. Here too the polemic draws on exactly the values disclaimed by "liberals" (whether Jewish or not) in discussing Israel, but eminently suitable for the Arabs. And these values, however else they might be whitewashed, are racist values. The Arabs are depicted as backward, enmeshed in the fantasies of their language, entitled only to a condition of subservience, incapable of facing a reality (Israel) whose existence of twenty years has assumed the position of undisputed historical fact with timeless standing.

It is no accident, I think, that in America the representation of the Arab in accounts of the modern Near East relies so heavily on a simple, though to my mind seriously defective and malicious, conception of fact. One of Dwight McDonald's most trenchant essays in *Against the American Grain,* "The Triumph of the Fact," characterizes and attacks this peculiarly American tendency to dignify so-called facts with indisputable authority, a tendency that ignores the intersubjective origins of a fact. To call something a fact means one accords to it an ultimate sort of privilege, but at the same time the label regrettably conceals a fear of dealing with the ambiguous, the nuanced, the in-between, and the precarious. Israel is a fact and that, the argument runs, is what the Arabs cannot or will not face; and that also is a fact about the Arabs. Yet it is precisely the Arab sense of fact that is being denied in this argument, that sense which sees Israel, funded without limit from abroad, displacing a whole population into a limbo that now seems, factually, to be their fate without limit of time. All facts are equal, but facts about Israel are more equal than those either perceived by or about Arabs. And, in this, it is not only the popular press or television which are to be faulted, but also the academic or enlightened liberal view, not to mention the Israeli view of the Arabs as well. Compelled into the strait jacket of "regional studies" institutes that were designed to serve the Western, or at least the American, sense of *fact* about other parts of the world, the Arab becomes simply an observable collection of factual statistics based on rigidly frozen cate-

8

gories of population, climate, trade, and so on. To say, therefore, that the Arab is a victim of imperialism is to understand the statement as applying not only to the past, but also to the present, not only in war and diplomacy but also Western consciousness. There are signs, however, that with much of the Third World, the Arab has now fully recognized this as his predicament: he is demanding of the West, and of Israel, the right to reoccupy his place in history and in actuality.

Jerusalem:
Its Place in Islam
and Arab History

When in A.D. 638 the second caliph 'Umar Ibn al-Khaṭṭāb accepted in person the capitulation of Jerusalem, the city had been for centuries first Roman and then Byzantine in character. Exactly five centuries earlier, Hadrian had obliterated the last vestige of Jewish life in the city. It was in fact completely destroyed and the site ploughed up. In its place rose the Roman colony of Aelia Capitolina with an altar for Jupiter where the last Temple once stood. The Jews were forbidden, under pain of death, to enter it.[1]

Following the adoption by Constantine of Christianity as the state religion, and as a result of his and his mother's zeal, the city was covered with Christian monuments including the Church of Resurrection, better known as the Holy Sepulchre. It was by Helena's orders that Roman pagan monuments in Jerusalem were dismantled. But it was on scriptural authority that no new building on the site of the old Temple was allowed. According to Matt. 24:2, thus spoke Jesus to the disciples as He was leaving the Temple: "Verily I say unto you, There

---

1. This study is based on original sources and official documents. While it is written from an Arab and Muslim point of view, special care has been taken to ensure factual accuracy. Because I hope it would reach a wider circle than the few specialists, I have dispensed with footnotes as distracting attention. My sources, however, include the Bible; the Qur'ān; Ibn Hisham's *Biography of Muhammad;* Tabari's *Annals;* Ibn Khallikan's *Biographical Dictionary;* the several Muslim travelers and geographers quoted in the text; the several Jewish travelers quoted in the text; Mujir' -ud-Dīn al-'Ulaimi, *History of Jerusalem and Hebron;* Rustum, *Documents on the History of Syria during the Egyptian Occupation;* Le Strange, *Palestine under the Moslems;* diplomatic and consular papers of the British Foreign Office from 1839 to 1920; Shaw [British] *Commission Report,* 1930; Löfgren [International] *Commission Report,* 1931; *Encyclopaedia of Islam; Jewish Encyclopaedia;* and the *Times* (London).

shall not be left here one stone upon another, that shall not be thrown down." According to Luke 19:43–4, Jesus prophesied a similar fate for Jerusalem itself: "For the days shall come upon thee, that thine enemies . . . shall lay thee even with the ground, and thy children within thee; and they shall not leave in thee one stone upon another."

It is asserted, however, that Constantine relaxed the Hadrian ban on the Jews. Once a year, on the anniversary of the destruction of the last Temple, those who paid a fee were allowed in for lamentation, apparently on the Mount of Olives overlooking the site of the Temple. The number of Jews who survived successive disasters in Palestine was a few thousand, mostly in Galilee. They saw a flicker of hope in the Persian invasion. Not only did they welcome the invaders but helped them as scouts and volunteers. In A.D. 614 the Persians captured Jerusalem, massacred thousands of its Christian inhabitants, and plundered and destroyed its churches. Fourteen years later Heraclius drove the invaders out and recovered the land and the city. He wreaked a terrible vengeance on the Jews.

At that time Muḥammad was preaching the new monotheistic religion of Islam in Mecca as God's last prophet and messenger to mankind. He preached the divine message piecemeal, as and when it was revealed to him. It is remarkable that the Byzantine discomfiture in Palestine was specifically mentioned in the divine revelation with a forecast of the reversal of fortune (the Qur'ān 30:1):

> The Byzantines have been vanquished in the nearer part of the land; and, after their vanquishing, they shall be the victors in a few years.

More important is the allusion in chapter 2, verse 143, to Jerusalem, in the direction of which Muḥammad and the early Muslim community used to turn their faces in prayer. It was by divine command that the direction was changed to Mecca.

Still more specific and fundamental mention of Jerusalem in the Qur'ān occurs in the first verse of chapter 17, and is in connection with Muḥammad's miraculous nocturnal journey to Jerusalem and then his ascension therefrom to heaven:

> Glory be to Him, who carried His servant by night from the Holy Mosque to the Further Mosque [al-Masjid al-Aqṣā], the precincts of which We have blessed, that We might show him some of our signs.

11

The interpretation of this verse and the explanation of this miraculous experience are to be found in the standard commentaries on the Qur'ān, in the collection of prophetic traditions, and in the near contemporary biography of Muḥammad by Ibn Hishām. According to these sources the experience was either through the body or the spirit. Its main features are as follows: Escorted by the Angel Gabriel and mounted on a mysterious winged animal called Burāq, the Prophet was carried by night from Mecca to Jerusalem. On arrival at the "Further Mosque," the Burāq was tethered at a spot which inevitably acquired its name to this day, and is commemorated by a mosque. Then on the site of the old Temple close by, Muḥammad led former prophets in prayer. According to some commentators, verse 44 of chapter 43 of the Qur'ān was revealed in Jerusalem at this very moment: "Ask those of our Messengers We sent before thee—Have We appointed, apart from the All-merciful, gods to be served?"

Later on Muḥammad with his escort ascended, by means of a celestial ladder, to heaven. The ascent was from a rock over which now stands the Dome of the Rock. Muḥammad was led by stages to the seventh heaven, until finally he experienced the supreme delight of the Beatific Vision. The descent and return to Mecca were accomplished before dawn during the same night.

Those readers with spiritual insight and poetic imagination need no reminder that this is symbolism refined to the highest degree. Small wonder that some of the unlettered Arabs were incredulous when Muḥammad related his experience. More educated and perceptive generations later enriched the story with details of exquisite vertuosity and fine poetic imagery. (According to a Spanish priest, who was Professor of Arabic at Madrid University, the Islamic story with its vivid description of paradise and hell served Dante as prototype for his *Divina Commedia*.)

2.

Such was the established Christian character of Jerusalem, and such was the place it newly acquired in Islam when, after winning a decisive battle against the Byzantines, the Arabs appeared before its walls. After a prolonged siege Patriarch Sophronius offered to surrender the city but only to the caliph himself. 'Umar was then in Syria conferring with his military commanders at al-Jābiyah in Jaulān. But mindful

12

that Jerusalem deserved special consideration, and anxious himself to visit the city, 'Umar acceded to the patriarch's request. The encounter between the two men was dramatic and conclusive. The coarse raiment of the caliph contrasted sharply with the splendid vestments of a Byzantine prelate. But in an age of intolerance and cruelty the terms of surrender were generous and humane:

> In the name of Allah, the Merciful the Compassionate. This is the covenant which 'Umar, the servant of Allah, the Commander of the Faithful granted to the people of Aelia. He granted them safety for their lives, their possessions, their churches, and their crosses . . . they shall not be constrained in the matter of their religion, nor shall any of them be molested. No Jew shall live with them in Aelia. And the people of Aelia shall pay the poll-tax . . . whoever leaves the city shall be safe in his person and his property until he reaches his destination.

'Umar's next concern was to identify the places hallowed by the Prophet's nocturnal journey. Reluctantly Sophronius guided him to the desolation at the site of the old Temple which by then had no traces of its Jewish or pagan past. For this reason it was very difficult to locate the Rock, which after a diligent search was found concealed under a dunghill. 'Umar himself led the Muslims in uncovering it, but directed that no prayers be held on or near it until the place had been washed by rain three times.

The caliph led the Muslims in prayer on a clean spot to the south, approximately where the Maghāribah Mosque now stands. The call to prayer was sounded by Bilāl, the Prophet's *muezzin*. Since the death of his master he ceased to perform the function as a mark of respect to his memory. But on express orders of the caliph, Bilāl made an exception for the occasion.

A large number of the Prophet's Companions were in 'Umar's entourage. Two deserve special mention as an indication of the place Jerusalem was to occupy in Islamic learning. The first was 'Ubādah Ibn aṣ-Ṣāmit who had already been sent to Syria as "judge and teacher." 'Umar regarded any Muslim who held high office as a teacher, and therefore charged him in addition to his usual function with teaching. 'Ubādah was now made the first *qādi* (judge) in Jerusalem and died while holding that office. The second was one of several of Muḥammad's Companions who were to take residence in Jerusalem

13

out of religious motives. He was Shaddād Ibn Aus, renowned for his piety and knowledge of prophetic traditions. He, too, died in Jerusalem.

As to 'Umar, he caused, before leaving Jerusalem, a "mosque" to be erected on the spot where he led the Muslims in prayer, close as it was both to the Rock and to the place where the Burāq was tethered. The structure was very primitive, little more than its Arabic name originally meant—a place for prostration in prayer.

From this humble beginning to the rise, some fifty years later, of great monuments of Muslim architecture, Jerusalem's place as the third holy city in Islam was finally established. Its Roman name was dropped and it became al-Bait al-Muqaddas (the Holy House) in apposition to al-Bait al-Ḥaram (the Sacred House), the appellation of Mecca. A variant of the name was Bait al-Maqdis or simply al-Quds (the Holy City). Later still it became al-Quds ash-Sharīf (the Holy and Noble City).

Its association with the Prophet and 'Umar was no doubt in Mu'āwiyah's mind when he had himself proclaimed caliph in it rather than in Damascus his capital. For some time under his successors the city became virtually the religious capital, since Mecca and Medina were in the hands of a rival. 'Umar's makeshift mosque gave way to the Aqṣā Mosque, the reality of the figurative name in the Qur'ān. The Dome of the Rock commonly but incorrectly known to Europeans as the Mosque of Omar, rose over the traditional site of Muḥammad's ascension. The spacious area over which the two monuments rose became known as al-Ḥaram ash-Sharīf (the Noble Sanctuary), and henceforth referred to as al-Ḥaram.

These magnificent buildings owe their rise to 'Abdul-Malik Ibn Marwān, the fifth caliph after Mu'āwiyah. Much has been made of 'Abdul-Malik's political motives. Yet the motives themselves and the action had deep religious roots and rested on excellent religious authority. In asking his subjects to pray and perform the pilgrimage at Jerusalem, instead of Mecca and Medina, while these holy cities were in the hands of a rival, the caliph invoked the authority of the Prophet. In a well-known tradition Muḥammad named three places of *equal* merit to which the faithful could "journey" for prayer and pilgrimage: Mecca, Jerusalem, and Medina.

Even after the end of the emergency, when Mecca and Medina came under their control, the Umayyad caliphs continued to pay equal respect to Jerusalem. Thus Sulaimān, the son of the builder of the Dome of the Rock, arranged for his investiture with the caliphate in Jerusalem, not in Damascus, Mecca, or Medina. He was, moreover, very fond of Palestine, for he made ar-Ramlah his second capital, where he built a magnificent palace and a new mosque.

The eighth Umayyad caliph, who for piety and uprightness went down in history as 'Umar II, regarded the Dome of the Rock so sacred that he ordered all governors who held office under his predecessor to give account of their stewardships upon oath at this place.

Nor did the Abbasid caliphs pay less regard to Jerusalem, from their distant capital in Baghdad. At least three of the early caliphs of this dynasty visited Jerusalem as pilgrims. Al-Manṣūr, the true founder of the dynasty, visited it twice. On the first occasion he went first to Mecca, then to Medina, and then to Jerusalem; on the second he went directly to Jerusalem. Al-Mahdi visited the city specially to pray at al-Aqṣā Mosque, presumably accompanied by his son, the illustrious Hārūn ar-Rashīd. The name of Al-Ma'mūn is even more closely associated with Jerusalem, since by his orders major restorations were made in the Dome of the Rock, the building of which enthusiastic courtiers tried very crudely to ascribe to their master. Al-Ma'mūn's brother and successor as al-Mu'taṣim was then viceroy in Syria, and he took personal interest in the works of restoration.

3.

In the wake of caliphs the flow of pilgrims continued to increase from the days of 'Umar onwards. State functionaries apart, commentators on the Qur'ān, students of prophetic traditions, mystics, and pious men and women, in general, went to the city for pilgrimage, prayer, study, or residence. Those who chose to reside in the city out of religious motives were legion. A Muslim historian of Jerusalem fills thirty pages with their names. However, because the fact is little known the mention of two remarkable women among them is of special significance. The first was Umm ad-Dardā, who rejected the hand of Mu'āwiyah. She used to spend half the year in Damascus and the other half in Jerusalem "comforting the poor." The second was the renowned mystic Rābi'ah of Basra, who came to live until her death a life of piety and meditation in Jerusalem.

Equally significant was the flow of Christian pilgrims since the days of Saint Helena. Their flow was not interrupted when the Holy Land fell under Muslim rule. The story that Hārūn ar-Rashīd sent the keys of the Holy Sepulchre to Charlemagne may be fictitious, but it was by the caliph's grace and with Charlemagne's patronage that hostels for pilgrims were established in the Holy Land and nuns sent to serve at Jerusalem.

By the time of Hārūn ar-Rashīd, Islamic law had been codified and the administration of the empire ordered accordingly. An important element in this order was the special tolerance accorded to "the People of the Book," the Christians and Jews. It is little appreciated nowadays that, in an extremely intolerant age, Islam did not seek to eliminate its predecessors. Not only had it no positive policy of suppression, it had in fact one of coexistence.

An assertion gained currency in recent years that under Islam non-Muslims were "second-class citizens." This is fallacious, in the first place because it projects into the different and distant past the comparatively modern notions of citizenship and equality before a secular law, and in the second place because it does not relate the principle of Islamic tolerance to the theory and practice of its own times, stained as they were with fanaticism and persecution.

The Qur'ān insists that Islam is the last divine message to mankind, sent down to complete previous messages. This being so, absolute religious equality, which even in our own times is still a goal seldom reached, was contrary to divine ordinance. But far from resenting its application, the Christians and Jews who benefited from the principles of Islamic tolerance welcomed it as heavensent. There is ample evidence in the early history of Islam in Syria and Palestine that the Christians and Jews welcomed the Muslims as deliverers from injustice and persecution.

Under the new order, freedom of worship, inviolability of existing places of worship, safety of person and property, and above all communal autonomy were all guaranteed in return for the single obligation of paying poll-tax. It is an established historical fact that it was the tolerance, not the sword, of Islam that swelled the ranks of believers in Syria and Palestine and resulted both in Islamizing and Arabicizing the majority of the population, and in the survival of sizable Christian and Jewish minorities.

To these minorities, as well as to foreign Christian and Jewish pilgrims, the Islamic state, with remarkable few individual lapses, guaranteed religious freedom and free access to shrines. What, if not

16

Muslim tolerance, could have relaxed gradually and informally the strict ban on Jews in 'Umar's covenant with Sophronius? It is a fact that gradually a trickle of Jews was allowed to reach and live in Jerusalem. But there is no evidence in the standard works by Muslim historians, jurists, and others of any Jewish place of worship in the city. So far as could be discovered the earliest mention of such a place is by a Persian traveler who visited Jerusalem some fifty years before the Crusades.

The Christian and Muslim holy places are, however, abundantly described by pilgrims and diverse authors. To the Muslims and to the Arabs the passage of time served only to enhance Jerusalem's position in their tradition and history. An appreciation of that position is best seen through the eyes of two or three Muslim authors who wrote during the century preceding the Crusades.

The first quotation is from Ibn Ḥauqal, a merchant and traveler who flourished in the golden age of the caliphate, the tenth century. He describes the Ḥaram area and the relative position on it of the Dome of the Rock and the Aqṣā Mosque. Of Jerusalem itself he says: "The Holy City is nearly as large as ar-Ramlah . . . [but] greater than its Mosque there is none in all Islam."

It is appropriate that the second quotation should be from al-Muqaddasi who, as his name indicates, was a native of Jerusalem. His family was among the first Arabs to settle in the city after its conquest. His love and veneration of it are clear from these words:

> As to her being the finest city, why, has any seen elsewhere buildings finer or cleaner, or a mosque that is more beautiful? . . . And as to the excellence of the city, why, is not this the place of marshalling on the Day of Judgment? . . . Verily, Mecca and Medina have their superiority by reason of the Kaabah and the Prophet, but, in truth, on the Day of Judgment, both cities will come to Jerusalem, and the excellencies of them all will be united.

The third quotation is from the Persian traveler Nasir-i-Khusrau who visited the city in A.D. 1047. He confirms that in Syria and the neighboring part, Jerusalem was known as al-Quds (the Holy City) and writes:

> The people of these parts, if they are unable to make the pilgrimage to Mecca, will go at the appointed season to Jerusalem and there perform their rites, and upon the feast day slay the sacrifices,

17

as is customary to do at Mecca on the same day. There are years when as many as twenty thousand people will be present at Jerusalem during the first days of the pilgrimage month.

4.

Khusrau also mentions Christians and Jews who came to Jerusalem to visit "the church [*kalisa*] and the synagogue [*konisht*] that are there." He describes in great detail the Church of Resurrection, but says nothing about a synagogue or any other Jewish place of worship. As mentioned above, there was no such place at the time of the Arab conquest. It is true that the ban on the Jews in the terms of the city's surrender to 'Umar was gradually and informally relaxed, but so far as could be discovered Khusrau is the first Muslim author to mention the "synagogue." His reference to it, no matter how cursory, raises a legal puzzle which is very difficult to solve.

Under Islamic law a *new* synagogue was not allowed. This was a more fundamental question than permitting the Jews to visit or even to live in Jerusalem. The silence of Muslim sources on this subject suggests, if Khusrau's statement is to be accepted, that the Jews may have used a dwelling for the purpose of assembly or communal worship since canon law prescribes ten as the minimum for such worship. It is important, however, that neither Khusrau nor any of his predecessors made any mention of Jewish lamentation at the exterior of the western wall of the Ḥaram, known later as the Wailing Place or the Wailing Wall.

No mention of either a synagogue or wailing at a wall is made by al-Ghazāli who visited Jerusalem some fifty years after Khusrau, and occupied quarters in the Ḥaram area within an arrow's shot from the wall in question. But al-Ghazāli's pilgrimage is of such supreme importance that it requires more than a passing mention. He had been the principal of the Nizāmiyyah in Baghdad, the highest educational institution, when he resigned his post, donned the garb of a mystic, and proceeded to Jerusalem on the way to Mecca and Medina.

From the first days of Islam the pursuit of learning was regarded as a religious duty, the more so since all learning was, to start with, religious. Just as it is true to say that the first textbook in Islam was the Qur'ān, so it is true to say that the first school was the mosque. Naturally mosques of the three holy cities were from the beginning

18

seats of learning. In them preachers and teachers diffused education among all those who frequented their circles.

Al-Aqṣā Mosque was a particular seat of learning. In enumerating the merits of his native city, al-Muqaddasi says it had in his time "all manner of learned men" who delighted the hearts of all intelligent students. Scholars coming from distant lands had for their reception special quarters the upkeep of which was ensured by religious foundations. Most of these quarters were near the Ḥaram, and the most common type was the *zāwiyah*, properly a retreat for meditation and prayer by mystics, but also a hostel and an educational institution.

It was at such a place on the eastern side of the Ḥaram area that al-Ghazāli took residence in 1095, and here at al-Aqṣā Mosque that he began the writing of his magnum opus which was to perform in Islam a function analogous to that performed by the *Summa* of Thomas Aquinas in Christendom. The place was over Bāb ar-Raḥmah, the Gate of Mercy, which later tradition associates with the gate "in the inward thereof is mercy," mentioned in the Qur'ān 57:13.

Al-Ghazāli's discourse at al-Aqṣā Mosque had so impressed the worshippers that they begged him to write for their benefit a concise exposition of the Islamic creed. This he did and called it the Jerusalem Tract, a unique composition in insight, clarity, and comprehensiveness. It has recently been my fortune to publish an annotated edition of it with an English translation and introduction, under the auspices of the Islamic Cultural Centre in London.

Four years after al-Ghazāli's pilgrimage "the greatest calamity befell Islam" by the loss of Jerusalem to the Crusaders in 1099. This is not the place to dilate upon the Crusades. Their barbarity is one of the darkest chapters in human history. As a holy war it began in Europe by assaults upon, and massacres of, the Jews. And it celebrated its victory in the Holy City by wholesale and indiscriminate massacre of the Muslim population, men, women, and children, even those who took refuge in the Ḥaram and its mosques, which were desecrated and their treasures plundered. The small number of Jews who had not escaped before the city was besieged assembled for safety in their "synagogue" which the Crusaders burnt over their heads. Thus all the non-Christian inhabitants of the city were wiped out, their property looted, and their houses occupied by the invaders. The entire Ḥaram area was confiscated and handed over to a new order of knights. The anguish that pervaded the then disunited and weakened lands of Islam

19

was depicted by Abi-wardi in a long poem of which the following lines
are representative:

> Our blood we have mixed with overflow of tears
> When our line of defence was no more.
> A man's worst weapon is tears to shed
> When war is waged with cutting swords.
> Oh ye sons of Islam, behold
> Onslaughts on all sides!
> How can you close your eyes
> To a calamity that awakes the sound asleep?
> How long will Arab heroes endure such injury,
> And submit to disgrace from the barbarian?

The injury had to be endured for some ninety years until Saladin
reconquered the city in 1187. About twenty years earlier a Spanish
traveler, Rabbi Benjamin of Tudela, visited Jerusalem and wrote an
account of his journeys containing a brief description of the city, its
holy places, and its inhabitants. He mentions no Muslims among them,
but says that there were about two hundred Jews, some of whom
operated a tannery which they rented from the "king." Some ten years
after Benjamin another Jewish traveler, Rabbi Petachia of Regensburg,
found only one Jew in Jerusalem, a dyer.

There is no mention in Benjamin's account of any synagogue. The
one reported by Khusrau, whether actually a synagogue or a house of
assembly, was probably the same building set on fire by the Crusaders
over the heads of the Jews. Benjamin ascribes erroneously the erection
of the Dome of the Rock, then used as a church and named by the
Crusaders as *Templum Domini,* to 'Umar Ibn al-Khaṭṭāb. He says that
opposite the Dome to the west was one of the walls of the ancient
Temple, that it was called the Gate of Mercy, and that "the Jews"
resorted to it for devotion. (The Gate of Mercy was of course on the
eastern side.)

It is clear that Benjamin's topography is faulty. But his language
does not mean that "the Jews" were actually permitted by the Crusaders to pray at the doorsteps of what was then a church. Nor does he
say that he himself prayed there. Indeed, his factual errors suggest that
he did not visit the area, but obtained his information secondhand.

Nevertheless, Benjamin is significant as one of the earliest sources to
mention devotion at what became known as the Wailing Place or

Wailing Wall. Pious Jews continued to mourn the disappearance of the Temple, and since the days of Constantine did so intermittently in Jerusalem or on the Mount of Olives overlooking the old Temple area. But this was not a Jewish religious duty, individual or communal. Whether inspired by legend and tradition, or based on historical and archaeological evidence, there grew an assumption among devout Jews that a portion of the massive lower structure of the western walls of the Ḥaram is a remnant of the walls of the old Temple.

It is difficult to establish when the custom of individual Jews resorting to the exterior of the western walls of the Ḥaram for devotion assumed more formal or communal character. Most probably the transition was gradual and to the Muslim authorities imperceptible. The restoration of some Jewish life in Jerusalem after 1187 was due entirely to Saladin. In his empire, wrote the well-known Jewish historian Graetz, the Jews found "a safe asylum from persecution." The decline of their number in Jerusalem to a single inhabitant under the Crusaders was followed by a gradual increase under successive Muslim rulers. Since the Crusades down to our own times the movement of Jewish refugees was from Christian Europe to the lands of Islam of which Palestine and Jerusalem received a small fraction.

5.

Saladin was not less generous or humane even to his enemies who had butchered the Muslim population of Jerusalem. To the successors of "chivalrous" knights who, according to their historian, waded knee-deep in the blood of Muslim women and children, Saladin guaranteed safety of life, property, and passage to the coast on payment of a moderate ransom. He exempted the aged men and women, and gave gifts to widows and orphans. He answered the plea of noble and common women whose men were captive by releasing them free. His brother al-'Ādil, with Saladin's consent, freed a thousand captives without ransom.

The recovery of Jerusalem by Saladin figures larger in Islamic history than its first acquisition by 'Umar five and a half centuries before. That Saladin's entry into the city fell on Friday, 27 Rajab, A.H. 583, the anniversary of the Prophet's nocturnal journey, was regarded by Muslims as providential. But it was too late to perform on that day the ritual and communal midday prayer. The Dome of the Rock and the

Aqṣā Mosque had first to be cleansed of defilement. For a whole week noble and learned men took part with humble folk in washing the floors seven times with water, thoroughly cleaning the walls, and liberally sprinkling the buildings with rose water.

On the following Friday, Saladin with his victorious army and a large number of ulema and notables gathered from all over the land for the midday prayer in the Aqṣā Mosque. The usual sermon was preceded by a much longer oration delivered by the qādi of Damascus appointed for the occasion by Saladin himself. After dwelling on the exalted status of Jerusalem in Islam by recounting in detail its place in the Qur'ān, Islamic history, and tradition, the orator cautioned and exhorted the Muslims in these words:

> Oh servants of God! Let Satan not deceive you into believing that this victory was due to your swords, for by God victory comes only from Him. . . . Beware lest you disobey Him who has honoured you with this victory. . . . Fight in His way! Obey His commandment and He will give you more victories. . . . Eradicate the enemy and purify the land from his filth.

Saladin was the first to obey the call, but military duties did not preclude him from attending to the tasks of peace. He ordered a complete restoration of the Ḥaram area to its pristine condition. The fact is to this day inscribed on beautiful tiles inside the cupola of the Dome over the Rock. The city had also to be repeopled by Muslims, at least to the same extent as before the Crusades. Where no relatives or descendants claimed Muslim houses now vacated by the Franks, Saladin deliberately assigned them to clans from well-known Arab tribes.

He was particularly anxious to restore to the city its character as a seat of Islamic learning. Apart from the resumption of normal worship and study at the Aqṣā Mosque the precincts were covered by new educational and charitable institutions. Saladin himself endowed a new *madrasah* (high religious school), two hostels for scholars and mystics, and a hospital. Two of his lieutenants followed his example by establishing similar institutions.

To his successors and their lieutenants goes the credit for a number of monuments, two of which in the Ḥaram area deserve special mention. In 1193 Saladin's son, al-Afdal, built the Maghāribah

Mosque in the southwest corner of the area near the gate by that name, and dedicated the land without the gate as *waqf* (religious foundation) for the mosque and pilgrims and scholars from North Africa. The choice of site for mosque and foundation had excellent reasons. Tradition had long associated the ground outside and inside the Maghāribah Gate with Muḥammad's nocturnal journey. Hence the Gate is also called the Prophet's or the Burāq's Gate, and the spot of tethering the Prophet's mount is commemorated by a chamber in the Ḥaram wall inside the Gate to the left which is often called the Burāq Mosque.

Another monument belonging to Saladin's era is also on the Ḥaram area and connected with the Prophet's nocturnal journey. In 1200 the governor of Jerusalem had the Dome of Ascension completely rebuilt on the spot which tradition identifies as the place where Muḥammad prayed before his ascension to heaven.

Saladin himself was responsible for yet another measure that raised the status of Jerusalem still higher. Seeing that the vandalism of the Crusaders had swept away a number of the graves of famous men who died in the city, he ordered the burial of the heroes of his campaign near the walls of the Ḥaram by the Gate of Mercy. The ground was named "the cemetery of the holy warriors." This place had already been the burial ground of famous men and women. Here were buried the two Companions of the Prophet, 'Ubādah and Shaddād, mentioned above. Here, too, was buried Fāṭimah, the daughter of Mu'āwiyah. Some famous men who died elsewhere were, by their wish, buried in Jerusalem. This was the case of two rulers of Egypt and Syria before the Fatimids, one of whom died in Cairo and the other in Damascus.

The restoration of Jerusalem to the fold of Islam brought to it a greater stream of pilgrims and scholars. It inspired numerous books on the city, its Ḥaram, and their place in Islam. The original historical facts and traditions were reinterpreted not merely to stress the sacred character of Jerusalem but to extend it to Palestine and indeed to the whole of Syria (ash-Shām).

A representative list of these works is before me as I write. The mere recurrence of the word *faḍā'il* (virtues) in the titles is noteworthy, for it is used in reference to Jerusalem or the Aqṣā Mosque or Syria as a whole. The earliest work in this class is by a contemporary of Saladin; its author is Ibn 'Asākir, the son and editor of the famous historian. One of the latest is by 'Abdu'l-Ghani an-Nābulusi, the mystic and theologian who died in the first half of the eighteenth

23

century. A number of these works, including Ibn 'Asākir's, were written in Jerusalem or delivered as lectures in the Aqṣā. All of them extol the pilgrimage to the city.

Like the pilgrimage to Mecca, the visit (ziyārah) to Jerusalem was now according to prescribed rites to be performed at the Dome of the Rock, the Aqṣā Mosque, and other spots sanctified by tradition in or near the Ḥaram area. But unlike the pilgrimage to Mecca, the visit to Jerusalem was not on a fixed date, and if performed in the same year as the former it may precede or succeed it according to the pilgrim's circumstances.

6.

The Crusades continued long after the reconquest of Jerusalem by Saladin. But he kept it open to Christian pilgrims, even those coming from enemy territory. He kept it open also for the Jews, travelers as well as refugees. For the Crusades, even before the expulsion from Spain, drove Jewish refugees to the lands of Islam, from Morocco to Syria. Under Saladin and his dynasty, as under Mamluk and Ottoman sultans, these lands afforded refuge for persecuted Jews.

Most of those who reached Palestine were destitute, particularly those who chose to live in Jerusalem on the charity of their kinsmen abroad. A few wealthy European Jews visited the city and wrote accounts of their visit which are remarkable for their brevity and vagueness, in contrast to similar accounts by Christian or Muslim pilgrims. This was perhaps inevitable, since a Christian or a Muslim found much to write about while a Jew had little more than memory.

Thus when the Spanish Kabbalist Isaac Ben Chelo visited Jerusalem about 1334 he merely reproduced Benjamin of Tudela and said so. He mentions no synagogue, nor does he say that he visited or prayed at the Wailing Place or the western wall. About a century and a half later two rabbis visited the city separately and wrote brief accounts of their visits. In 1481 Meshullam Ben Menahim of Volterra reported 250 Jewish householders in the city, but says nothing about a synagogue or his praying anywhere. His reference to the Ḥaram, which incidentally corrects some of Benjamin's errors, is worthy of note:

The Temple, may it be restored speedily in our days, is still surrounded by a wall, on the east side are the Gates of Mercy. . . .

24

The Gates are closed, and on the sides of the Gates are Muslim graves.

Some ten years later the Italian Rabbi Obadiah Jaré da Bertinoro reported about seventy Jewish families in Jerusalem. He says he "made enquiries" concerning the Temple, which suggests that, like his predecessors, he did not come near it. Nor does he say he prayed at the Wailing Place or the western wall, which he describes as "composed of large, thick stones." But he specifically mentions a synagogue—"large, narrow, and dark, the light entering it only by the door . . . quite close to it stands a mosque."

This statement is confirmed by a Muslim contemporary, Mujīr-ud-Dīn, who later became the qādi of Jerusalem and author of a learned book on it. As we have already suggested, and as Obadiah's description indicates, the building must have been used as a synagogue surreptitiously. The three hundred or so Jews lived, according to Mujīr, in a quarter separated from the walls of the Ḥaram by purely Muslim quarters including that of the Maghāribah (North Africans) along the western walls. The mosque mentioned by Obadiah was contiguous, not simply near the synagogue.

Hence in 1473 the existence of the synagogue was challenged before a Shāfi'i judge. The judge ruled that as Jewish property the building could be used as a dwelling house or shop but as a synagogue it was an unlicensed innovation. Some zealots misinterpreted this ruling and proceeded to demolish the building. The Jews appealed to the Sultan Qaitbai in Cairo, who was angry that the zealots took the law in their hands. Not only did he punish some of the suspected instigators, but also sanctioned, after legal consultation, the rebuilding of the synagogue, despite an anonymous accusation he received from Jerusalem that the Jews had paid money into his treasury to secure the concession. (The *Jewish Encyclopaedia* confirms that "a large sum of money" was actually paid.)

The concession was clearly made by a confident sovereign for the assurance of a powerless and very tiny religious minority. The evasion of the law by a few hundred Jews was condoned by him probably because the local authorities must have tolerated for some time the existence of a synagogue next door to a mosque. But it is singular how a tiny minority, entirely dependent on the goodwill and hospitality of

Muslim rulers, could so stealthily contravene Islamic law and obtain an advantage therefrom!

This episode is yet another example of Arab and Muslim tolerance. It was by the grace and favor of Arab rulers that the terms secured by Sophronius from 'Umar banning the Jews from Jerusalem were gradually relaxed. It was also by the grace and favor of Muslim rulers that the Jews, completely eliminated by the Crusaders, were readmitted. These favors have now been crowned with the great indulgence over the question of the synagogue.

Nevertheless, the concession was very unpopular, and the Ḥanafī judge delegated by the sultan to execute his order went down in history as "the judge of the synagogue." To the best of my knowledge this is the earliest occasion since the Arab conquest that a synagogue was authorized in Jerusalem.

7.

Qaitbai was by all accounts a pious sultan, and Jerusalem was an object of his special attention. In 1475 he went on pilgrimage to Mecca and before returning to Cairo visited Jerusalem and performed the prescribed rites. He sat in the Aqṣā Mosque and listened, according to ancient custom, to complaints against his officials. The controversy about the synagogue was still raging. To conciliate religious opinion he ordered the reestablishment on a grand scale of a school, al-Madrasah al-Ashrafiyyah, inside the Ḥaram close to the Aqṣā Mosque. According to Mujīr, the building of the school was "a third jewel" in the Ḥaram area. Its endowment provided for a staff of jurists and sufis as well as quarters for scholars.

Nor were other Mamluk sultans less generous patrons of learning in Jerusalem or less assiduous in adding to or embellishing its religious and public buildings. For they covered the city with more endowed schools and hostels for scholars and mystics. They enriched the Ḥaram area with four minarets and added more cloisters around it. They certainly deserved the honorific titles they assumed as "servants and guardians" of the holy places in Mecca, Medina, and Jerusalem. It was they who checked the Mongols in a decisive battle in northern Palestine, and achieved the final expulsion of the Crusaders from their last stronghold in the Holy Land.

As champions of Islam, the Ottoman sultans were worthy suc-

26

cessors. Syria and Palestine were conquered by Salim I, who, on entering Damascus ordered the building of a shrine over the tomb of the mystic Ibn al-'Arabi. And before joining his army which had advanced along the coast as far as Gaza he specially made a detour to Jerusalem, performed the rites of a pilgrim, and took formal possession of the city. By the end of January, 1517, his army entered Cairo, where he received a delegation from the sharifs of Mecca. Salim had thus succeeded to the titles of the Mamluks as the "servant and guardian" of the holy places of Mecca, Medina, and Jerusalem.

Salim's successor, Sulaiman the Magnificent, gave Jerusalem substantially all the superstructure of its present walls, a new water supply, five water fountains on or near the Ḥaram area, and carried out extensive repairs in the area and in the Dome of the Rock. He continued the practice of his Muslim predecessors by establishing a hostel for mystics and a religious school.

It is not necessary to enumerate the pious acts of successive Ottoman sultans. These are recorded in the religious court in the city and inscribed where appropriate on the buildings in the Ḥaram area and elsewhere. But it must be recognized that, coinciding with a decline in Ottoman power, anarchy crept into provincial administration, and educational establishments and some foundations were neglected to such an extent that many of the schools actually disappeared.

The Ḥaram itself was never neglected. The sultans who erected magnificent mosques in Constantinople never forgot the ancient mosques in Jerusalem, Mecca, and Medina. The maintenance and embellishment of the mosques in Jerusalem were a source of pride to successive sultans. It would be sufficient in this place merely to refer to those who reigned during the nineteenth century when major restorations were undertaken by Maḥmūd II and his two successors, 'Abdu'l-Majīd and 'Abdu'l-'Azīz. So major were these restorations that they amounted in places to rebuilding. The last-named sultan is known to historians for his extravagance, and few if any of them give him credit for his lavish spending on the Dome of the Rock and the Aqṣā Mosque.

Greater attention was paid to Jerusalem, together with Mecca and Medina, in the last decades of the nineteenth century when Ottoman sultans began to emphasize their roles as caliphs. None of them was more assiduous in cultivating this idea than 'Abdu'l-Ḥamīd II. He

27

completed the work of restoration begun by his predecessors and had the floors of the mosques all covered with valuable Persian carpets.

Under these four sultans radical if gradual changes took place in Jerusalem. In the early decades of the nineteenth century the city was still within the walls. Except for monks and guardians of holy places, Franks were not allowed, since the days of the Crusades, to reside in it, not even as diplomatic representatives. Pilgrims and travelers were admitted, but for limited periods during certain times of the year. An exception was made in favor of Jewish refugees who came at first mostly from Spain and rather later from central and eastern Europe. Most of them lived in abject poverty, huddled in a small quarter. Many were aged who came to die in the city, and many others were perpetual students of the Talmud who with most of the other Jewish inhabitants lived on the charity of their kinsmen in Europe.

As a result of the Egyptian occupation of Palestine and Syria in 1831, the slow process of change was accelerated. Lawlessness was stamped out, and the country was opened to European merchants, missionaries, and travelers. The Egyptian administration was particularly tolerant toward Christians and Jews. A British consulate, the first of its kind, was opened in Jerusalem. Among its tasks was the "protection" of the Jews. An Anglican bishop was installed in the city with a mission that sought their conversion to Christianity. Great Britain placed the sultan under great pressure until he allowed the building of a new Protestant church just inside the city wall near the citadel.

When exactly the Muslim authorities did allow the Jews to pray at the exterior of the western wall of the Ḥaram is very obscure. It must have come about gradually and imperceptibly without formal authority, as in the case of the synagogue described above. Evidently it was by the same Muslim indulgence, which had sanctioned a synagogue next door to a mosque, that the Jews were permitted to wail and pray at the doorstep of the third holy place in Islam.

8.

During the Egyptian occupation there were two main Jewish communities in Jerusalem, mutually hostile to each other. The Sephardim, who came principally from Spain, formed the vast majority and were Ottoman subjects. By careful use of adjacent buildings they converted the only synagogue into four, but under one roof. One of their rabbis was recognized by the Turkish authorities as the spokesman of the community, and was later on promoted to the official post of chief rabbi.

The other community, the Ashkenazim, were recent arrivals from Prussia, Austria, Poland, and Russia and formed a small minority. Most of them retained their foreign nationalities, and under the system of capitulations were virtually beyond the reach of Ottoman law. A further complication was introduced by the instructions to the newly opened British consulate "to afford protection to the Jews generally." Accordingly many European Jews who were not British subjects sought and received British consular protection.

Exploiting the advantage of foreign protection, European Jews employed some elaborate stratagems to secure permission to acquire immovable property, to erect a new synagogue, and, most ambitious of all, to gain a prescriptive right over a sacred Muslim property. Under Ottoman law foreigners were still debarred from acquiring real estate anywhere in the Empire. And the Egyptian administration, though established as a result of a rebellion against the sultan, recognized him as the legal sovereign, and upheld his laws as well as Islamic law in general. Hence Muḥammad 'Ali had no hesitation in refusing permission to foreign Jews to buy land in or near Jerusalem. (Other Jews, the vast majority, were as Ottoman subjects free to do so.)

More cunning was the attempt in the autumn of 1839 by Jews under foreign protection to acquire a vested interest in the Wailing Place. A British consul approached Ibrāhīm Pasha, the Egyptian commander-in-chief, with the news that a British Jew had made a votive offering for paving the Wailing Place, and with the request for permission for his protégés to undertake the work. Ibrāhīm himself gave a favorable reply, but when the proposal was laid before the consultative council which he himself had set up in the city, a firm refusal was recommended. The recommendation was buttressed by a vehement protest from the Shaikh of the Maghāribah.

It will be recalled that the land without the Maghāribah Gate of the Ḥaram, including the ground of the Wailing Place, had been dedicated as a Muslim religious foundation (waqf) by Saladin's son. In the course of time the area became the exclusive resort of Maghāribah (North African) pilgrims, divines, and scholars. In 1303 a zāwiyah was founded on the land under a new bequest. A more important foundation, with a zāwiyah and dwelling houses on the original waqf land, was instituted in 1320 by Shu'aib Abū Madyan al-Ghauth, himself a Maghribi. So close had the association of North African

Muslims with the Ḥaram and its precincts become that the Sultan of Morocco, 'Ali Ibn 'Uthmān al-Marrini, wrote the whole Qur'ān with his own hand on parchment and sent the copy in 1352 to the Aqṣā Mosque, with another Abū Madyan as guardian. In 1630 the land and its amenities was re-registered in the Muslim religious court as a *waqf*.

Thus the North Africans had been in possession under three bequests for over six centuries when in 1839 they were shocked by Jewish pretensions. The Shaikh of the Zāwiyah of Abū Madyan wrote on behalf of his community that their quarter was adjacent to the walls of the Ḥaram where the Prophet's Burāq was tethered. He concedes that the Jews had been allowed to visit a section of the wall, but in a seemly manner without raising their voices. In the last few years, however, they came in greater numbers and caused annoyance by raising their voices as if the place were a synagogue. Now, he concludes, they wish to pave the ground "preliminary to their ultimate aims."

The consultative council substantiated these statements and added in their report that the Wailing Place was a narrow lane leading to and ending with the *zāwiyah,* which, together with the neighboring houses and the lane itself, were embraced by the Abū Madyan foundation. All the papers were referred to Muḥammad 'Ali in Cairo. The result of a thorough examination is contained in an order to the governor of Jerusalem dated 24 Rabī' I, A.H. 1256 (May 26, 1840):

> The deliberations of the consultative council in Jerusalem show that the place the Jews petitioned to pave is adjoining the wall of al-Ḥaram ash-Sharīf as well as the place of tethering the Burāq, that it is included in the *waqf* [foundation] of Abū Madyan (may God sanctify his spiritual mysteries), and that the Jews never repaired such things in that place. It has also been found that the petition is inadmissable under the *shar'* [Islamic law]. Therefore the Jews must not be allowed to pave it. They must be warned against raising their voices and other ostentations, and must be forbidden from doing so. They are only allowed their visits as before.

9.

So far as could be ascertained this was the earliest occasion for an authoritative statement of the conditions under which the Jews were permitted to resort to the wall of a Muslim holy place for devotional purposes. During the rest of the nineteenth century the Jews, particularly those under foreign protection, benefited from the liberal reforms introduced by two imperial decrees. Thus in 1854 the Ashkenazim in Jerusalem sought, with the support of the British consul, permission to "rebuild" a ruined place which they claimed was an ancient synagogue.

I have seen no mention of such an ancient synagogue in the accounts of Christian, Jewish, or Muslim travelers and other writers on Jerusalem. The fact that the document submitted by the Ashkenazim described the place as *dair* (monastery) raises serious doubts as to its real past. Furthermore, the dates and the language of these documents raise more doubt as to their authenticity. But the matter was not for historians to decide. The same British ambassador who had a decade earlier exercised great pressure to obtain a permit for a new Protestant church was now able to extract a permit for what was represented as merely rebuilding an old synagogue.

Thus each of the two main Jewish communities had now its own authorized synagogue. But there existed other places of worship which required no formal authority. These were strictly places for the study of the Talmud, but their premises, no matter how poor and unhygienic they were, according to contemporary eyewitnesses, served also for assembly and prayer.

The number of Jews then in Jerusalem cannot be ascertained. Official Turkish statistics are lacking, and the Jews themselves resisted on religious grounds (*vide* 1 Chron. 21:1 ff.) attempts to hold a census even by such a distinguished Jew as Sir Moses Montefiore in 1849. Hence different sources give widely different estimates. In 1874 the British consul estimated their number at three thousand. Much higher figures were given two or three decades earlier. One explanation of the difference is that both immigration and emigration were periodic, depending on Jewish circumstances abroad and their means of livelihood in Jerusalem.

Be that as it may, most of the Jews who had hitherto come to Jerusalem were destitute. Their aim was purely religious: to end their days in the Holy City. A radical change in the character and aims of immigrants began to appear after 1881, following Russian legislation and the pogroms.

This is not the place to give even a brief account of the origins of Zionism. Suffice it merely to state that before it gave a *political* color to Jewish immigration, the Turkish government and the Arab population

31

had for centuries continued a traditional practice of affording asylum for persecuted Jews. The foregoing pages will have shown the great lengths to which the Muslim authorities went in order to facilitate Jewish worship and devotion, even at the doorstep of the third holy place in Islam.

And yet despite the political character of Zionism, the first change in this attitude was not strictly political. On the part of the Turkish government it was due to the influx of Russian subjects who sought and received foreign consular protection; on the part of the Arab population of Jerusalem, to the competition of a new type of Jewish immigrant: craftsman, peddler, and shopkeeper. Gradually both the government and the local population began to resent and suspect the exclusiveness and separate existence which Jewish immigrants studiously maintained, often under foreign protection.

In 1887 the Ottoman government issued orders which, while allowing European Jews to enter the country as pilgrims or visitors, forbade their settlement, particularly in Jerusalem, where the Jewish quarter was overcrowded and unhygienic. Similar orders were issued banning such Jews from acquiring land in Jerusalem and the rest of Palestine. The British consul was the first to protest against these measures, although he had the fewest number of protected Jews on his list compared to the Russian and Austrian consuls.

The measures were, however, ineffective more because of an inefficient administrative machinery than of foreign consular opposition. Foreign Jews did in fact continue to settle and buy land. Within a decade their presence caused an economic crisis in Jerusalem in which the Muslim population suffered most. In 1891 they sent a formal protest to the grand vizier. That no energetic action was taken during the next two decades is clear from a debate in the Chamber of Deputies in Constantinople in 1911 on "the storm of Zionism."

The year 1911 was significant in the history of Jerusalem in yet another way. Since the official ruling of 1840 concerning the Wailing Place and the pavement in front of it, the number of Jews had greatly increased in the city, and correspondingly greater numbers visited the Wailing Place. Gradually individual devotion at the place led to what might be called communal prayer which at any rate needed no more than ten persons.

All attempts to bring to the place certain articles such as chairs were invariably followed by protests from the guardians of the Abū Madyan foundation, and orders from the Turkish authorities to maintain the old practice unchanged. But the Jews persisted in trying until the matter was once more covered by an authoritative decision similar to that of 1840. On November 12, 1911, the Administrative Council passed the following decision to the governor of Jerusalem for ratification:

The guardian of the foundation of Shu'aib Abū Madyan al-Ghauth (may God sanctify his spiritual mysteries) has submitted a petition that members of the Jewish community who had been accustomed to visit the wall of the Burāq outside al-Ḥaram ash-Sharīf to the west, provided they stood during the visit on their feet, began lately and contrary to custom to bring chairs to sit on during the visits. Since the Burāq is the property of the above mentioned foundation, and is in a blind alley, the guardian asked for this development to stop, lest the Jews claim in future ownership of the place.

The petition was considered by His Eminence the Mufti, the Department of Religious Foundations, and the Religious Courts, and they pointed out that this particular property belonged to the dwelling houses adjacent to the wall of the Noble Aqṣā Mosque on the western side, that it was a blind alley within the property of the foundation in question, that according to Islamic law it was absolutely illegal to place chairs, or a screen or such other articles, or introduce any innovation which might lead to the claim of possession of the wall of the Noble Aqṣā Mosque, and that steps must be taken to prevent the Jews from introducing the innovation.

After deliberation the Council decided not to allow the placing of any articles that might be construed as evidence of ownership, neither at the said property of the foundation nor at the wall of al-Ḥaram ash-Sharīf, to give no opportunity for anyone to introduce such articles, but strictly to maintain the ancient custom.

That was the position on the eve of the outbreak of the First World War which led to the end of long Muslim rule and the beginning of British occupation.

10.

The above is essentially a factual account of the place of Jerusalem in Arab and Muslim history. It has made little attempt to describe its place in the heart of the Muslim, or to portray its evocative and emotional associations in the mind of the Arab, be he Christian or Muslim. To do so, history would need to borrow from religion its deep feelings, and from poetry her sweet tunes. And these alas have no place in the scheme of this essay.

Although clearly not concerned with the place of Jerusalem in Jewish tradition, a great deal of space has been allocated for Jewish association with the city during thirteen centuries of Muslim rule interrupted only by the Crusades. The facts speak for themselves, and any fair-minded historian cannot fail to observe that successive Muslim governments of the land continued to play hosts to Jews persecuted elsewhere. Even when the Jews occasionally abused the hospitality afforded to them, they were treated with patience and tolerance. From the episode of the first synagogue at the end of the fifteenth century to the repeated attempts to change the *status quo* at the Wailing Place in our own times, the Jews were merely corrected, not punished for their abuse of hospitality.

A great change took place after 1914. In that year the number of Jews in all Palestine was variously estimated between sixty and eighty thousand. A sizable majority of them lived in Jerusalem.

During the First World War both the Arabs and the Zionists secured certain British promises. The Arabs, who rose in revolt against the Turks and allied themselves with Britain, were promised independence in the McMahon Letter of October 25, 1915, which they always understood to include Palestine. The Zionists were promised in the Balfour Declaration of November 2, 1917, "a national home in Palestine" which they always intended to convert into a national state.

Various means, including appeal to religious sentiment, were used by the Turks to counteract the Arab revolt. Having lost Mecca to the Arabs, and with Medina besieged by them, the sultan-caliph controlled only the third holy city, Jerusalem. Here Jamal Pasha, the commander-in-chief, had the religious school established by Saladin revived as a center of Islamic propaganda. He was no doubt aware that the Indian Muslims were not sympathetic to the Arab revolt on religious grounds, and that they protested at a series of articles in the *Times* which described the British advance in southern Palestine as a crusade.

Jamal Pasha tried to wean the Arabs from a British alliance, not simply by offering political terms, but also by appealing to common religious sentiments. The British army, he wrote, would not have been on its way to Jerusalem, the city secured for Islam by Saladin, had the

34

Arabs and Turks remained united in the defense of their heritage. So pained and embarrassed was the sharif of Mecca, the leader of the Arab revolt and the staunch ally of Britain, that he refrained from sending congratulations on the capture of Jerusalem, much to the disappointment of the British government. But he also was disappointed for their failure to invite his son Faisal, who commanded the Arab army in Transjordan, and protected the right flank of the British advance, to be present on the entry into the city.

A proclamation, carefully prepared by Lord Curzon and approved by the Cabinet with a view to allaying the fears of Indian Muslims, was read in the presence of General Allenby, the commander-in-chief, on his formal entry into the city. Here is an important paragraph of it:

> I make known to you that every sacred building, monument, pious bequest, or customary place of prayer, of whatsoever form of the three religions, will be maintained and protected according to existing customs and beliefs of those to whose faiths they are sacred.

It is now possible to reveal for the first time, on the basis of official and hitherto secret British documents, how the Jews, and the Zionists in particular, sought to nullify the solemn British promise to maintain the *status quo* in the holy places in Jerusalem.

Even while half of Palestine was still in Turkish hands and final British victory still a year ahead, the Zionists began to challenge, secretly and openly, the spirit and the letter of Allenby's proclamation. They persuaded the British government to accept a token detachment of two battalions in the British army in Palestine. And one of the first acts of this detachment on arrival early in 1918 was to hold a "public service" at the Wailing Wall on March thirtieth. Ten days later the Zionist Commission under Weizmann did likewise.

On its way to Palestine the Commission was acquainted of the political and religious apprehensions of the Arabs and Muslims. The Sultan of Egypt expressed to the British authorities Muslim fears that the Jews had designs against the Ḥaram in Jerusalem. Dr. Fāris Nimr, the Christian Arab Lebanese who edited the pro-British *al-Muqaṭṭam,* conveyed the same fears to the British liaison officer with the Commission who, however, dismissed them as anti-Semitic propaganda. This is belied by Weizmann himself. He sought "authority to deal with this question as soon as possible" in a letter he wrote from Tel Aviv on May 30, 1918, to Balfour:

THE HANDING OVER OF THE WAILING WALL. We Jews have many holy places in Palestine, but the Wailing Wall—believed to be a part of the old Temple wall—is the only one which is in some sense left to us. All the others are in the hands of Christians or Moslems. It is surrounded by a group of miserable, dirty cottages and derelict buildings, which make the whole place from the hygienic point of view a positive danger, and from the sentimental point of view a source of constant humiliation to the Jews of the world. Our most sacred monument, in our most sacred city, is in the hands of some doubtful Moghreb [sic] religious community. . . . We are willing to compensate this community very liberally, but we should like the place to be cleaned up; we should like to give it a dignified and respectable appearance. [p. 10, item 3 in the letter]

Ronald Storrs, the military governor of Jerusalem, undertook the very delicate task of sounding Kāmil al-Ḥusaini, the Mufti of Jerusalem, regarding a purchase of the land and houses adjacent to the Wall, but apparently he said nothing about the Wall itself which Weizmann wanted to be "handed over" to the Jews.

Storrs's approach met with the expected reply: any property of a Muslim religious foundation, especially this particular one in connection with the third holy place in Islam, cannot be sold for any amount of money even to a Muslim. How could it be sold to the Jews who had revealed designs on the western wall of the Ḥaram? Storrs used all manner of inducements and even pressure without avail. The Zionists themselves made another move directly. A Moroccan Jew was sent to the Shaikh of Abū Madyan foundation with handsome offers of money.

According to an official British report this move caused among the Muslims "something like a panic." Storrs had to suppress two attempts at public demonstration, but agreed to receive written protests. One was signed by 'Ārif Pasha Dajāni and fourteen dignitaries representing the leading Muslim families. They quoted Allenby's proclamation and hinted that, since the Jews were involved, there was "a particular objection." The other protest was on behalf of three educational societies, the only organizations allowed by the military authorities. This protest, too, refers to Allenby's proclamation, but adds more explicitly that "we, with all the Muslims, will not allow the exchange [for money] of such a holy place."

All the papers were referred with a warning from Allenby's chief political officer to Balfour that since the Muslims now feared attempts

36

on the Ḥaram itself it was "dangerous" to proceed. The Foreign Office issued instructions for the matter to be dropped. But the damage had been done; Arab antagonism to Zionism assumed a religious in addition to a political character.

But the Zionists were not deterred. On the first anniversary of the Balfour Declaration they were not content with an indoor celebration but insisted on a public procession in Jerusalem. Once more the British military authorities, who sanctioned this Zionist demonstration, banned and threatened to stop by force any Arab counterdemonstration.

To make matters worse, the behavior of the two Zionist battalions in the British army had increasingly become so provocative on visiting Jerusalem and the Wailing Wall that the military authorities placed the city out of bounds to them. The order was disobeyed by an officer who marched his men into the city in the direction of the Wall. They were of course court-martialled, and fifty-eight were sentenced, and the Zionist detachment itself disbanded.

In April, 1920, the first major clash between the Arabs and Jews occurred in Jerusalem with loss of life on both sides. A few days later shots were fired at the house of the Mufti of Jerusalem. The chief military administrator believed the culprits were members of the disbanded Zionist detachment. Accordingly he wrote to the Zionist Commission asking, but in vain, for their cooperation to apprehend the offenders.

When, later in April, the mandate for Palestine was assigned to Britain, and the government nominated a British Zionist, Sir Herbert Samuel, as high commissioner, there was alarm in the Arab camp and increased aggressiveness in the Zionist and Jewish camp. The chief military administrator wrote to the Foreign Office of "disquietening portents." On May 16 he received a letter from Weizmann's deputy in which he said that "the Wailing Wall was a possession of the Jews throughout the world." On May 30 he received another letter from the chief rabbi in which he asked the government "to entrust the Wall to the care and control of the representatives of Jewry."

This was an inauspicious beginning of the British mandatory regime: a tiny minority of about 8 percent of the population claiming, with the protection of British bayonets, not only political dominance over the vast Arab majority, but also possession of part of a Muslim holy place.

11.

Under a mandate of the League of Nations, Britain assumed responsibility for maintaining the *status quo* in the holy places, and, subject to the approval of the Council, for appointing a commission to "define and determine the rights and claims" of different religious communities. In the meantime the question of the holy places was withdrawn from the jurisdiction of the courts in Palestine, and the duty of giving rulings on any claims devolved on the British high commissioner subject to directions from London.

With a favored position under the British mandate, the Jews resumed with great assurance the attempts at the Wailing Place, which they had furtively begun in the later years of Ottoman Turkish rule. They tried to bring to the Wall such articles as chairs, benches, and screens. Every time they did so the guardian of the Abū Madyan foundation complained to the Mufti of Jerusalem, who in turn made representations to the government. On two important occasions in 1925 and 1928 the government issued rulings forbidding the introduction of such articles, and did in fact authorize the police in 1928 to remove them when introduced in defiance of orders.

On this occasion the Jews, and in particular the Zionists, raised a storm of protest at this "interference" with Jewish religious worship. The Zionist propaganda in Palestine and abroad was such as to remove the matter from the domain of religion to that of politics. Until political Zionism gave it a national twist, Jewish interest in the Western Wall was religious, limited largely to orthodox and devout Jews. An indication of this limited appeal may be seen in the fact that the *Jewish Encyclopaedia,* published in 1901, does not include an article on the Wall either under its Hebrew or other names. But the *Universal Jewish Encyclopaedia,* published in 1939, after the matter had become a major political issue, carries an entry of a tendentious nature under "Wailing Wall," and the Hebrew name is mentioned only in the text.

Indeed, photographs of the pre-Zionist period show the votaries as predominantly elderly, clad in oriental flowing robes or caftans and fur-trimmed hats. The "emancipated" young Jew, in ordinary European clothes, is conspicuous by his absence. And yet most of the postwar agitation was led precisely by this type of nationalist who eventually hooked in the orthodox Jew. The question was no longer one of ensuring the ancient custom of access to and devotion at the Wailing Place, but also of gradually extending Jewish claims to the extent of physical possession of the ground if not also of the Wall.

It was this possibility that the Muslim Arabs genuinely feared. Accordingly, as president of the Supreme Muslim Council, the Mufti of Jerusalem warned the Palestine government of the grave consequences of the Jewish and Zionist campaign, conducted, as he stated, "with a view to influencing the British and other governments, as well as the League of Nations, in order to take possession of the Western Wall of the Aqṣā Mosque known as the Burāq, or raise claims over the place."

Let us note that the phrase "take possession" in the Mufti's protest is precisely the same as that used by the responsible Jewish and Zionist authorities in their secret demands quoted above. The Mufti was thus neither misrepresenting the real Jewish and Zionist designs nor even exaggerating them. He cited twelve written protests submitted previously against attempts to change the *status quo* by the Jews. The history of the case traced above confirms his reminder that the Jews had converted "a mere favour" into a right, not merely of access but also of ultimate possession.

While their secret representations to the British government remained secret, the Zionists made bold to deny, as indeed they have publicly denied their plan for a Jewish state, any designs on the Aqṣā Mosque and the Dome of the Rock. But they said nothing in their denial about the Western Wall and the ground in front of it, the immediate subject of dispute. The Council of the Jews in Palestine issued a similar denial, but reaffirmed their right of worship at the *kothel maaravi* (the western wall), as if this were in dispute. The two official bodies thus left open the question of the Wall itself and the pavement in front of it.

In November, 1928, the British government issued a White Paper endorsing the action of the local authorities in removing the articles introduced by the Jews at the Wall as contrary to the *status quo*. Because of the vehemence of Jewish and Zionist protests, however, the Palestine government invited the two parties early in 1929 to submit documentary evidence in support of their points of view. The Supreme Muslim Council returned a prompt reply with documents including those of 1840 and 1911 cited above, but the Chief Rabbinate failed, despite repeated reminders, to reply.

39

By the summer of 1929, and as a result of press campaigns among
the Arabs and Jews in which religion and politics became hopelessly
entangled, feelings ran high on both sides. As the chairman of the
Council of Jews in Palestine told the officer administering the government in August, Jewish feeling was "getting worked up over the
Wailing Wall." The sixteenth Zionist Congress was then sitting at
Zurich. It passed a resolution that the *kothel maaravi* was "the place of
prayer sanctified by an unbroken tradition of centuries," and that "it is
the unalterable right" of the Jews to comply at it with their religious
ordinances.

In plain language this compliance meant an insistence on bringing to
the Wall the articles forbidden by the legal government of the country.
Plainer language was used in English by the *Palestine Weekly,* and
plainer still in Hebrew by the right-wing *Doar Hayom* which called
upon all Jews in and outside Palestine not to rest "until the entire Wall
has been restored to us . . . Those of us who are here will not rest
until that relic, which has always been ours, . . . has been restored to
us."

Two days later, the eve of the anniversary of the destruction of the
Temple, some six thousand members of the Haganah and smaller
paramilitary organizations demonstrated in Tel Aviv, and passed a
resolution calling for "the redemption of the Wall." Three days later
still, a few hundred youths from Tel Aviv arrived in Jerusalem with the
declared intention of holding a demonstration, with or without official
permission, at the Wailing Wall. The demonstration had to pass
through Arab and Muslim quarters. At the Wall, the Zionist flag was
hoisted, the Jewish national anthem was sung, and some cries were
raised such as "the Wall is ours."

Needless to say this caused a great stir among the Arabs. The
following day was a Friday, and the eve of the Prophet's birthday.
After the midday prayer the shaikhs of al-Aqṣā Mosque led the
worshippers to the Wall and back in a protest demonstration. The
Mufti fulfilled a promise to the government that he would restrict the
demonstration to that route and not let it go even through purely Arab
and Muslim quarters.

On August 23 widespread disorders broke out in Jerusalem and
elsewhere in Palestine. The Shaw Commission came to investigate the
disorders later in the year and visited the Wailing Place. Their report
states that the ground on which the Jews had been accustomed to stand

40

in front of the western wall of the Ḥaram for devotion was eleven feet in width and its total area 120 square yards. The ground was surrounded on the other three sides by dwelling houses belonging to the Abū Madyan foundation. The Jews gained access to the ground only from the north side through a narrow lane. In 1929, and before the disturbances broke out, the Abū Madyan Zāwiyah on the south side, between the Wailing Place and the Maghāribah Gate of the Ḥaram, was revived. On the western side of the eleven-foot wide Wailing Place there were two doorways leading to houses inhabited by the beneficiaries of the Abū Madyan foundation.

With the political recommendations of the Shaw Report we are not directly concerned. The commissioners, however, regarded the Wailing Wall question as of such importance as to urge, in anticipation of their report, the early appointment of an *ad hoc* commission as provided for in the mandate to determine the rights and claims.

Accordingly the appointment of an international commission under the chairmanship of Eliel Löfgren, former Swedish minister for foreign affairs, was approved by the Council of the League of Nations. The commission heard evidence from the Arabs and Jews in Palestine and submitted its report in December, 1930.

It is important to record that the Jews formally asked the commission to recommend measures to be taken for the evacuation of the inhabitants of the Maghāribah quarter and their settlement elsewhere. Without specifically saying so, the Jews repeated in 1930 Weizmann's offer in 1918 to "buy" an inalienable land, the property of an ancient religious foundation. The commission made no such recommendation, but they insisted on the imperative necessity of banning all speeches and political demonstrations at the Wall. On the main issue they reached two conclusions:

1. The Western Wall was an exclusively Muslim *waqf* property and part of a Muslim holy place, al-Ḥaram ash-Sharīf area. The pavement in front of the Wall and between it and the Maghāribah quarter was also a Muslim *waqf* property and formed part of a legally constituted religious foundation.
2. The Jews have the right of access to the Western Wall for devotion on the pavement, and should be permitted on specific occasions to bring specified articles pertaining to acts of Jewish devotion.

These conclusions confirm the Muslim legal right of ownership and the Jewish customary right of access. But they limited the former by extending the latter, through the recommendation of allowing certain articles which the Jews had tried for decades to introduce. However, the acceptance of the commission's report, with these conclusions, by Britain and the League of Nations made it legally binding as an international document. By an order-in-council, 1931, it became law in Palestine.

12.

No sooner had the question of the Wailing Wall been adjudicated than the fears of the Arabs of Palestine for their political future were aroused to a greater extent than at any time since 1917. Following the rise of the Nazi party to power in Germany there was an alarming increase in Jewish immigration. An average of nine thousand per annum during the first decade of the mandate rose to nearly sixty-two thousand in 1935. The Arab leaders saw that at this rate a Jewish majority, and all that it entailed, was a real possibility in some fifteen years' time. With no constitutional means for safeguards against eventual subjugation to Jewish rule, the Arabs rose in a revolt which lasted nearly three years and required two divisions of British troops to suppress it.

A belated British attempt to do justice to the Arabs was defeated by the combined forces of Zionism, influential British politicians including Winston Churchill, and powerful pressure groups in the United States. The postwar attempts were even less successful, since Zionism had now become more powerful following the adoption of the United States instead of Britain as the guardian of its interests. Thus a scheme of partitioning Palestine was strongly supported by the United States, and it was largely due to American influence that partition was adopted by the United Nations General Assembly in November, 1947. Under the scheme of partition Jerusalem and Bethlehem with their environs were constituted as an international enclave to be placed under a high commissioner appointed by the United Nations.

But this was not to be. Immediately after the scheme of partition was adopted, and for six months preceding the British withdrawal and the proclamation of Israel, the Arabs and Jews became locked in a deadly struggle, the former to prevent and the latter to enforce partition. It is to the discredit of those who honor Jerusalem that they did not shrink from making it a battlefield. Their failure in this matter recalls the action of the much maligned German Emperor, William II, who on perceiving in 1917 that the British advance on Jerusalem could not be beaten off, expressed a wish to the Turkish high command to spare the Holy City the horrors of war. It was largely to gratify this wish that the Turks retired without fighting near or in Jerusalem.

In the spring of 1948, when the scale of Arab-Jewish hostilities demonstrated to the United Nations that partition could not be executed peacefully, the idea of a trusteeship for Palestine as a whole was suggested. Simultaneously, and in response to world concern for the holy places in Jerusalem, the Security Council adopted a unanimous resolution calling for a truce. But the representative of the Jewish Agency refused to accept the call unless it did not prejudice the Assembly's resolution on partition and the establishment of a Jewish state.

He declared that without the "enforcement" of partition, the Jews would have to "defend" Jerusalem lest it should fall "under the tyranny of the infamous and impious Arabs." This was said when most of the city outside the walls, including purely Arab areas, was in Jewish occupation, and when about seven hundred members of the Haganah and terrorist groups were entrenched inside the walls in the Jewish quarter which had been cleared except for a few civilians. Seen in the light of these facts the Jewish refusal to accept the truce concealed an intention to attack the Arab parts of the city within the wall where all the holy places were located.

On the other hand, the Arab League issued a statement accepting the truce in Jerusalem and undertaking to safeguard the holy places within the walls and to extend the truce also to the Mount of Olives. The statement called attention to the past Arab record in recognizing and safeguarding the holy places of all faiths in Jerusalem.

But meanwhile the balance of military strength in Palestine was shifting in favor of the Jews who proceeded to "enforce" the establishment of the state even while the country was still under British control and the Arab states unable to interfere. From the first week in April the Arabs in Palestine began to lose the initiative, largely owing to the panic which the Jews created among the civilian population. It was enough to blow up by dynamite an Arab village here, and to massacre the entire population including women and children of another there, to cause dislocation and to start a stream of refugees.

43

Thus before the end of the mandate, and while Britain had the right of sovereignty and the duty of maintaining law and order, a great deal of Arab lands and villages, outside the boundaries assigned by the United Nations for a Jewish state, were occupied by the Jews. Small wonder that their leaders turned a cold shoulder to the British high commissioner who was actively trying to negotiate a truce with them. Moreover, they rejected out of hand the Red Cross suggestion to convert the old city of Jerusalem into a hospital.

When the British mandate came to an end on May 15, 1948, the expected Jewish attack on the old city began immediately on three sides, in a determined effort to link up with those entrenched in the Jewish quarter and to take the city by storm. This was prevented in the nick of time by the intervention of Transjordan. Apart from national and political considerations, King Abdullah was deeply involved on the religious and personal levels. No one knew better the place of Jerusalem in Islam than he, the son of the sharif of Mecca, a descendant of the Prophet. Indeed, the Sharif himself, who died in exile as King Ḥusain of Hijaz, was, by his own wish, buried in a special chamber in one of the cloisters on the west side of the Ḥaram.

If Jerusalem, especially the old city, became a battlefield, it was not by Abdullah's choosing. He came to the rescue after, not before, the Jewish attack and the Jewish refusal of a truce. The besieged Jewish garrison fought his army desperately even from the main synagogue. They surrendered only after it had been destroyed over their heads. This fact needs to be underlined, for Zionist propaganda blames the Arabs for the destruction of this synagogue. (It must not be forgotten that during the British mandate the police discovered a virtual arsenal in the basement of the great synagogue in Tel Aviv.)

Those who show such scant respect to their own places of worship can scarcely be expected to behave better toward the places of worship belonging to other communities. Thus after the proclamation of Israel, the Ḥaram was repeatedly attacked with mortar, machine gun, and rifle fire. Sixty bombs fell on the area in a single attack. As a result of these attacks four worshippers were killed and five wounded including one of the shaikhs of the Ḥaram. The Dome of the Rock was hit in several places, and some of the matchless mosaic and the stained glass in the windows was destroyed. The Aqṣā Mosque, on a lower level than the Dome, was less exposed to direct hits but nevertheless sustained

44

material damage. One bomb made a hole in the roof and several windows were broken.

Nor did the Holy Sepulchre and other Christian holy places escape unscathed. Thus in their attempt to seize the holy city, the Jews spared none of the Christian and Muslim holy places, nor indeed their own places of worship.

When the armistice lines were agreed, the old city remained in the Jordanian sector, but as subsequent events proved, the Zionists never ceased to entertain the ambition of one day taking old Jerusalem and the rest of Palestine. The opportunity came on June 5, 1967, when Israel began a simultaneous and surprise attack on three Arab states, Egypt, Jordan, and Syria. At eight minutes past 8 A.M. an official Israeli communiqué, in a characteristic Zionist fashion, thus misrepresented the facts to the world:

> Since the early hours of this morning there has been fierce fighting against armoured units and the air force of Egypt which attacked Israel. Our troops went into action to repulse them.

How different the truth turned out to be is now common knowledge. The communiqué said nothing about Jordan or Jerusalem. But according to Randolph Churchill, a notorious pro-Zionist who was permitted to reproduce the official Israeli military diary of events in Jerusalem on 5 June:

> at 0800 air-raid alarms were sounded by the orders of General Narkis.
> at 0910 Narkis spoke on the telephone with the mayor of the Israeli sector, and told him: "It is war. . . . You may as well be mayor of a united Jerusalem."
> at 0911 Amman Radio announces that Jordan was being attacked.

Churchill's story, based entirely on Israeli military sources, confirms that the Jordanians fought like lions against overwhelming odds outside the city walls, but did not fight inside the old city where all the holy places were located. He also confirms that the Muslim quarter in the old city was shelled and that Israeli aircraft went into action when no resistance was being offered. The Jordanians in 1967, much the same as the Turks in 1917, retired before superior force out of respect for the holiness of the city.

On reaching the Wailing Wall on June 7 the Israeli minister of

45

defense repeated the old Zionist cry "The Wall is ours." A few days later a sign in Hebrew was placed at the foot of the Wall reading *Bet ha-Kenesset* (synagogue).

Meanwhile the United Nations called for a cease-fire, but Israel was bent on exploiting the initial advantage of surprise attack by occupying more and more Arab territory before complying. As regards Jerusalem, no time was lost by Israel in proclaiming its annexation, despite warning from friendly countries that this would prejudice the chances of a peace settlement. On July 5, therefore, the United Nations General Assembly passed a resolution by a majority of 99, with 20 abstentions, which declared Israel's measures in Jerusalem as invalid and called upon it to rescind them. When the resolution was ignored, another was passed on July 12, viewing with deep concern Israel's neglect to comply, repeating the previous call, and asking Israel to refrain from taking any measures for changing the status of Jerusalem.

Israel did not even attend the meeting. It is noteworthy that there were no votes against either resolution and that the United States abstained on both occasions. All the other great and major powers voted for the resolution. And in addition to the Arab states all the Islamic states, including secular Turkey, voted for it. Before the Assembly session was closed, the secretary-general reported that Israel had ignored the resolutions and declared moreover that its measures were irrevocable and the annexation of Jerusalem not subject to negotiation.

The two resolutions by the General Assembly adopted in July, 1967, were buttressed by a similar one taken by the Security Council on May 21, 1968. But Israel treated the Council with the same contempt with which it had treated the Assembly: it refused to respect any of their resolutions.

13.

Thus by force of arms Israel wishes to impose her sovereignty over the Christian and Muslim holy places. Zionist propaganda has now made the Western Wall of the Ḥaram, confirmed as the third holy place in Islam by the League of Nations, a main pivot of Israel's claim to a city overwhelmingly Christian and Muslim Arab in population, and containing only Christian and Muslim holy places and no Jewish.

The assault on the Ḥaram by the chief rabbi of the Israeli army and his holding of a public Jewish prayer not at the Wailing Wall, but inside the Ḥaram area, was perhaps a feeler. But it confirmed the worst fears of the Muslims: first prayer at the Wall, then the Wall itself, and finally the restoration of the old Temple.

A more concrete assault was made by the government of Israel on the area to the west of the Wailing Wall, an area hallowed by the Prophet's nocturnal journey, and thrice dedicated as a Muslim religious foundation, the first by the son of Saladin. This is precisely the inalienable *waqf* property of which the Zionists did their utmost to obtain possession since 1918. Now the inhabitants, beneficiaries of such ancient Muslim religious foundations, have been forcibly removed, their houses leveled, and the land confiscated "with compensation." Never has Islam been flouted in Jerusalem, and never has an inalienable property of a Muslim religious foundation in it been confiscated, since the days of the Crusades.

The modern Crusaders even more than the old abide only by the rule that might is right. They have never forgiven the tenacity of the Maghāribah since 1840. Their shaikh then felt that the Jews had "ultimate aims." Despite repeated denials, time proved him right, and his successors and their families have now to pay the maximum penalty for resisting Jewish encroachment.

I cannot help recalling, in conclusion, a lone voice raised in 1919 at the Foreign Office in London. Like the shaikh of the Maghāribah, the head of the Middle East section saw the ultimate consequences of the Zionist policy of the British government. The occasion was a recommendation by Balfour of a certain course of action favorable to the Zionists. One civil servant minuted that the proposal would put the Jews in a privileged position from the start. But the head of the section, who had called attention to that before without effect, now wrote in despair:

> Take action as required. . . . I understand that the Zionist wolf and the anti-Zionist lamb have decided to lie down together in the fat pastures of Jordan, and whether the lamb finishes inside the wolf is no concern of ours.

The lamb was, of course, *forced* to consort with the wolf, and ended where foreseen. The wolf, brought up by Britain, and declared to have attained the age of majority by the United Nations, has since shown no gratitude to the former and little respect for the latter. No member state which owed its legal existence to the United Nations has repeatedly disregarded its resolutions more than Israel. No other member state has to its discredit so many resolutions by the Security Council condemning its conduct.

Toward Islam and the Muslim religious foundations, Israel showed now and since 1948 no respect for religious or even international law. By occupying Palestine the modern Crusaders have earned the enmity of all Arabs; by seizing Jerusalem that of all Muslims. Are the modern Crusaders bent on forcing history to repeat itself?

Prelude to War:
The Crisis of
May–June 1967

In early May, 1967, certain indications led many observers to believe that Israel was preparing for massive military action against Syria. Retaliatory action had been carried out a month earlier against Syria when Israeli air strikes were made on April 7 only a few miles from Damascus. On November 13, 1966, massive action had been taken against the Jordanian village of Al-Sammū‘, in which a number of Jordanian civilians and soldiers were killed and a large part of the village was leveled. The cause of these attacks, according to official Israeli statements, was increasing Arab guerrilla activity on the Israeli side of the armistice line.

The crisis took shape as intelligence reports began to come in about Israeli troop deployment along the Syrian-Israeli border. On May 8, two Syrian intelligence officers arrived in Cairo and informed President Nasser of an impending Israeli attack against Damascus. Information concerning troop movements was corroborated by Lebanese sources. By May 10, according to Eric Rouleau, *Le Monde*'s Cairo correspondent, President Nasser had become convinced that Israel was in fact making preparations to attack Damascus and overthrow the Ba‘th regime. His view was confirmed when the Russians informed him that the Israelis had timed a swift strike at the Syrian regime for the end of May "in order to crush it and then carry the fighting over into the territory of the U.A.R." In Tel Aviv, Israeli leaders, including General Rabin, spoke publicly of attacking Damascus and demanded the immediate cessation of guerrilla activity. The *New York Times* correspondent in Tel Aviv reported on May 12 that Israeli authorities had already decided that the use of force against Syria "may be the only

49

way to curtail increasing terrorism." President Nasser believed, according to Rouleau, that the Israeli attack would take place within the next few days, on or about May 17.

In retrospect, it is ironic to note how Israel's actions in May, 1967, served to intensify precisely those conditions which they were supposed to alleviate. Israel was determined to put an end to the nascent Palestinian guerrilla movement. The Israeli leaders had begun to realize that the Palestinian Arabs were engaged in a serious effort at organizing themselves as an independent force and that a Palestinian revolutionary movement was afoot. Al-Fateh, the Palestinian liberation movement, now appeared as more than a mere handful of "infiltrators" and "terrorists." Israel, by persistently attributing resistance activity to Syrians, Egyptians, and Jordanians, had succeeded in obscuring the real nature of this activity as an autonomous Palestinian revolutionary movement. Israel's policy has been to refuse to acknowledge the existence of the Palestinian Arabs, referring to them simply as "the Arab refugees." This has enabled Israel to fight the guerrillas by means of retaliatory action against its neighbors in accordance with its basic strategic principle of always waging war on Arab soil, never on its own.

It is probably in large part because of the new dimension which the Palestinian guerrilla movement represented (as an *internal* movement of resistance it violated the fundamental principles upon which the concept of Israeli "defense" was based) that the reaction to increasing activity by Al-Fateh was so strong in early 1967. Israel's theory of punitive retaliation underwent radical transformation both in structure and goal. It was no longer sufficient to "teach its neighbors a lesson"; it was now necessary for Israel to impose its explicit will on them. Thus the retaliatory raid gave way to military strikes aimed at repressing or overthrowing recalcitrant and undesirable regimes. With this new policy Israel could kill two birds with one stone: it could destroy the Palestinian resistance movement in embryo and maintain "peace" and "stability" in the surrounding regimes. In May, 1967, the crisis gathered momentum as a direct result of Israel's intention to do something about the Ba'th regime in Damascus. This marked not only an escalation of Israel's political and military aggressiveness but also a self-conscious expansion of its role in the broader context of a United States–Soviet confrontation in the Middle East.

Seen in this light, the situation in May looked ominous, even by Middle Eastern standards. For Israel's immediate neighbors it appeared that unless something were done they might have to submit to a new kind of threat from Israel. Their first obligation, however, with regard to Syria was to suppress the Palestinian movement in their midst.

Israel's new attitude implied another and equally serious warning. The U.A.R., as well as the other "progressive" states, was convinced that the overthrow of the Ba'th regime would seriously upset the balance of forces in the Arab world in favor of Zionism and its allies, the "conservative" regimes and colonialism. There was a general consensus among all revolutionary elements in the Arab world that the American-Israeli offensive in the area would have to be arrested. Syria was not the real issue but rather the symbol and immediate cause of the confrontation.

As in past years when collectively threatened, the Arabs turned to the U.A.R. and Gamal Abdul Nasser for guidance and leadership. In the U.A.R. events followed rapidly. The armed forces were put under a state of emergency on May 16; later the same day the commander of the United Nations Emergency Force (UNEF) in Sinai was handed a letter from General Fawzi, the chief of the Egyptian Armed Forces, asking him "to withdraw all U.N. troops immediately" from the Egyptian-Israeli border and from Sharm el-Sheikh. On May 18, U Thant gave orders to UNEF to withdraw from the U.A.R. He said he had serious misgivings about this move but could not refuse the U.A.R. "without putting into question the sovereign authority of the government of the United Arab Republic within its own territory." Foreign minister Mahmoud Riad explained the same day to the representatives of the nations with troops in UNEF that the emergency force had completed its tasks and was no longer needed in the Gaza Strip and the U.A.R.

On the following day, May 19, Israel conveyed to the Western powers that it would fight any move to close Aqaba and cut off shipping. It maintained that former president Eisenhower had agreed that such an event would entitle Israel to rectify the situation with U.N. support. On May 22, in a speech given at air-force headquarters in Sinai, President Nasser announced the closure of the Straits of Tiran to all ships flying the Israeli flag or carrying strategic materials to Israel.

51

We are now face to face with Israel and if they want to try their luck without Britain and France we await them. The Israeli flag will not pass through the Gulf of Aqaba and our sovereignty over the entrance to the Gulf is not negotiable. If Israel wants to threaten us with war they are welcome.

On May 30 Jordan (followed later by Iraq) concluded a mutual-defense pact with the U.A.R.

It was probably at this point, or perhaps a day or two earlier, that the Egyptian president decided that the Israeli threat to Syria had abated sufficiently to allow him to de-escalate Egyptian military pressure. At a press conference on May 30 attended by representatives of the world's major newspapers and news agencies, he declared that the U.A.R. did not want war but that if attacked it would have to repel aggression. He suggested that the Palestine Mixed Armistice Commission be revived to supervise the phased withdrawal of Egyptian and Israeli forces from the armistice lines and offered to take the question of the Straits of Tiran to the International Court of Justice for adjudication. In an interview on June 3 with Anthony Nutting he emphasized that so far as the U.A.R. was concerned the Middle East crisis had eased and no further escalation was planned. He was reported to have given the impression that he shared the Soviet and French view that war should definitely be avoided.

At the time that Nasser, and behind him the U.S.S.R., was seeking a way to avoid war Israel had apparently opted for war.

In Amman on June 4, King Hussein warned Britain and the United States that they stood to lose their friends in the Arab world "forever" if they fell into the "Zionist trap." And in Tel Aviv the appointment of Moshe Dayan as defense minister was welcomed by the Israeli army with the expectation that they would see more action. In Washington on June 4, a warm Sunday afternoon, the atmosphere was alive with rumors of an impending explosion in the Middle East.

In Tel Aviv, as well as in Washington, sufficient intelligence had been available to show with certainty that a pre-emptive strike by Israel would result in a swift Israeli victory which within days would bring about the collapse not only of the Ba'th regime in Damascus but also of Nasser in the U.A.R. When Israeli planes attacked shortly after sunrise on Monday, June 5, a new chapter was being written in the political life of the Arab world.

52

2.

Looking back at Egyptian military and diplomatic moves in May and early June, one is struck by their overwhelmingly deterrent character. Note, for instance, the theatrical aspect of Egyptian troop movements through the main streets of Cairo in the middle of the day. A near-festive mood was generated by blatant broadcasts reporting every move of Egyptian troops in Sinai. From the beginning of the crisis the U.A.R. was making signals to dissuade Israel from going through with its threats against Damascus. The U.A.R. was addressing not only Israel but also the United States.

In May and June of 1967 the U.A.R. was not prepared to go to war. Some 50,000 Egyptian troops were committed to Yemen, including some of the best-trained soldiers. President Nasser had no illusions as to the military capability of the Arab world. Earlier at Port Said he had put it plainly:

> I am not in a position to go to war; I tell you this frankly, and it is not shameful to say it publicly. To go to war without having the sufficient means would be to lead the country and the people to disaster.

Nasser had read the report put out by the Institute for Strategic Studies in 1965 and probably agreed with its conclusions. In armor the Israelis could expect to knock out at least two Arab tanks for every one of their own, and in the air the "kill ratio" was two or three Arab planes to one Israeli plane.

The Israelis said they would regard the closing of the Gulf of Aqaba to Israeli shipping as an act of war. From the Egyptian standpoint this act was not considered to be irrevocable nor was it thought to be an act that would inevitably lead to war. Nasser's judgment was that he enjoyed room to maneuver without getting too close to the brink. The problem of sovereignty over the gulf was far from settled by American assurances to Israel in 1957. At a news conference on July 16, 1957, Secretary of State John Foster Dulles had acknowledged the questionable status of the gulf.

> There is and always has been a difference of opinion about the international status of the Gulf of Aqaba. The Arab countries believe that

the six-mile limit applies rather than the three-mile limit; and that, since the position of Israel on the Gulf is not fixed by any permanent boundary decision, Israel does not have the right to claim a voice in the access to the Gulf; and that, if the countries which do have permanent boundaries to the Gulf, namely, Egypt, Jordan, and Saudi Arabia, agree to close the Gulf, they think that they have the right to do it. There is a certain amount of plausibility from the standpoint of international law, perhaps, to those claims. This is not the view of the United States.

On May 24, 1967, President Nasser outlined to U Thant in Cairo the following points: the Straits of Tiran should be recognized as Egyptian territorial waters, Israel should fully accept the provisions of the 1949 armistice agreement, the U.N. should be responsible for policing *all* frontiers and demarcation lines, and Israel should strictly observe the demilitarized zones. Nasser's intention was not to restore the *status quo ante bellum* obtained before the Israeli attack of 1956, but that of 1948. As his hand seemed to grow stronger, Nasser thought more and more in terms of the totality of the Palestine problem. In a speech to the Pan-Arab Workers Federation on May 26, he declared that "the Arabs insist on their rights and are determined to regain the rights of the Palestinian people"; and on May 29 he told the members of the Egyptian National Assembly that "the question today is not of Aqaba nor is it the Tiran Straits or the United Nations Emergency Force. It is the rights of the people of Palestine."

President Nasser had achieved a diplomatic victory and was ready to negotiate a political settlement. It is not certain whether the Israeli leaders (or the White House for that matter) fully appreciated this element in the crisis. Now, perhaps for the first time since 1948, the Arab side was in a position to tackle a political settlement of the Palestine problem. The Egyptian president, spokesman for all the Arabs, was at this point capable not only of entering into negotiations but also of contemplating concessions hitherto unthinkable. The central problem was, of course, connected with the rights of the Palestinians. Nasser publicly made it clear that all other problems (including passage through the Suez Canal) were ancillary to the acknowledgment of the rights of the Palestinian Arabs.

As late as June 4, Charles Yost, United States special envoy to Cairo, observed, "there does not seem to have been any intention in Cairo to initiate a war." In an interview two days earlier (broadcast in part in the United States on the evening of June 4) President Nasser told British MP Christopher Mayhew that if the Israelis do not attack, "we will leave them alone. We have no intention of attacking Israel." The U.A.R. sent firm assurances to the United States to this effect and maintained a dialogue with Washington until the hour of the Israeli attack. During this week agreement was reached on a proposed visit by U.A.R. Vice-President Zakaria Mohieddin to Washington and a subsequent return visit by Vice-President Hubert Humphrey.

According to Eric Rouleau, the *Le Monde* correspondent in Cairo, all the U.A.R. required to withdraw its troops from the frontiers was a public declaration by Israel renouncing its intention to attack Syria.

It is probably true that both Washington and Tel Aviv were aware of this fact, but neither seemed willing to leave the U.A.R. with a strong hand. It is now obvious that for Israel the real problem was not one of security: a country which has demonstrated that it can dominate its neighbors militarily could not have entertained serious fears about its security. It seems certain that the Israeli leaders had full knowledge of the U.A.R. military condition (certainly the White House had), and Israel's military superiority was indisputable. It is also probable that the report submitted in late May to President Johnson by Pentagon analysts contained a forecast very close to the events which actually took place in the week of June 5.

In this light, the events of the preceding days of crisis had favored Israeli interests. Indeed, the situation was slowly building up in a way that was giving Israel increasing freedom of action. In retrospect it is evident that Israel's real intention was not to "damp" the crisis or to "de-fuse" it. The problem for Israel's leaders was to choose the appropriate moment to strike. This decision was tied to certain preconditions. What were these preconditions? One, certainly, was a favorable world opinion siding with a "beleaguered little country" defending itself against numerically superior forces. On the diplomatic level, another was a disunited and neutralized United Nations. United States backing, or at least tacit approval of Israel's policy, was an essential precondition.

Did the United States give the green light to Israel? Was there American-Israeli collusion? And, after the outbreak of war, was there American assistance, or a promise of assistance in case things went wrong? Of course, definite answers to these questions cannot be given

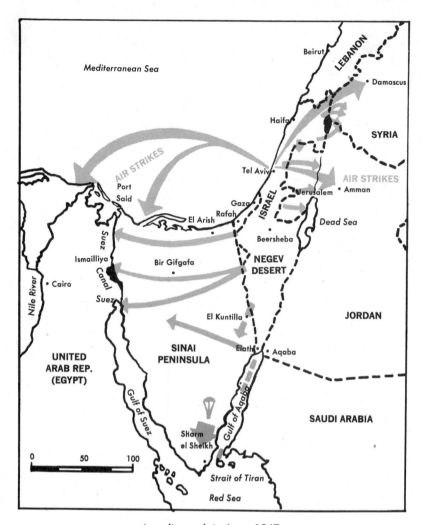

Israeli attack in June, 1967

now and will have to await revelations which only time will make possible.

It is not surprising that President Nasser's signaled promises—withdrawal of troops, adjudication of the Aqaba question, political settlement of outstanding issues—were ignored. From Israel's standpoint, the anticipated rewards of military action certainly exceeded those of diplomatic negotiations. Israel acted, not spontaneously in fear or in anger, but calmly, in the light of careful calculations based on exten-

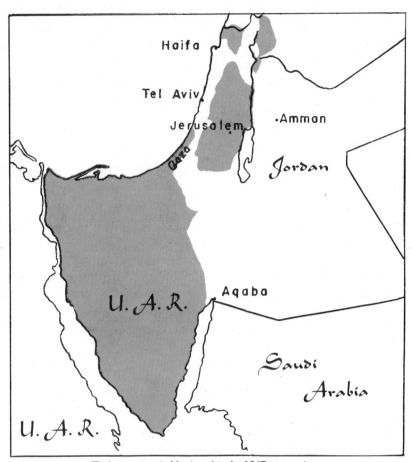

Areas occupied by Israel in the 1967 aggression

sive intelligence and highly sophisticated analysis of the overall political and military situation. For the Arabs, the cost was enormous: a crushing military defeat, with some 20,000 soldiers killed; over 500,000 new refugees, including 120,000 Syrians and 250,000 Egyptians; and occupation of the entire area from the Suez Canal to the Jordan River as well as the Syrian Golan Heights, some thirty miles from Damascus.

How did the war start? Ambassador Yost expressed the view of many observers when he stated, "no government plotted or intended to start the war." The war was the product of circumstances beyond the control of any of the parties involved. But what were the conditions

57

under which the situation went out of control? Why did Israel spurn a political settlement when this was possible? How can we explain Israel's overnight transformation from a supposedly threatened, helpless country to a conquering military power?

The answers to these questions are to be sought not in the crisis itself but in an analysis of Israel's overall strategy.

3.

Israel, like the United States, bases its strategy on the principle of total preparedness, on the theory of total force. It is a policy predicated on the belief that the all-consuming passion of a country's enemy is to destroy it; only the enemy's realization of Israel's invincibility and of its own vulnerability prevents it from doing so. Hence the overriding concern of this policy is to determine the costs required to maintain military superiority and to preserve a correct estimate of the enemy's awareness of and responses to this military position.

Israel can have only an aggressive policy, not just because of strategic considerations (small territory, long borders, population size, etc.) but also because it is rooted in a movement of colonization. It acts with the knowledge that in the eyes of its adversaries it is not a "state" but a usurper of conquered land. Its relationship with its adversary is thus based solely on force—a relationship which precludes any objective grounds of legitimation that might allow for bargaining in terms of a mutually acceptable "maximum." Settlement for Israel has to be enforced. In its view, the adversary should have only one position from which to bargain, that of the conquered. And precisely because of the lack of any binding legitimacy the adversary has to be kept in a condition of constant and effective threat. This position necessitates an offensive posture not only in war but also in peace; a dominating diplomacy becomes the condition of every non-military approach. What are the aims of this diplomacy? They are, simply, to keep the adversary constantly on the receiving end, where he will always be eager to receive but always incapable of determining the price of what he receives. This is the substitute for legitimation which sets the relation between conqueror and conquered on a level where enforced equilibrium provides for the conqueror the promise of progressively increasing stability.

A distinctive characteristic of Zionist strategy is that it is directed

58

not at resolving conflict but at protracting it. The resolution of conflict would necessarily require concessions and the relinquishing of gains forcibly acquired; it threatens not only to stifle an expansive orientation but also to undermine Israeli strategy at its inception. Thus a primary tactic of Zionist diplomacy is to bring about those conditions which would temporarily suspend conflict but which would introduce no radical change in the *status quo*. By disengagement, by creating distance and blocking or channeling contact, a *modus vivendi* is created out of a violently accomplished fact, and the conditions for an equilibrium which in time would bring about a sense of mutual benefit are set up. For the conquered the payoff is necessarily assessed in relative terms, hence every little gain would represent a bonus and an incentive to acquiesce.

To Israel, attitudes of compromise on the Arab side (from the Geneva Protocol of 1949 on) have always been a source of embarrassment and have always been spurned. President Habib Bourgiba's conciliatory position regarding the Arab-Israeli conflict, far from bringing relief to Tel Aviv, provoked profound discomfort in Israel's leadership circles. A compromising attitude on the part of Israel would require a radical transformation in its diplomatic-military thinking and a shift from offensive to conciliatory strategy. Israel is not yet prepared to make such a shift. It is probably correct to say that Israel needs some fifty years of friction and tension to enable it to build itself economically and establish strong and stable institutions capable of bringing about conditions of permanent equilibrium. Thus, from the standpoint of Israel's dominating diplomacy the final resolution of conflict is possible only when the tactics of protracted conflict reach their limit and become irrelevant. This goal cannot be achieved until a position of domination has been reached and continuing conflict is no longer required to sustain equilibrium.

This diplomatic-military strategy must assign high priority to the policy of territorial expansion. Expansionism is an expression of a policy of force, but it is also a reaction to a "yielding environment." As Arthur Koestler (a former Zionist) put it, "A yielding environment acts as a vacuum, a constant incentive for further expansion." It may be necessary to add that beyond a certain point it would be disadvantageous for Israel to expand. What is the limit of Israeli expansion? Its final determination will depend mainly on the outcome of the diplomatic-military conflict. But the general outline of the territorial extent of the Jewish state has been adumbrated by various spokesmen since 1919. One of the more recent statements was made by the Israeli prime minister following the war of 1967 (as quoted by Rouleau in *Le Monde*):

> We are not disposed to give up one inch of our territory; negotiations must begin from the recognition of the existing territorial *status quo*. Palestine was cut up in the course of the First World War by the Sykes-Picot Agreement; it was divided a second time by the creation of Transjordan by Churchill; and it was divided a third time in 1948. We cannot accept a fourth amputation. . . . No more than 20,000 kilometers are left of old Palestine. It is our hope that in the next few decades millions of Jews will be able to emigrate from Russia, Europe, and the United States.

The Suez Canal in the U.A.R., the Litani River in Lebanon, the Jabel Druz in Syria, and the eastern boundaries of Jordan are the frontiers of a greater Israel which would be acceptable to all Israelis, from Gahal to the Zionist faction of the Communist Party. Israel's optimum policy would aim to surround itself with a ring of weak and subservient states—a Maronite state, a Druze state, a "Palestinian state," a Kurdish state—extending from the Persian Gulf to the Mediterranean and to enforce a *Pax Judaica* over the entire region.

A cardinal principle of the hard strategy which is at the basis of all Israeli political and military thinking is the necessity always to carry "defensive" war outside Israel's boundaries and never to allow its boundaries to be penetrated. (Guerrilla warfare and a "people's war of liberation," since they are not subject to this principle, are threats which require a different strategy.) Thus defensive war is necessarily preventive war. Israel cannot allow itself to give up the incentive to preempt territory. For it equates its security with the capacity at all times to anticipate and thwart the enemy's power of pre-emption. An important corollary of this strategic thinking is related to the problem of boundaries. So long as the objective possibilities for pursuing a hard strategy exist, Israel will seek to adjust its boundaries through territorial expansion. It has no other choice, given the external conditions of surrounding Arab weakness. Next to military preparedness, the question of boundaries constitutes the most important element of Israeli diplomatic-military strategy.

Under what conditions, in terms of this hard strategy, would Israel consider itself compelled to engage in all-out "defensive" (preventive) war? Precisely when the fundamental principles on which its hard strategy is based are violated: for example, when the U.A.R. (or any other neighboring Arab state) acquires new weapons which might upset Israel's position of unconditional viability; when its real or "distant" boundaries are seriously threatened as they were by Egyptian action in the Straits of Tiran; or when a nationalist revolutionary government takes over in Jordan or Lebanon. In the future Israel may also feel it necessary to launch a "defensive" war against its neighbors in order to put an end to Palestinian guerrilla activity. During periods of peace Israel has depended on circumscribed retaliatory expeditions following punitive threats as a primary weapon of limited action. In this situation the threat is to be regarded as a diplomatic weapon decisive in the process of bargaining. Diplomacy, as a system of threats (and promises), gives way to retaliation or war only when it fails or when it breaks down. Short of military action, the threat of war, "punitive" or "defensive," is the crucial element dominating the course of conflict.

What makes the Israeli threat convincing and therefore effective? Or, viewed from the Arab standpoint, what makes the Israeli threat credible? To carry out a threat one must have the means at one's disposal and the will to use those means. If a threat is to be credible, a sufficient proportion of threats made must be carried out—enough that the party threatened will take all threats seriously. The efficacy of threats then lies in their power to elicit or at least greatly influence the performance of the threatened party in the desired manner.

Israel's strategic position focuses on four different levels: the first is concerned with Jordan, Syria, Lebanon, and Iraq; the second with the Arab states in general, including those of North Africa; the third with the U.A.R.; and the fourth with the Palestinian Arabs. The latter two may be regarded as decisive at least for the foreseeable future.

Israel's relation to the Palestinians is that of an occupying power and a conquered people. Dispossessed and in disarray, the Palestinians have lost all viability as a people. But out of total negation there has arisen a resistance which has now taken the form of organized total revolution. (In contrast, Arab opposition to Israel in North Africa and Arabia is still only potentially effective and in its present state stands at the opposite pole to the urgent actuality of Palestinian resistance.) Israel's position vis-à-vis Jordan, Syria, Lebanon, and Iraq is one of strength with the potential for domination. Only with respect to the U.A.R. is Israel's superiority conditional, placing the two states in a relationship of conditional viability toward one another. It is this mutually conditional viability which tends to make the Arab-Israeli conflict (on the formal military and diplomatic levels) primarily an Egyptian-Israeli conflict. The only real military threat to Israel is the U.A.R. Similarly no decisive political action can be undertaken by Israel with respect to any other Arab state without the U.A.R.'s participation or tacit consent.

It is worth noting here that there exists a factor which could radically transform Israel's position with regard to the U.A.R. and its other Arab neighbors, but not necessarily with regard to the Palestinian guerrilla fighters. If Israel were to acquire an effective rocket system (for example, the MD680) together with a nuclear tactical weapons system it would become unconditionally viable and at the same time its neighbors, including the U.A.R., would be reduced to virtual impotence.

What would be the political consequences of such a situation? The acquisition of a similar weapons system by the U.A.R. would restore the balance of arms but would create a new situation—though still in Israel's favor. The neutralization of the conflict militarily would set it permanently against a strictly political background. Under these conditions the *fait accompli* becomes the core of the *status quo* and with time solidifies into permanent structures. It is at this point that Israel's hard strategy reaches its final limit and is transformed into a conciliatory strategy. The need for protracted conflict would no longer obtain.

4.

Self-criticism after the Arab defeat tended to begin with the premise that in order to confront Israel the Arabs must acquire an advanced scientific and technological culture. The theoretical validity of this principle is obvious, but it lacks practical relevance to immediate problems. The situation of conflict is a concrete historical situation to which any desideratum, whether of mental attitude or of technological proficiency, is related only theoretically and in an abstract way. What is decisive to the outcome of conflict, particularly to a political-military conflict having immediate bearing on the fate of millions of people, is not *potential power* but rather available *actualized* power. Certainly, to be effective, especially in war, one has to modernize and acquire the requisite technological know-how, but can the Arabs modernize while they are locked in unequal combat? Can they, when their freedom of social and political action is threatened daily, plan even for modernization?

The Arabs' shortcomings are near at hand and can be seen plainly without much recourse to theoretical analysis. On the technical level the Arabs suffered in the June War from such things as miscalculation, faulty intelligence, inability to convey messages, and inadequate communication. Necessity may still bring to bear the required funds and energies to insure needed reforms. Response here is not to a desired goal that one sets up but to vital necessity. There is a qualitative difference in action animated by the will to survive and mere incentive to reform. The revolutionary element is set into motion by the first, the second comes in its train. In the end what is *available* in will, energy, and material resources is decisive for revolutionary change. Thus what is concretely accomplished, and that alone, will determine Arab viability in the continuing conflict.

Three interrelated aspects of Arab diplomacy have contributed to the success of Israel's hard strategy. In the first place, the Arab side, by the nature of its position, has had restricted or limited freedom of action on both the diplomatic and military levels. This is plainly illustrated by the decisions and events of the critical days preceding the Israeli attacks on the U.A.R., Jordan, and Syria in June, 1967. The Arabs, incapable of devising a unified strategy, were incapable of carrying out a rational military plan. Because they could not admit the principle of compromise in the diplomatic field, they were always forced into a position of inflexibility and retreat before the highly mobile diplomacy of their adversary.

The Arab side denied itself the advantage of the political and diplomatic offensive by placing itself in a position where it could not make fundamental concessions. Israel, basing its policy on a hard strategy which also precluded basic concessions, was able to use Arab inflexibility to appear always willing to reach a reasonable settlement. The same structural limitation which has prevented the Arabs from seizing the political and diplomatic initiative has prevented them from seizing the military initiative. In the May–June crisis President Nasser's hand was from the very beginning greatly weakened by his adversary's knowledge that the U.A.R. was not likely to pre-empt a strike.

63

Arab diplomacy has always given Israel's hard strategy optimum advantages in both war and peace. In peace it has contributed to Israel's capacity to sustain the stable disequilibrium which always worked in its favor, for it served to consolidate the *fait accompli.* And in war it enabled Israel to engage in "punitive" and "defensive" strikes which have hitherto allowed Israel to expand territorially and to establish the effective system of retaliatory threats that have safeguarded its gains.

Secondly, one must consider the inescapably "irrational," or at least only partly rational, character of the decisions and choices of Arab diplomacy. What we call the Arab side does not in reality constitute a single entity; it has no coordinated organizational arrangements, no unified political or military structure, no adequate communications and information systems. Inherent in Arab agreements is a multiplicity of conflicting decisions, desires, intentions; formal collective agreements lack substantive content and as a result have little practical import. Israel's dependence on this fragmentation of Arab will, and on its corresponding practical ineffectiveness, figures significantly in Israeli strategic thinking and action.

Finally, the Arab position is bound to a "radical" view of the Palestine question; this is at once a source of great strength and of great weakness. Arab opinion, official as well as popular, is founded on right as the basis of all claims to Palestine. From this perspective it is difficult to separate the ancillary problems from the central problem of right. Zionism, on the other hand, takes as its starting point the opposite position. It assumes a given *status quo* and ignores all historical perspectives. For the Arabs, all military effort ultimately aims at "restoring Arab rights in Palestine." In the Israeli perspective, this is equated with driving the Israelis into the sea. All Israeli effort, both military and political, seeks to preserve, consolidate, and expand Zionist presence. It necessarily turns away from fundamental claims and focuses on the singular problem at hand. It knows that its cause is tactically best served by concentrating on individual problems— boundary adjustments, transit rights, shipping, hydraulic claims.

The May–June crisis thus signified different things to Arabs and Israelis. It was (as President Nasser put it) not the Gulf of Aqaba, or the Suez Canal, or any other limited problem which was behind the crisis but the "right of the Palestinian Arabs to their land and homes." For the Israelis this was not the issue, for in the logic of Israel's hard strategy all this belonged, as the question of Jerusalem does now, to the non-negotiable category of the conflict. What from the Arab standpoint constitutes the heart of the matter, for the Israelis constitutes the settled and non-negotiable aspect of it. Their position on "right to land and home" has forced the Arab states to view problems ultimately in terms of fundamental human rights. While as a principle of political orientation this has greatly restricted Arab maneuverability, it has also preserved intact the Arab claim to Palestine. On the psychological level, and on the level of legality, this constitutes a major source of strength for the Arab side.

One minor point remains to be disposed of. American writers every now and then advise the Arabs that they should submit to the facts of life and reconcile themselves to the existence of the Zionist state "however unjust its creation appears to them" and that they would do well "not to threaten and harass . . . [Israel or] . . . arouse among their people false hopes about its dissolution." Arab writers have noted with irony that such advice comes from people whose country, to safeguard its security and prosperity, has seen fit to engage in wars thousands of miles away from its coasts. The war against Zionism, these writers say, far from aiming to preserve "security and prosperity" aims to prevent a new and vicious type of colonialism from enslaving the Arabs at home; furthermore, they point out, Arabs are defending themselves not in some distant land, but on their own invaded soil.

Israel's
Arab Policy

M ost students of the Middle East agree that the Palestine conflict, and in consequence the Arab-Israeli conflict, represents a long drawn-out struggle for the ultimate possession of Palestine and the final disposition of the Palestinian people. The hostilities of June, 1967, were simply another eruption of that struggle. Depending upon their perspectives and the facts at their command, scholars are prone to attribute somewhat different causes to these periodic eruptions. Each outbreak, it is true, represents a different configuration of precipitating factors and to that extent scholars are justified in dealing with each separately. For a proper comprehension of the total conflict, however, it is imperative to place each eruption in perspective, and thus an assessment here of the forces that generated the 1967 outbreak of hostilities between Israel and the adjacent Arab states cannot but be incomplete.

For purposes of this essay, we are concerned with Israel's Arab policy insofar as that policy may have constituted an important and a precipitating factor in Israel's attack on the adjacent states on June 5, 1967. However, the reservation noted above applies with equal logic to a consideration of Israel's Arab policy in relation to the outbreak of that conflict. Although there may have been slight shifts in Israel's Arab policy in the mid-1960s which ultimately led to conflict, that policy and its accompanying shifts should be placed within the context of the totality of Zionist premises concerning Palestine.

Two factors—namely, ideology and practical exigencies—guided the Zionists in their behavior toward the Palestinian community and subsequently guided Israel's policy toward the Arab states. Accord-

66

ingly, to speak of Israel's Arab policy requires us to consider the ideological components of Zionism. We must not assume, however, that ideology alone determines external relations. It is obvious that foreign policy is frequently related to national interests, even when these contravene the ideology of the regime.

Israel's relations with the Arab states are no exception. From the very beginning, one can isolate the ideological factors inherent in Zionism which made it imperative for all Zionist groups, regardless of their differences, to adopt a specific policy toward the Palestinian community. That policy's principal objective was to denigrate the cultural and national affinities of the Palestinians and ultimately to excise them from Palestine. But as time passed the increasing complexity of the situation required Zionists and Israelis to adopt certain courses of action in order to attain limited objectives at particular junctures of history, even though these apparently deviated from the ideological stance.[1]

Those who assert that conflict is a permanent feature of relations between Zionists and Palestinians, and consequently between Israelis and Arabs, derive their conclusions chiefly from the ideological components of the Zionist movement. If these are the sole or determining elements there can be no real resolution to the conflict short of the political elimination of one or the other protagonist—a conclusion that has already been advanced by some observers on the scene.[2]

On the other hand, if one assumes that conflict is not a permanent condition of the area but a result of competing aspirations and ambitions that can be accommodated in some other way, then conflict is related to a certain set of empirical factors which give rise to it. The hopeful among the observers—and there are many—contend accord-

---

1. The tactical modifications in the policies of the Zionist movement are noted in practically all literature on the Palestine conflict. For recent illustrations see Christopher Sykes, *Crossroads to Israel* (London: Collins, 1965); and Ibrahim Abu-Lughod, "The Arab-Israeli Confrontation: Some Thoughts on the Future," *Arab Journal*, V (1968), 13–23.

2. The leadership of the Palestinian community perceived this some time ago. Moshe Dayan made the Israeli perception explicit in "A Soldier Reflects on Peace Hopes," *Jerusalem Post*, September 30, 1968 (all references to the *Jerusalem Post*, unless otherwise indicated, are to the airmail weekly edition). Even a third party such as the pro-Israeli American Professors for Peace in the Middle East suggests this in its report on a mission to the area of conflict (*Jerusalem Post*, October 17, 1968, and November 11, 1968).

ingly that the way to avert further conflict is to solve specific problems and to settle specific areas of contention. Under this assumption one might define the Palestine "refugees" as an unresolved problem and advance certain programs which, if carried out, would not only solve the specific problem but would also facilitate further cooperation between the present protagonists. One can think of a number of similar specific problems that might be solved in a practical sense, if one views the conflict largely in terms of temporary exigencies.

Each of these approaches has a different implication. If the first view is maintained, then it follows that conflict is inherent in the relationship, regardless of the immediate issues of contention. Issues simply offer convenient pretexts at particular moments in history so that the conflict may be resumed. Accordingly, it becomes slightly irrelevant to consider the *casus belli* at any particular time. Furthermore, one can consistently blame the party one initially considers responsible for the conflict regardless of the details of each specific confrontation.

If, however, one adheres to the second view, one is in a better position to assess the forces precipitating each incident, to examine the specific issues of contention, and to judge the parties accordingly. Most of the literature dealing with the 1967 June War, especially that contributed by third parties to the conflict, has followed this course.[3]

In contrast, it should be noted that Arabs and Zionists alike more frequently adhere to the first position. Our premise in this essay is that there exist a number of ideological factors which if left unchecked tend to give credence to the first position; these factors encourage one or the other of the protagonists to adopt policies which lead to further conflict. At the same time, we recognize the presence of some specific situational factors that reinforce this basic tendency toward a renewal of conflict and others which may inhibit this impulse.

In the case of the recent war, one can see both ideological and

---

3. Ignoring the frankly partisan material published in the United States, certain types of serious analysis illustrate this approach: see Charles Yost, "The Arab-Israeli War: How It Began," *Foreign Affairs*, XLVI (January, 1968), 304–20; John Badeau, "The Arabs, 1967," *Atlantic*, December, 1967, pp. 102–10; C. Ernest Dawn, "The Egyptian Remilitarization of Sinai," *Journal of Contemporary History*, III (July, 1968), 201–24; and Alan Horton, "The Arab-Israeli Conflict of June 1967," *Northeast Africa, American Universities Field Staff Reports* (September, 1967).

situational factors working together to produce conflict. These factors are related to three basic elements: first, the underlying Zionist premises concerning the Arab and how he should be dealt with; second, Israel's specific internal problems in the mid-1960s (which made an aggressive policy toward the Arabs particularly attractive to certain policy makers in Israel); and finally, Israel's evaluation of the appropriateness of the regional and international climate within which to launch its attack on June 5, 1967.

The Arab-Israeli confrontation in June, 1967, represented an inevitable conflict between Arabs and Zionists that, at least in part, grew out of Israel's Arab policy. While this policy has been more or less manifest from the inception of the Zionist movement, each eruption of conflict has represented a somewhat different combination of factors. Thus, as background to a discussion of the June conflict, one must briefly delineate the historic development of that policy.

2.

Three distinct phases in Zionist-Palestinian and Israeli-Arab relations can be easily recognized. The first phase began with the introduction of the mandate system in Palestine and ended with the emergence of the state of Israel. During this period two principal objectives of the Zionist movement were to gain acceptance of their efforts to establish a Jewish state in Palestine and to remove the Palestinians from areas essential for the growth and development of that state. However, from the very beginning of the mandate, the Palestinian community would not acquiesce to the fate envisioned for it by the Zionist movement. Accordingly, a policy of direct military confrontation was adopted by both protagonists. The aim of the Zionists was to surmount Palestinian opposition to the establishment of a Jewish state, while the Palestinian objective was to frustrate the Zionist goal. At no point during the period of the mandate did either of the protagonists alter its position with regard to the other.

The outcome of that confrontation is well known and need not detain us at this point. The emergence of the state of Israel in Palestine signified the initial success of the Zionists. However, that success was only partial, for two basic problems remained: the territorial objectives of the Zionist movement were not fulfilled by the *de facto* frontiers of

69

Palestine Mandate

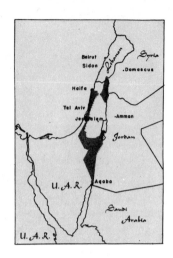

Partition Plan

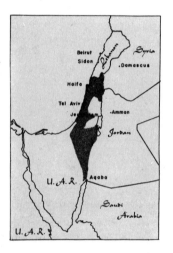

Areas conquered 1949

Area occupied 1956

Palestine 1919-1967

 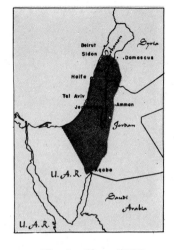

Area occupied 1967   **Zionist Plan 1919**

the new state of Israel, and the Palestinian community did not sur-render. These two problems, plus a number of questions arising from Israel's unique experience as a foreign-supported state, led to the second phase of Israel's Arab policy.

This phase began with the commencement of relations governed by the armistice agreements between Israel and each of the adjacent states. This second phase of Israel's Arab policy had a trifold objec-tive: first, to break the back of what remained of Palestinian resis-tance; second, to serve notice to the adjacent states that, should they harbor Palestinian resistance movements in territories under their jurisdiction, they would automatically invite intervention by Israeli armed forces in their domestic affairs; and third, to maintain a high but tolerable level of tension on Israel's frontiers in order to serve the internal political purposes of the new state—namely, strengthening the bond of its citizens and consolidating its hold over external supporters.[4]

---

4. The psychic need for a certain degree of opposition to consolidate Zionism and Jewish nationalism was recognized by Theodor Herzl in *The Jewish State* (New York: American Zionist Emergency Council, 1946), pp. 79, 92.

The latter would assure the flow of capital badly needed to sustain the new state.

This interpretation of the underlying motives of Israel's actions toward the Arab states is not one to which most Israelis would subscribe. An Israeli observer would not disagree with the factual account itself, namely, that a high degree of tension characterized the relations between Israel and the adjacent states, but he would attribute this tension solely to Arab "irrationality," "aggressive designs," and continued Arab "harassment" of Israel.

Regardless of which view a third party might hold, he could not deny the existence of the tension. Within the second phase of Israel's Arab policy, we discern a simple pattern of continued violence. Until about 1953–54 this violence was concentrated along the Israeli-Jordanian armistice lines where large-scale villages and settlements, made up of Palestinians indigenous to the area or those displaced by Israel, were located. Although the Palestinian community had been defeated in the war of 1947–48, it had not capitulated to Israel nor had its resolve to liberate its homeland been weakened, and naturally it continued its defense measures. By the same token, it was natural for the Israelis to continue their measures of harassment in an attempt to convince the Palestinians that their efforts could not succeed. The conflicting tendencies of both communities led to continuous friction along the Jordanian armistice line. Intermittently large-scale military adventures were undertaken by Israel's armed forces resulting in repeated condemnation by various bodies of the United Nations.[5]

It should be noted that during that period there was also some tendency on Israel's part to think in terms of the conclusion of a peace treaty that would legitimize its previous conquests. For quite some time the Jordanian government exhibited receptivity to Israel's pressures, but the assassination in 1951 of King Abdullah of Transjordan, who was the principal architect of that accommodation, brought this tendency to an abrupt halt in Jordan. Israel's "Arab experts" then suggested an alternative approach, namely, systematic coercion. The Israelis presumed that the only language which Arabs could under-

5. For this period see E. H. Hutchinson, *Violent Truce* (New York: Devin-Adair, 1956); Earl Berger, *The Covenant and the Sword: Arab-Israeli Relations, 1948–1956* (Toronto: University of Toronto Press, 1965); E. L. M. Burns, *Between Arab and Israeli* (London: Harrap, 1962).

stand was the language of force.[6] Israel therefore applied force systematically in the hope of compelling Jordan to sue for peace. A basic assumption of that period was that peace with Jordan would lead to peace with the rest of the Arab states.

By 1953 it had become clear that Israel's principal assumptions were mistaken. The resistance of the Palestinians did not decline. Further, Jordan's willingness to accommodate Israel was limited and, after the assassination of King Abdullah, no official in the Jordanian government would risk a similar fate. Finally, Israel's strong measures against Jordan produced the opposite of what Israel's "Arab experts" had predicted. Jordanians recognized Israel's superior armed strength, but this stimulated measures for their own defense. Instead of suing for peace, they began to undertake more seriously the task of arming the Jordanian population, particularly in those areas adjacent to Israel.

Israel then shifted the direction of its pressure. The failure of Israel's Jordanian policy, coupled with international exigency, produced this shift which was recognized by Zionist as well as non-Zionist observers of the Middle East.[7] The scene of continuing violence shifted from the Jordanian lines to Israel's southern armistice lines with Egypt. One reason for this increased involvement on the Egyptian frontier was that the Palestinians who had settled in the Gaza Strip, although not as numerous as those on the West Bank of the Jordan, were equally determined to continue the resistance. The trauma of their exodus in 1948 had for a while left them paralyzed, but by 1953 they were recovering their capacities and were beginning to undertake measures of defense that were quite clearly inimical to Israel. Secondly, Israel's "Arab experts" recognized that any kind of Arab-Israeli accommodation would have to start with Egypt, which by that time had already succumbed to the growing Arab revolution. Thus, Israel

---

6. For typical illustrations of this assumption see Walter Eytan, *The First Ten Years: A Diplomatic History of Israel* (New York: Simon & Schuster, 1958); and the round-table discussion organized by the Israeli newspaper *Maariv* and recorded as "How to Speak to the Arabs" in the *Middle East Journal*, XVIII (Spring, 1964), 143–62. See also Aharon Cohen, "How to Talk to the Arabs," *New Outlook*, VII (January, 1964), 10–15; and Michael Bar-Zohar, *The Armed Prophet: A Biography of Ben-Gurion*, trans. Len Ortzen (London: Arthur Barker, 1967), particularly p. 212.

7. On this shift in Israel's object of attack and the underlying reasons for it, see Leonard Binder, "The Middle East as a Subordinate International System," *World Politics*, (April, 1958), p. 422; Uri Avnery, *Israel without Zionists* (New York: Macmillan, 1968), pp. 110–12; Ernest Stock, *Israel on the Road to Sinai: 1949–1956* (Ithaca: Cornell University Press, 1967).

was faced with two options. On the one hand, it could wait until the Arab revolution had completed its course; then, hopefully, Egypt would come to terms with Israel. On the other hand, there was danger that the Arab revolution would succeed in strengthening the capacity of Egypt to withstand mounting pressures from Israel.[8] Neither of these outcomes could be predicted accurately, but an early analysis led Israeli leaders to conclude that should the Arab revolution succeed it would improve the posture of Arab defense and reduce their inclination to accept Israel's terms for peace. A third reason for the shift in the direction of Israeli military pressure was that Israel was at a stage in its internal development which required a certain amount of friction with Egypt. Israel was interested in developing its external trade with Asia and Africa, but Israeli ships were barred from the Suez Canal. Israel at that time was still working to complete its port at Elath.

Fortunately for Israel, France was then in the midst of its suppressive acts in North Africa (a program which was to end in the bloodiest of revolutions). The militarists of Israel and France suddenly discovered that they had much in common, and they developed a working relationship which had the destruction of the new revolutionary system in Egypt as its object. It should be pointed out that, although the militarists pushed for the alliance, it was David Ben-Gurion who called attention to the utility of working in concert with France at that time.[9]

The deterioration of the frontier situation in the south of Palestine is now part of history. It led ultimately to the tripartite invasion of Egypt in 1956.[10] By then Israel had a set of limited objectives which no longer included a peace treaty. Israel hoped (1) to gain freedom of navigation for Israeli ships in the Suez Canal and the Gulf of Aqaba,

---

8. Uri Avnery, a member of the Israeli Knesset, calls attention to this aspect of Israel's dilemma in *Israel without Zionists,* p. 103.

9. Michael Bar-Zohar, *Suez: Ultra Secret* (Paris: Fayard, 1964) and *The Armed Prophet,* p. 200; see also *Israel Government Year-Book 1959/60,* (Jerusalem: At the Government Printer, 1960), pp. 71–77.

10. The most important books that deal with the tripartite attack on Egypt in 1956 are Terence Robertson, *Crisis: The Inside Story of the Suez Conspiracy* (New York: Aetheneum, 1965); Erskine Childers, *The Road to Suez* (London: MacGibbon and Kee, 1962); Anthony Nutting, *No End of a Lesson: The Inside Story of the Suez Crisis* (New York: C. N. Potter, 1967); Hugh Thomas, *Suez* (New York: Harper & Row, 1967); and Kenneth Love, *Suez: The Twice-Fought War* (New York: McGraw-Hill, 1969).

since by that time Elath was completed and ready to receive ships; (2) to suppress the Palestinian resistance that was mounting in the Gaza Strip; (3) to destroy Egypt's capacity to utilize the arms it had bought; and (4) to undermine President Nasser's increasingly central position of leadership in the Arab world.

Israel managed to accomplish some of these objectives in the 1956 campaign. Freedom of navigation in the Gulf of Aqaba was acquired *de facto*. Tranquillity on the southern armistice lines was obtained, largely through the separation of the combatants by the interposition of the United Nations Emergency Force. And Egypt's defensive capability was significantly retarded by the heavy blow inflicted on its armed forces and by the capture of a good deal of its armaments. These were important gains for Israel, but certain frustrations remained. It became increasingly obvious that President Nasser had lost none of his charismatic qualities; indeed his central role in the Arab community was accentuated as a result of the attack. Navigation in the canal was not obtained by force nor, interestingly enough, was it subsequently sought through accepted peaceful channels such as the International Court of Justice. Relations between the Arabs and Israelis assumed greater rigidity.

The world-wide condemnation of Israel which followed this attack launched in concert with old-fashioned imperialists, and the limited gains which resulted from the attack, may account in part for the relative quiet that characterized the frontiers in subsequent years. At that time Israel and the adjacent Arab states were quite preoccupied with problems of internal development. These preoccupations, together with the force of world opinion, restrained them from colliding with one another for some time to come. And certainly the presence of United Nations forces inhibited incidents that could have escalated into major operations.

3.

For the next ten years, then, the armistice lines remained reasonably tranquil, considering their potential explosiveness. Such incidents and countermeasures as occurred contrast quite sharply in terms of their intensity and frequency with pre-1956 conditions. The relative lull of the ten-year period was the result of a mutually satisfactory, although temporary, desire on the part of both protagonists to establish *modus vivendi.*

The Arabs believed that they had succeeded in effecting a *de facto* containment policy which, in its simplest form, accepted the existence of Israel within the confines of the armistice agreement but in no way assisted Israel in its attempt to grow and expand; hence the economic boycott assumed a more important role. Palestinian activity within Israel's territory faced increasing opposition from Jordan, out of fear that such activity might precipitate a premature and highly undesirable confrontation. Also, during this period, whether as a rationalization of an immediate weakness or a reflection of a genuine belief, there developed an attitude concerning a solution to the Palestine conflict. Increasingly, an articulate segment of the Arab intelligentsia and certain Arab government circles asserted that the Palestine conflict would not be resolved favorably from an Arab standpoint until the Arab revolution was consummated in each of the Arab countries. The solution to the Palestine conflict was made dependent on the economic, social, and political transformation of the Arab community. This dictated the logical strategy of concentrating attention on the Arab community and away from Israel. It was during this ten-year period following the tripartite attack on Egypt that the most fundamental programs of social and economic reconstruction were initiated in the Arab world at large. It was also during this period that the Arabs attempted, with limited success, various forms of political unification.

From Israel's standpoint, the situation likewise demanded a cautious course of action vis-à-vis the Arabs. Israel was still absorbing immigrants. Its economic development was (as it still is) dependent on external support—whether from governmental sources, such as German reparations or official United States support, or from private Jewish contributions. The domestic tasks facing Israel were many and had to be accomplished in relative peace. Thus, for ten years the basic ideological premises of both parties were submerged and not permitted to interfere with the concrete implementation of public policies and the concerns of pressing environmental realities.

Some observers interpreted the lull as signifying a potential for peace in the future. Increasingly, possible approaches were put forth for the resolution of the endemic conflict between Arabs and Israelis. Proposals for conflict resolution made up to as late as 1966 received favorable publicity in the Israeli periodical *New Outlook*.[11] But in 1967 the realities suddenly emerged, and another confrontation seemed imminent. Either the earlier diagnosis had been illusory or a new congruence of factors was impelling the parties to an unavoidable conflict.

At this juncture it is perhaps impossible to give a completely accurate picture of the imperceptible changes in Arab-Israeli relations that took place in the mid-1960s and that led ultimately to conflict. It might be asserted that conflict was actively sought at that particular moment because it served a specific purpose. In evaluating events, two things should be kept in mind. On the one hand, the intermittent activity of the Palestinians in the preceding years had not appreciably disturbed the relative stability along the armistice lines nor had it affected the major orientation of either protagonist. On the other hand, there was what seemed to be a sudden shift which sought to destroy that *de facto* lull and to create conditions that would lead to an armed clash. Two expressions of the contradiction illustrate its empirical reality. The mission of the French philosopher Jean-Paul Sartre to the region in the hope of bringing about a dialogue between Arabs and Israelis symbolized the belief that the time had come that the two protagonists could initiate steps which might lead to a peaceful resolution.[12] Almost simultaneously, throughout 1966 and 1967, the secretary-general of the United Nations was sounding alarms that tension was mounting. His warnings had a specific reference, namely the Syrian-Israeli armistice lines. The two interpretations symbolized different conditions. One referred to the past; the other to the future. Sartre's mission focused on the ten-year abatement of the conflict and optimistically envisaged further amelioration. U Thant's apprehensions were based upon a more realistic assessment of the events which were likely to result from the basic reorientation of policies then occurring

---

11. The reader is reminded that this hope seems to have been shared by the U.N. Palestine Conciliation Commission which dispatched Mr. Joseph Johnson, president of the Carnegie Endowment for World Peace, to the Middle East for another attempt at conciliation in the early 1960s. Though his report remains "confidential," his comments at the time suggested that a mutually acceptable settlement was as remote then as it had been in previous periods. See also *New Outlook*, VII (June, 1964), 16–24.

12. *New Outlook*, VIII (January-February, 1965); *ibid.*, VIII (March, 1965); and *ibid.*, IX (May, 1966). The publication of a special issue of *Les Temps Modernes*, "Le Conflit Israelo-Arabe," (June, 1967) was conceived in that light.

on the part of the protagonists. It is to these that one must turn to explain the eruption of conflict in June, 1967.

4.

Again, the reader is reminded that two factors underlie Arab-Israeli relations: the ideological and the situational. By 1965, both factors were again united to propel Israel to shift emphasis in its relations with the Arabs. The empirical reality which pressed itself on the Israeli government and demanded some kind of solution was the result of Israel's unilateral diversion of the Jordan River. This action, which was undertaken in violation of the principles of international law, had not yielded the anticipated results. For purely technical reasons, Israel was unable to benefit fully from the water it had fought so hard to divert, a fact reported at the time in the *Jerusalem Post* and the *New York Times*.[13] To deal effectively with the technical failure, Israel needed control of the headwaters of the river, but these were located in the territory of a sovereign state, Syria. A second situational factor was that Israel was still not permitted to use the Suez Canal. Significantly, Israel had not sought during the intervening period to put its proclaimed right to use the canal to a legal test, even though the U.A.R. had accepted the compulsory jurisdiction of the International Court of Justice with regard to this issue. Nevertheless, the canal problem remained.

Israel's policy makers had to contend with other temporal problems. One in particular was immediately relevant to the eruption of the June, 1967, conflict. Although Palestinian resistance to Israeli occupation in those portions of Palestine not granted to Israel by the Partition Plan of 1947 continued intermittently throughout the post-1948 period, in 1965 a new development began to affect the type of resistance being waged. By then, the semiorganized resistance assumed greater cohesion and attracted wider support from a young generation who had become active members of the Palestinian community in the intervening period. These youths had come of age by 1965 and were conceiving important ways of recovering their homeland as well as organizing more effectively the struggle for their rights. Several major organizations assumed

---

13. *Jerusalem Post*, April 14, 1965 (daily edition), p. 4; *New York Times*, April 17, 1965, p. 2.

a leading role in channeling resistance to Israeli occupation of Palestine; these commanded a high level of support from the Arab community at large as well as from Arab governments. The Palestine Liberation Organization, the Popular Liberation Front, and the Front for the Liberation of Palestine asserted their presence and, although only the PLO received legal recognition from the Arab states, the other two were no less active nor were they denied some measure of public support from certain states in the region.[14] By 1965 it had become obvious that the Palestinian people—whom the world had relegated to oblivion and had classified as passive refugees allegedly being used as a "political football" by the Arab states—were determined to continue their resistance with even greater tenacity and discipline. The increasing number of confrontations with Israeli occupation forces across the demarcation lines was becoming a fact with which the Israelis were reluctant to live.

Along with the changing nature of objective relations between Israelis and Arabs, Israel was undergoing important changes at home, and its outlook on the Arabs as well as the world was being altered. While we cannot go into the details of this fundamental change in the internal structure of Israeli politics or institutions, we can single out some issues of immediate relevance to the 1967 June War.

The German reparations payments, so important in terms of their contribution to Israel's economic development during the preceding ten years, had come to an end by 1965: a substitute source of funds had to be found. Although Israel continued to accept support from Jewish capitalists throughout the world, its economic needs required an even greater inflow of foreign capital. The increasing recession in Israel's economy, a matter of public and international knowledge, reached alarming proportions in the year 1967. Israelis and Zionists debated causes as well as remedies, but it was obvious that a surgical operation of major proportions was needed to halt this economic decline.[15] It

---

14. While these developments in themselves call for investigation by serious students of the Middle East, our task here is simply to show the relevance of this development to the 1967 conflict. Malcolm H. Kerr, *The Arab Cold War, 1958–1964: A Study of Ideology in Politics* (New York: Oxford University Press, 1965), p. 151, calls attention to the implications of the PLO not only to inter-Arab politics but to the whole nature of the official relations between Israel and the Arab states.

15. The reader's attention is called to the dismissal by the Israeli government of the English Zionist Jon Kimche, editor of the *Jewish Observer and Middle East Review,* for his frank discussion in March, 1967, of the artificial economic policies that

was during this period that some peculiar solutions to the economic problems of Israel commended themselves to certain Israeli policy makers. These solutions were in the direction of an armed conflict that would attain certain economic objectives.

Short of an immediate conflagration between the protagonists, some relief from economic problems could be gained through increased commercial transactions with markets in the immediate vicinity of Israel. Increasingly, it became evident that there was no substitute for a normalization of trade with the adjacent Arab states, especially since the projected increment of trade with African markets was in fact illusory. Although a certain amount of trade went on between Israel and Africa, its volume was low, and its proportion of the Israeli export market remained negligible and was, in fact, declining despite the improvement in Israel's relations with several African states.[16]

There were other situational factors which contributed to Israel's shift in policy in the mid-1960s. Although established by Western powers and considering itself a Western nation, Israel nevertheless had entertained the idea of belonging to the wider Afro-Asian world, even if its actions often did not correspond to the idea. International politics precluded serious identification and, by the mid-1960s Israel had gone as far as it could in establishing viable relations with powers that counted in the Third World. It was quite clear to Israelis, their allies, and their adversaries that the Third World viewed Israel with a good measure of ambivalence.

5.

By the end of 1965, the time was appropriate for a total reevaluation of Israel's regional and international relations. A major debate on this question indicated that something was stirring in Israel, especially since that debate engaged all the leading public figures. Moshe Dayan; Shimon Perez, former secretary-general of the Ministry of Defense and

---

led to the Israeli recession. See also "Israel's Economy Slows Down," *New Outlook,* IX (June, 1966), 9–18; and "Anatomy of a Crisis," *New Outlook,* X (March-April, 1967), 21–25.

16. A summary of Israel's trade problems with African countries can be found in Stuart Schaar, "Patterns of Trade and Aid in East Africa," *East Africa, American Universities Field Staff Reports* (March, 1968). Also highly informative is Odeyo Ayagu, "Africa's Dilemma in the Arab-Israeli Conflict," *Pan-African Journal,* Vol. I, No. 2 (1968), esp. p. 114.

one of the architects of the French-Israeli alliance of the 1950s; and Abba Eban, at that time deputy prime minister of Israel, were some of the spokesmen who publicly discussed the challenge to Israel's foreign policy in the next decade. Two major positions emerged which, while not in fundamental disagreement, differed in their approach. Before examining the areas of difference and contention, we might summarize the broad areas of agreement, since these undoubtedly entered into the subsequent formulation of Israel's policy.

Both parties agreed that Israel's relations with the outside world were as good as could be hoped for. All derived satisfaction from the close working relationship between Israel and the European-American community. Although the United States and Western Europe had in the past stood solidly behind Israel and had assisted it extensively in its efforts to surmount difficulties in the region, the relative power of each member of this community had undergone important changes. In the previous decades the alliance between Britain and Israel, and later the alliance between France and Israel, had served Israel's needs satisfactorily. But by the sixties it was apparent that Israel's aspirations would require the support of the senior member of that alliance, namely, the United States. Their future course of action must of necessity see the United States committed legally and morally to Israel's strategies.[17]

There was a compelling consensus among the debaters that Israel's Arab policy not only had made no progress since 1948 but in fact had suffered serious rigidification. In certain periods in the past Arabs and Israelis had at least spoken with one another—for example, during the negotiations at Rhodes, Lausanne, and in other European centers. Intermediaries had shuffled back and forth. Negotiations of sorts had been conducted through the Mixed Armistice Commissions along the armistice lines, and some gifts had even been exchanged between responsible Arabs and Israelis.[18] Yet all these interchanges had come to an end by the mid-1960s, and the protagonists, while appearing peaceful had hardened sufficiently so as to preclude serious discussions. The policy debate acknowledged that Arab-Israeli relations had in fact regressed. There was substantial agreement among the participants that

---

17. Jon Kimche stresses the need for a new alliance to replace the former Zionist-British alignment in *The Unromantics* (London: Weidenfeld & Nicholson, 1968), p. 82.
18. See Avnery, *Israel without Zionists*, pp. 105–6; *New Outlook*, VII (October, 1964), 45–46; and *ibid.*, VII (November-December, 1964), 78–89.

the greatest challenge to Israel's foreign policy in the next decade remained in its immediate environment. Israel's energies would have to be directed to that region so that its long-range objective of a settlement with the Arabs could be attained.[19]

There was then a broad consensus, but due to their private perspectives and varied predilections Israeli leaders differed about a course of action. Two general lines of action were proposed.

Perez, Dayan, and others of their persuasion bluntly stated that there was only one way to solve the problem conclusively, and that was to defeat the Arabs so decisively in battle that they would be forced to accept a dictated settlement at the conference table. This view was based on the premise, so fondly nurtured by various Israeli "Arab experts," that force was, after all, what Arabs understood best.

An alternative diagnosis and prescription was offered by Abba Eban. While its outcome was not fundamentally different from the Perez-Dayan proposal, its strategy was subtler, requiring a greater degree of skill in execution. Eban looked at the Arab scene and perceived that events tended to disunite the Arabs and to propel each state to a greater attachment to its separate sovereignty and that the Arabs were leaning toward a recognition of Israeli legitimacy. If this spirit were to prevail, ultimately Israel could be accepted by the Arab states within the framework of separate sovereignties in the region, all associated with one another voluntarily and for mutual benefit. He noted that the attempt by one Arab state to influence others, let alone merge with them, had been seriously undermined in recent years and that further fragmentation could be anticipated in the region. Eban recommended that this trend be encouraged; if it were to become dominant Israel's problem with the states of the region would be eased considerably. Until that occurred, however, Israel's security and safety would have to be assured. Given this interpretation, whatever pressure could be exerted on the Arabs to move them to accept a peace settlement with Israel ought to be encouraged. Accordingly, in Eban's view

---

19. It is useful to point out in this connection that a relevant contribution to this discussion by the late Moshe Sharett, perennial foreign minister and at one time prime minister of the state, was resurrected and given a certain degree of circulation. The substance of his argument was that Israel's problems with the Arab states will continue until Israel recognizes the rights of the Palestinian community and the harm inflicted by Israel on that community. See the *Jerusalem Post*, October 18, 1966 (daily edition).

Israel's foreign policy should be directed toward organizing pressure on the Arabs to normalize their relationship with Israel while at the same time making it crystal clear that under no circumstances would the Arabs ever be in a position to bring about a solution other than one envisaged by Israel. This policy, properly encouraged by international pressure, would lead the Arabs to accept Israel's terms for the conclusion of peace. Eban's diagnosis did not preclude the use of force; it merely drew attention to the importance of a judicious use of international pressure as a preliminary and necessary step prior to its use.[20]

This, in brief, was Eban's assessment, the assessment which seems to have carried the day. The question was, what concrete mechanisms could be employed to bring about the necessary international pressure? It will be recalled that when Eban made this speech he was deputy prime minister. Soon thereafter, in January, 1966, he became foreign minister and was in a position to implement his plan of action with the approval of the cabinet. His "task force" committees undoubtedly helped clarify problems and specify means for implementing his policy. Not long afterwards, the actual plan of action emerged.

6.

Eban's plan of action assumed, first, that direct negotiations with the Arabs were not yet possible. The second assumption was that the road to a Middle East settlement must pass through Washington and Moscow and, to a lesser extent, London and Paris. These powers had to be persuaded that peace in the Middle East was of direct concern to them and that they would have to take certain initiatives to bring it about. It would be suggested that peace could be attained by two means: (1) positive influence could be exerted on the Arab states, with Moscow pressuring the progressive regimes and Washington influencing the conservative ones, and (2) negative sanctions could be imposed, for instance arms could be withheld from the major powers'

---

20. Eban's views and assessments are to be found in various issues of the *Jerusalem Post* and *Israel Digest;* see, for example, *Jerusalem Post* of October 17, 1965, January 3, 1966, January 28, 1966; and *Israel Digest* of January 14, 1966, February 11, 1966, February 25, 1966, and January 27, 1967; see also his "Reality and Vision in the Middle East," *Foreign Affairs,* XLIII (July, 1965), 626–38.

respective Arab allies, thus depriving them of the capacity to counter Israel's power.

While it appeared then that the major powers had the means to hasten a settlement, at this time these same powers were scarcely concerned with the Middle East. Preoccupied as they were with an immediate conflict elsewhere and lulled into false security by the relative tranquillity along the Arab-Israeli armistice lines, they more or less ignored the Middle East. Although verbal reminders to the major powers of the problem would have had some influence, Eban thought a graphic demonstration of the potentially explosive character of Arab-Israeli relations was necessary.

Two types of activities were simultaneously undertaken by Israel. On the diplomatic level, prominent Israeli leaders made extensive tours of various world capitals throughout 1966. At the same time "incidents," particularly along the Syrian-Israeli armistice lines, intensified. Through escalation, Israel sought to increase its military offensive capability and it succeeded in obtaining additional arms, primarily from the United States. By the systematic application of diplomatic pressure and by escalating the military situation along the Syrian-Israeli armistice lines, Israel succeeded in realerting the major powers to the explosiveness of the situation in the region. The major powers, however duly impressed, did not seem to share Israel's confidence that they could exert pressure on the protagonists. Significantly, the United States government, particularly President Johnson, thought that such an opportunity could be utilized for a purpose other than the one Israel intended. Apparently President Johnson decided to assist Israel at that time—not only diplomatically but militarily as well—in return for certain support which he needed in the Vietnam conflict.

In 1966, President Johnson was not winning the war in Vietnam, but instead of seeking an immediate end to that conflict, he sought further intensification. There was a considerable amount of internal opposition to the Vietnam war—opposition that transcended ethnic or religious lines. Evidently, by 1966 Johnson considered the American Jewish community unduly critical of the war. Why he singled out this community to chasten for criticism of his war effort in Vietnam is an interesting question in itself. According to Johnson's logic (which may or may not have been faulty), America's war in Vietnam resembled Israel's in the Middle East. He argued that American Jews continually exerted pressure on various administrations to commit the United

84

States government to Israel, and he reminded them that they expected the U.S. to stand by its commitments. How could the Jews then oppose similar commitments to South Vietnam? Thus, he sought to undermine the American Jewish community's opposition to his war effort.

The exact timing of this strategy is not known, but President Johnson raised the question of Vietnam with Mr. Eban during the latter's visit to the president in February, 1966. It is certain that offensive weapons were promised Israel following this visit, that Israel increasingly supported the U.S. effort in Vietnam, and that Eban ultimately supported U.S. proposals for "peace" in Vietnam in his speech before the General Assembly of the United Nations on October 4, 1967. Almost simultaneously with this reorientation of Israel's policy toward Vietnam—a reorientation that was supposed to culminate in Israeli recognition of South Vietnam—the *New York Times* reported the gist of letters exchanged between President Johnson and leading members of the American Jewish community. On September 11, 1966, it reported that President Johnson had sent a letter to Mr. Malcolm Tarlov, president of the Jewish War Veterans, in which he criticized Jewish opposition to the war and pointed out the inconsistency of this position with regard to Vietnam and Israel. The *New York Times* also reported that this question was raised with Israeli leaders and with leading members of the American Jewish community. Conveniently for Israel, it was then in the midst of negotiations for the delivery of American arms, particularly missiles and aircraft, as well as atomic-powered desalinization plants. These negotiations were rather successful. The price may have been that Israel, and its supporters in the United States, agreed to work to muzzle Jewish opposition to the war in Vietnam.[21]

Obviously, this crude maneuver by the president did not go unchallenged. Leading members of the American Jewish community, including Rabbi Joachim Prinz, then president of the Conference of Presidents of Jewish Organizations, as well as Jay Kaufman and William

---

21. The full documentation of the link between Israel and Vietnam, insofar as President Johnson's view is concerned, is not yet part of the public record. The reader can get an insight into it by consulting the *New York Times* of September 11, 13, 14, 15, 18, and November 2 and 7 of 1966. The delivery of American arms to Israel, subsequent to Mr. Eban's visit to President Johnson on February 3, 1966, by which the U.S. sought Israel's support for war in Vietnam, was revealed on July 24, 1967, by the *New York Times*.

Wexler, president and vice-president of the B'nai B'rith, demanded an immediate explanation. Ultimately they were given one by Mr. Arthur Goldberg, then chief of the American delegation to the U.N. Presumably, after several conferences the Jewish organizations "understood" the aims of President Johnson.

What those aims were and what commitments were made in the process still remain shrouded in secrecy. Certain consequences, however, are now part of the public record. The link between Vietnam and the Arab-Israeli conflict was thus forged between the United States and Israel. The link was further strengthened by the visits of Mr. Dayan (who held no official position in Israel at that time) to Vietnam and of General Westmoreland to Israel.

But this was not enough. Beginning in July, 1966, and continuing throughout 1967, the escalation of hostilities—intended to call attention to the Middle East—proceeded. Israel's constant attacks on Syria, each time under a convenient pretext, became a permanent feature of the Middle East scene and resulted in frequent condemnations of Israel by the United Nations, all of which heightened U Thant's periodic alarm.[22]

The concert of action between the U.S. and Israel had more than a specific reference; it should be pointed out that the period following the assassination of President Kennedy witnessed a major offensive by the United States against the nonaligned nations of the world. In the context of this general offensive, the Johnson administration hoped to remove President Nasser and strike a crippling blow against the U.A.R. A careful student of American policy in the Middle East would be struck by the increasing degree of hostility which the Johnson administration exhibited against the U.A.R.—the central power in the Middle East, as well as one of the world's most active promoters of nonalignment. Within the Middle East, American policy actively en-

22. The reader will recall at least three major attacks in 1966 and 1967: two air attacks on Syria and one against Jordan. The reader is also reminded of the visits to Israel by three important figures in the Johnson Administration: Lucius Battle, assistant secretary of state for Near Eastern affairs; Mr. Harold Sanders, White House advisor on Near Eastern affairs (intelligence); and Mr. Townsend Hoopes, assistant secretary of defense, visited Israel, and on March 14, 1967, had a conference with Eshkol. On March 24, General Rabin, former chief of staff of the Israeli armed forces, declared that the arms balance had definitely tipped in favor of Israel and it would continue to be so in the future. Significantly, he added that there was no chance for a peaceful settlement with the Arabs and that in case of war Israel would win (See *Israel Digest,* April 7, 1967, p. 7).

couraged the polarization of those willing to accept America's leadership and those following an independent line. The independents were increasingly identified as part and parcel of the Communist camp.

The conclusion drawn in the United States from this polarization was that peace and stability in the region were in fact being threatened not by the unresolved Arab-Israeli dispute but by the policies pursued by the United Arab Republic and its allies in the area. The reader will recall, for example, the hearings held by the Congressional Subcommittee on Peace in the Middle East which, in April, 1967, gathered testimony from diverse sources. It concluded that peace in the Middle East was in fact threatened by the progressive policies of the United Arab Republic and its allies, which, it was thought, were affecting American and British interests in the area adversely and were promoting the cause of Communism.[23] By the spring of 1967 a major offensive against the progressive regimes in the Middle East, which appears to have been linked to both Vietnam and Israel, was already underway. This new American foreign policy assumed that Israel would play a dominant role in the next phase.

7.

The situational factors discussed above with regard to Arab-Israeli relations served, during this particular period, to propel the parties to military confrontation as a major form of policy. By the spring of 1967 specific issues were pressing Israel into a more aggressive policy. In addition, the regional and international climate of opinion was construed by Israeli leaders as favorable to that policy. Finally, Israel's ideological drive was not in conflict with the situational factors leading to the confrontation.

These complex factors as they appeared by the spring of 1967 may be summarized as follows: the immediate problem revolving around

---

23. Senator Joseph Clark's *War or Peace in the Middle East* was offered as testimony to that committee. The brochure is quite "frank" in its conclusions, namely that the obstacle to "peace" in the region is the U.A.R. and its progressive orientation. Accordingly, Senator Clark called for the destruction of the progressive regimes in the Arab world and a greater commitment to Israel as the bulwark of American interests in the region. The increasing hostility of the U.S. under President Johnson has been documented by the former chargé d'affaires at the American Embassy in Cairo, Mr. David Ness, in "The June War in the Middle East" (Lecture given at Boulder, Colorado, 1968).

the sources of the River Jordan (Israel's unilateral diversion of the river was not interfered with by the Arab states, despite the threats they had earlier voiced); navigation in the Suez Canal; the disposition of the Palestinian people, especially since their resistance was assuming an increasingly organized form; and Israel's need to open new markets.

An important aspect of Arab-Israeli relations at that time was the fact that although Israel had predicted increased fragmentation of the Arab world, the opposite was true. For the first time in centuries, Arabs were in a position to determine the kind of political, social, and economic systems that would fulfill their communal aspirations. In this situation the underlying forces for unity were proving stronger than the surface indications of fragmentation. In short, for the first time in centuries Arabs were in a position to exercise their options; they rejected the concept of forced options.

Finally, Israel's underlying ideology was again coming to the surface. It should not be forgotten that the concept of *Eretz Israel,* so long a guiding principle for various sectors of Israeli society, had a territorial counterpart. While the exact extent of that territorial entity remains a mystery to most students of the politics of Zionism, the boundaries of the Partition Plan of 1947 and even the armistice lines of 1949 assuredly fell far short of the territorial ambitions held by even the most moderate of Zionists. Israel's commitment to adjust those frontiers is a matter of public record, even if the exact limits of these adjustments remain the most fluid part of Israel's design. Furthermore, Israel's commitment to the 'ingathering" of the Jews and the belief, unequivocally expressed, that the life of the Jew in exile is an impossible anomaly, has led Israel to generate various pressures to accelerate emigration of Jews from various countries of the world. The reader is simply reminded here of Israel's persistent demand throughout the year 1967 for increased immigration, particularly by American Jews, and for the "release" of Russian Jewry.

So much for the motivations; what of the feasibilities? In the first place, Israel needed some assurance that a war with the adjacent states would result in speedy and absolute triumph. Only if the quality and quantity of Israel's arms were thought adequate to inflict sufficient damage on its opponents would that triumph be guaranteed. Second, it needed a firm commitment from the United States—the one country whose interests in 1967 coalesced with Israel's. The U.S. administration at that time seems to have made some kind of commitment, the nature of which is still in dispute. What is not in dispute, however, is that the commitment made by President Johnson to Israel was legally as well as morally construed and that it enabled Israel to plan its attack on the adjacent states without the slightest fear of an adverse political or military reaction from the West.[24] Third, Israel needed to be certain that its adversaries were not in a position either to assume the initiative or to withstand a surprise attack. The U.A.R.'s preoccupation with the Arab revolution in Yemen and southern Arabia, plus its constant counsel to other Arab states to avoid a premature confrontation with Israel, were reasonably well known, not only to Israel but to the United States as well. If anything was clear by the spring of 1967, it was that the United Arab Republic was neither in a position to attack Israel nor to withstand a surprise assault.[25] That world public opinion was led to believe otherwise simply testifies to the skillfulness of Israel's public "misinformation" campaign.

The outbreak of the war and the events immediately following are not our concern at this point. Israel attacked the adjacent states, subsequently justifying and defending its actions by citing the insecurity arising from the U.A.R.'s declaration closing the Gulf of Aqaba and from the withdrawal of UNEF. These were, of course, convenient pretexts—perhaps *too* convenient. The precipitating events occurred toward the end of May, 1967, but the decision to go to war apparently had been made by Israel a few weeks earlier. The reader may recall Mr. Eshkol's statements of May 9 and May 12, in which he clearly outlined the objectives of Israel's next offensive. He declared that,

> We shall hit when, where, and how we choose. . . . Israel will continue to take action to prevent any and all attempts to perpetuate sabotage within her territory. Israel will continue to foil every scheme to divert the *sources* of the Jordan River and will defend its rights to free navigation in the Red Sea.[26]

---

24. Referring to the nature of the U.S. commitment to Israel, Senator Joseph Clark, endorsed by Senators Dirksen and Javits, announced following a briefing with Secretary of State Dean Rusk on June 6, 1967, that "legally, we are an ally of Israel." (*New York Times,* June 7, 1967, p. 18).

25. Despite their convoluted way of examining the various issues that led to the conflict in June, 1967, Michael Howard and Robert Hunter recognize this in *Israel and the Arab World: The Crisis of 1967,* Adelphi Papers, No. 41 (October, 1967), p. 11. See also Kerr, *The Arab Cold War,* p. 151; and Horton, "The Arab-Israeli Conflict," p. 4.

26. Howard and Hunter, *Israel and the Arabs,* p. 14; *Israel Digest,* May 19, 1967, p. 5 (italics added).

The reader is reminded that this statement was made following a declaration by Israel's chief of staff that the Arabs would never be allowed to interfere with the sources of the river. It was made *before* any discussion had taken place concerning the withdrawal of UNEF and before there had been any interference with Israeli shipping in the Gulf of Aqaba.

On the basis of Israel's own assessment, then, the time was ripe indeed to effect a crippling blow to the combined capabilities of the adjacent states and, at the same time, to deal effectively with the resistance of the Palestinian community. The decision to go to war seems to have been taken some time in early May; various groups sympathetically affiliated with Israel seem to have been informed.[27] There cannot be the slightest doubt that the United States was informed of that decision. Certainly, by June 1 the United States already anticipated the attack, for on that day all American F-104 jets sold to Jordan and placed there with their American pilots (who were "training" their Jordanian counterparts) were ordered out of Jordan for safety.[28]

A new phase in Arab-Israeli relations began with the cease-fire of June 9, 1967. It does not promise to be any more peaceful than previous ones. Ominously, Israel's Arab policy is already assuming a shape that is bound to lead to further situations of conflict.

---

27. In the light of Eshkol's bellicose declarations of May 9 and May 12, 1967, top American Jewish leaders seem to have been instructed to proceed for "urgent" consultations with Israeli leaders. Between May 15 and May 25 many of these descended on Israel and were taken on a tour of the front. Two conclusions were "drawn" from that visit, at least by Rabbi Herbert Friedman, chairman of the United Jewish Appeal: first, that war is the "only solution," and second, that it would be necessary to launch an Israel Emergency Fund in the United States, Canada, and England to finance the war (see the *Jerusalem Post,* July 3, 1967). On May 29, 1967, Eshkol announced, "The Israel Defence Forces are capable today of meeting any test with the same capacity that they demonstrated in the past—*and knowing the situation as I do, I would say even more* (italics added); see *Israel Digest,* June 2, 1967.

28. *Aviation Week and Space Technology,* July 3, 1967, p. 21.

Some Legal Aspects
of the Arab-Israeli Conflict

This article will touch upon some of the legal aspects of the Arab-Israeli conflict. It is not an ontology of the whole problem. Particular emphasis is placed on those issues which are proximately connected to the events leading to the 1967 June War. Facts and issues which bear upon those events but which are grounded in the history of the conflict will be dicussed but not analyzed in depth.

International law derives from four sources: international custom as evidence of a general practice accepted by law; international conventions; general principles recognized by civilized nations; and development and acceptance of doctrines and judicial decisions. But it should be noted that the customs and practices embodied in world law are of European origin. International conventions which have contributed to the formulation of international law were negotiated or imposed by European governments. In practice, "civilized nations" has meant European or European-affiliated states. American contributions to world law must be included in this category because the customs, traditions, and political institutions of the United States have all been derived from European sources. The customs and traditions of non-European states have made virtually no impact on international law.

Israel must be regarded as representative of the European cultural tradition despite its geographic setting. The Arab countries, then, deriving their concepts and traditions from a non-Western culture, find themselves engaged in a contest for which their adversaries have written all the rules. Arab circles have represented their position as one based on right—legal and moral—foreswearing considerations of a purely political nature. For the Arabs, Israel is itself the original wrong, and the Arab position proceeds on the theory that a poisonous tree can produce only poisonous fruit. From the Israeli viewpoint, Arab conduct is judged on the basis of each separate act without relation to the chain of events or the original illegality of the Israeli position.

The state of Israel, proclaimed in 1948, was born from the Zionist claim that the Jews of the world constitute a separate nation entitled to a land of their own and sovereign statehood. The demand for the creation of a Jewish "homeland" in Palestine was pursued by the World Zionist Organization, which was founded in Basel, Switzerland, in 1897. When Turkey entered World War I as an ally of Germany, the Arab people seized the occasion to align themselves with Great Britain and secure their independence. The 1915 MacMahon Agreement with Sherif Hussein of Mecca confirms this fact. But the Sykes-Picot Agreement, made later the same year between Britain and France, and the November 2, 1917, Balfour Declaration revealed the emptiness of the British alliance with the Arab people. The first steps toward the realization of Zionist ambitions to take over Palestine may be dated from the Balfour Declaration of 1917 in which British Foreign Secretary, A. J. Balfour, with the support of the Allies, proposed "the establishment in Palestine of a national home for the Jewish people." The Balfour Declaration was accorded international recognition when it was incorporated into the preamble of the League of Nations agreement assigning Palestine to Britain as a mandated territory. The Treaty of Lausanne of 1924 and the League of Nations Council confirmed the Middle Eastern mandates of Great Britain and France embodying the Sykes-Picot Agreement and the Balfour Declaration.

The World Zionist Organization may be said to have won recognition as an international body under world law when it was invited to take part in the drafting of the mandate agreement. Under the terms of the mandate, the British government was to encourage Jewish immigration into Palestine. The right, however, of the League of Nations under international law to approve a British-protected Zionist invasion of Palestine is as questionable as the subsequent attempt of its successor, the United Nations Organization, to apportion Palestine into Arab and Jewish states in the 1947 Partition Plan. The wishes of the people whose home had been in Palestine for 1,300 years were totally disregarded, and their right to self-determination was never considered.

(It is important to note that the British government, before adoption of the mandate, had detached that portion of Palestine east of the Jordan River and established the emirate of Transjordan within which Britain asserted the terms of the Balfour Declaration would not apply.) The mandate created the Jewish Agency (which was financed by the World Zionist Organization) to represent Jewish interests in Palestine and the Arab Higher Committee to serve Arab rights there. Both agencies were very clearly intended to function under direct British control and possessed no international juridical status *per se*. No Arab state was at that time a member of the League of Nations, and no authorized Arab representative ever consented to the League's decision to allow Zionist immigration into Palestine.

The following facts reveal the progression of the British-sponsored Zionist invasion of Palestine in the interwar period.

Up to 1920 the population of Palestine was approximately 90 percent Arab; after 1920 the allowed rate of European Jewish immigration was set at 10,000 persons annually; by 1930 the Jewish population rose to 19 percent; by 1940 it became 30 percent of a total population of 1,530,000. Even though Great Britain in a 1939 White Paper pledged to keep the population ratio at one-third Jewish and two-thirds Arab, the displacement of Jews in World War II resulted in a massive influx of those whom the rest of the world was refusing to accept. The price of European atrocities was now to be paid by the Arabs in exchange for their efforts to help the Allies defeat Germany and its allies in both World Wars.

It should be noted that on June 3, 1922, Great Britain restricted the intent of the Balfour Declaration by stating that it did not contemplate "the disappearance or subordination of the Arabic population, language or customs in Palestine" or "the imposition of Jewish nationality upon Palestinian Arabs."[1] In May, 1939, Britain reasserted this view in a White Paper on Palestine and pledged that Jewish immigration would be limited to a total of 75,000 during the ensuing five years. At the end of this period no immigrants were to be admitted without specific Arab approval. Meanwhile the high commissioner for Palestine was authorized to regulate, limit, or prohibit all further transfers of land to Zionist ownership. There were then about 500,000 Jews in the

---

1. Great Britain, Foreign Office, *Documents on British Foreign Policy 1919–1939*, ed. by E. L. Woodward and R. Butler (London: H.M.S.O., 1946).

country—some were citizens but many were not lawful residents—and approximately one million Arabs. Zionists owned about 12 percent of the land.

This White Paper precipitated a direct confrontation between the Zionists and the British. In New York on May 11, 1942, the American Zionist Organization adopted a manifesto that quickly became known as the Biltmore Program.[2] It posed four demands: (1) the mandate over Palestine must be terminated; (2) Palestine must be recognized as a sovereign Jewish state; (3) a national Jewish army must be created; (4) a Jewish government must be established for Palestine. In Jerusalem, the Jewish Agency denounced the Balfour Declaration and adopted the Biltmore Program as official Zionist policy.[3] This action by the Jewish Agency amounted to a renunciation of its function as an arm of the mandate administration (its only legal basis) and would appear, therefore, to have terminated its status as a public body under international law. Surrender or abrogation of its status as an agent of the mandate left the Jewish Agency with only *de facto* existence. The time had come, however, for the Zionists to reap the benefits of the disguised invasion by openly seeking statehood, and the administrative structure of the Jewish Agency was to form the core of the provisional government of the state of Israel.

2.

In 1945 hundreds of thousands of hopeless, stateless Jews lived in hastily built displaced persons camps in Western Europe. No Western nation was ready to receive more than a token handful of them. With an eye on its own domestic politics, the United States government demanded that Britain disregard its earlier Palestine policy and accept 100,000 refugees into Palestine at once. Britain refused. The growing spirit of revolt in the Arab empire made Britain unwilling to increase Arab anger. Openly encouraged by Washington and financed almost entirely by private American gifts, Zionists smuggled great numbers of Jews from Europe into Palestine past an ineffective British blockade.

By 1947 there were approximately 700,000 Jews in Palestine and a

2. *New York Times,* May 12, 1942.
3. William Yale, *The Near East* (Ann Arbor: University of Michigan Press, 1958), pp. 404–6.

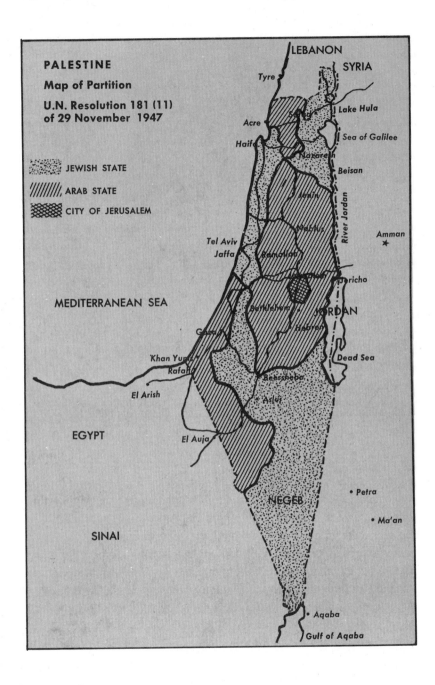

PALESTINE

Map of Partition

U.N. Resolution 181 (11)
of 29 November 1947

JEWISH STATE

ARAB STATE

CITY OF JERUSALEM

LEBANON

SYRIA

Tyre

Lake Hula

Acre

Safad

Haifa

Sea of Galilee

Nazareth

Beisan

Jenin

Nablus

River Jordan

Amman

Tel Aviv

Jaffa

Ramallah

MEDITERRANEAN SEA

Bethlehem

Jericho

JORDAN

Gaza

Hebron

Khan Yunis

Rafah

Dead Sea

El Arish

Beersheba

Asluj

EGYPT

El Auja

NEGEB

Petra

Ma'an

SINAI

Aqaba

Gulf of Aqaba

secret army, the Haganah (together with Irgun Zvai Leumi and the Stern Gang), operated against both the Arab population and the British administration. In February, 1947, Britain announced that it was "not prepared to govern Palestine" any longer under those conditions.[4] On April 2, 1947, she invited the United Nations General Assembly to "make recommendations under Article 10 of the Charter for the future government of Palestine."

Five Arab states asked the Assembly to recognize Palestine as an independent Arab nation. Both the General Committee of the Assembly and the Assembly itself refused to put the Arab proposal on the agenda. The Assembly instead named a Special Palestine Committee, which reported two suggestions on September 7: a majority recommendation for the creation of separate Arab and Jewish states in Palestine and a minority proposal for one federal state with autonomous Arab and Jewish regions. Both called for an international zone to include Jerusalem and its immediate vicinity in recognition of Jerusalem's importance as a Holy City for Jew, Muslim, and Christian. On November 29, 1947, the General Assembly adopted the majority proposal, recommending, with Solomonian justice, the partition of Palestine into two states. The Zionists accepted the plan and the Arabs rejected it. Arabs still owned over 80 percent of the land, either privately or by public domain, but the partition granted the Jewish minority—at least half of whom were neither citizens nor lawful residents, having been illegally smuggled into the country—56 percent of the territory of Palestine. After an international zone was set aside, the Arab majority was asked to be content with what was left. (When the Arabs rejected this historically unprecedented and legally unjustifiable solution and when hostilities started, Israel, after declaring its independence, annexed 23 percent more of Palestine, thus increasing the share allowed by the partition by almost 45 percent.)

In a draft resolution presented to the Security Council on November 11, 1947, before the Partition Plan was adopted, the Arab states posed a series of legal questions and asked that they be referred to the International Court of Justice. The chief points were those of (1) the legal right of the United Nations to dispose arbitrarily of Arab territory and (2) the inherent right of an indigenous population to determine its own constitution and government. Other legal problems

---

4. *New York Times*, February 13, 1941.

were posed including that of the legal effect of promises made to Arab leaders by Britain and France during World War I for the establishment of a free Arab state, that of the legal status of the Balfour Declaration and the Palestine mandate which were created without Arab participation or approval, the question of British authority in Palestine under a mandate from a league that no longer existed, and the related question of the authority of the United Nations to deal with Palestine on the basis of that mandate. The Arab resolution failed adoption by 20 to 21, with 13 abstentions. The then European majority control in the U.N. in the name of international law had unilaterally abrogated the Palestinians' right to self-determination—a tragic lesson in practical world politics.

3.

Britain pulled out of Palestine on May 14, 1948. On that same day a provisional government in Tel Aviv proclaimed the state of Israel. Barely minutes after that announcement, President Harry S Truman extended American recognition to the new state. It may be properly asserted, however, that Israel's creation was not sanctioned by international law. Recognition by other states was and is a political, not a legal, decision. Such recognition has no more significance in world law than the decision of the United States *not* to recognize mainland China.

Since an advisory opinion of the International Court of Justice on the Partition Plan had not been obtained the extent of protection of the Arab population required under article 80 of the U.N. Charter was left to a political rather than to a legal determination, and the question of the legality of a Jewish state remained. It seems clear, however, that the partition was a violation of the rights of the Arab population protected by the League of Nations mandate, of the Trusteeship articles of the U.N., and of article 80 which provides that in no manner can a trusteeship under the U.N. alter the existing rights of peoples.

The partition had resulted in the displacement of Arab peoples and outright usurpation of their property, as well as violation of the right of the people to self-determination. The Arab people were thus authorized to refuse acceptance of the partition. The illegality of the partition likewise would give no rights to the Jewish population to set up their state on illegally appropriated territory.

Israel's only claim to the territories it holds—either those originally incorporated in the newborn state of 1948 or those seized in the Arab-Israeli conflict of 1967—rests solely on military conquest. The principle has long been accepted in international law that military conquest does not confer lawful sovereignty—*jus ex injuria non oritur,* rights do not arise from wrongs.

Given the illegality of the Israeli position, the ensuing struggle with the Palestinian Arabs must be regarded as civil strife and not war. A question arises under international law as to foreign third-party intervention; but regardless of the validity of the Arab states' intervention, the foundation of the state of Israel remains either an illicit act by the U.N. or an invalid declaration of independence on usurped territory. Neither case would afford a legally valid basis for what is today a state recognized by the U.N. and most countries of the world.

The assertion by the Arab states that a state of war continues presupposes its original existence. If the initial conflict between Palestinian Arabs and Jews aided by non-Palestinian Jews who entered the land illegally were a civil strife, then Israel would today be the state successor of Palestine. All rights and obligations of the former state would, therefore, inure to the latter. If Israel's right to sovereignty (as a state and a nation) is denied, then a state of war could not legally exist with a nonstate entity. Niceties of that sort could produce interesting academic arguments. A state of military confrontation has existed and still exists between opposing contentious parties, and all the effects of war have resulted from this confrontation. The issues raised by the creation and existence of Israel are still relevant to the present context. (The Egyptian position on the right to visit and search vessels using the Suez Canal, for instance, represents an exercise of the rights of a party in a state of war.)

On May 11, 1949, the General Assembly voted to accept Israel as a member of the United Nations. Paragraph 4 of the preamble to this resolution took note of the declaration by the state of Israel that it "unreservedly accepts the obligations of the United Nations Charter and undertakes to honour them from the day when it becomes a Member of the United Nations." But not only the obligations to which Israel would be bound as a successor state,[5] but also those which were

---

5. See, for example, A. B. Keith, *Theory of State Succession* (London, 1908), p. 5; G. H. Hackworth, *Digest of International Law* (Washington, D.C.: Government Printing Office, 1943), pp. 360–77; L. F. L. Oppenheim, *International Law: A Treatise,* ed. H. Lauterpacht, 8th ed. (London: Longmans Green, 1955), pp. 156–69, 571–73, 944–45.

specifically imposed upon it by the U.N. (especially the resolutions establishing the right of the Palestinians to return to their homes or to claim compensation and those regarding the status of Jerusalem) are flouted by Israel with impunity. The world community outlawed war as early as 1929,[6] and the U.N. Charter reiterates this prohibition. The world community and the U.N., however, have not, in the name of preserving peace, condoned the violation of the charter's decisions with respect to the preservation of the human and political rights of the exiled Palestinian people. The Arab states maintain their responsibility for the preservation of the Palestinians' rights on the same ground of kinship as that the Jews of Israel have claimed for their European brothers in faith.

As events unfolded, Israeli aggressiveness gave rise to the right of individual and collective Arab self-defense. Israeli expansionism was manifested by the gradual takeover of the rest of Palestine, its aggression on Egypt in 1956 and 1967, and other aggressive acts. The principles of state of war and justifiable self-defense are analogous to the story of the chicken and the egg. The Arab states and Israel justify their respective conduct by that of their opponent. If the vertical chain of events is to be logically followed, one would be back to the question of the validity of the creation and existence of Israel as a sovereign state and to its unfulfilled ensuing obligations.

4.

The boundaries of Israel are certainly a legal issue, but they are a derivative one. Their derivation is from the actions and issues pertaining to the very creation of the state. If the birthright of Israel is the 1947 partition, then the situation is clear; as we have seen, however, the question of the legality of the Partition Plan remains untested. But if the boundaries of Israel are set by its declaration of independence of 1948, then the territory it occupies must be regarded as wholly usurped or at least conquered. That Israel can declare the occupied territory as its own would be violative of international law if it were not for the color of legality assumed by the U.N. grant of the partitioned territory.

---

6. The Kellogg-Briand Pact of 1929. See Quincy Wright, "The Meaning of the Pact of Paris," *American Journal of International Law*, XXVII (January, 1933), pp. 39–61; and Wright, *The Outlawry of War and the Law of War,* 1953.

It should be noted, however, that Israel cannot consistently maintain its right to statehood based on the territorial grant of the U.N. and also claim historical biblical rationalizations for its conquest and declaration of independence.

The armistice demarcation lines, or cease-fire lines, can by no stretch of the legal imagination become the basis of permanently legal territory without the express approval of the Arab sovereign owners. Such territory as Israel occupies today is not *territorium nullius* but claimed territory upon which the sovereign Arab states exercised their jurisdiction and sovereignty—sovereignty which cannot be conferred upon an aggressor by reason of conquest. Israel cannot claim right to such territories beyond the questionably allocated territory of 1947, either by conquest or by prescription. Consequently no rights of sovereignty under international law inure to Israel from such forceful and illegal seizure of another (equal) sovereign state's territory.

Title to territory cannot be acquired through conquest in a legal order wherein war is outlawed. A state resorting to war or seizing territory belonging to another acts contrary to its obligation. Article 10 of the Covenant of the League of Nations established the inviolability of national sovereignty,[7] as did the Inter-American Convention on Rights and Duties of States (article 11), and the Draft Declaration on Rights and Duties of States (articles 9–10–11). This notion lies at the very heart of the Kellogg-Briand Pact of 1929 and the U.N. Charter (article 2, paragraph 4). It is part of American concepts of international law.[8] These principles are so well established in international law that the unanimous resolution of the Security Council of November 22, 1967, stated: *"Emphasizing* the inadmissibility of the acquisition of territory by war . . . , (i) withdrawal of Israeli armed forces from territories occupied in the recent conflict . . ."* is called for. The fact that the Arab states whose territory was thus taken refuse to recognize the state of Israel or claim belligerency does not warrant Israel's occupation and certainly not its usurpation of any such Arab territory.

Israeli refusal to withdraw from the occupied territory is in deliber-

---

7. See *American Journal of International Law Supplement,* Vol. XV, No. 1–4 (1921).

8. Ellery C. Stowell, "The Stewardship of Secretary Stimson," *American Journal of International Law,* XXVII (January, 1933), pp. 102–4.

ate violation of the U.N. order and is a clear indication of Israel's intention to pursue a course of territorial expansion at the cost of its neighbors and in disregard of the orders of the United Nations of which it is a member. Israeli intentions were made manifest in the 1967 occupation of Jerusalem by force and the subsequent annexation of Jerusalem as Israeli territory—an act which could not be accomplished under any rule except the rule of might. The U.N. reacted promptly and adopted resolutions on July 4 and July 14, 1967, the latter by 100 to 0 with 18 abstentions (including the U.S.), which declared Israel's action "invalid" and called upon Israel "to rescind all measures already taken and desist forthwith from taking any action which would alter the status of Jerusalem." This condemnation, however, did not deter Israel's implementation of its program of annexation.

5.

There are presently 140 nations in the world community, not one of which has been established with a people composed of disparate nationalities linked together by the vague contours of a political doctrine claiming to be based on religious premises.

The requirement under international law that a state have a composite population has always meant that it be constituted by the people already living on the land and linked by a concept of nationhood. Nowhere is there any precedent or justification for the implantation of other persons gathered literally from the four corners of the world who base their association on "race" or religion. Theoretically nothing precludes such an occurrence if we were dealing with a *territorium nullius,* which does not have an indigenous population. The Zionists did not "discover" Palestine, but came upon an existing entity declared by the League of Nations as provisionally independent with sovereign territoriality and an established population.

During the first phase of the Arab-Israeli war (1947–49), over 800,000 Palestinian Arabs fled or were expelled from their homes by Zionist military forces. They found refuge in Jordan, Egypt, Syria, and Lebanon, where the United Nations UNRWA undertook to assist them. Today there are 1,344,576 registered refugees.

In June, 1948, the United Nations General Assembly dispatched Count Folke Bernadotte, vice-president of the Swedish Red Cross, to mediate the Arab-Israeli armed conflict. He achieved short-lived truce agreements, and on September 19, 1948, he sent a report of his mission to the secretary-general of the United Nations, Trygve Lie. A substantial portion of that report referred to the plight and the rights of the refugees and read in part:

> The right of innocent people, uprooted from their homes by the present terror and ravages of war, to be returned to their homes should be affirmed and made effective, with assurance of adequate compensation for the property of those who choose not to return.
> The liability of the provisional government of Israel to restore private property to its private owners and to indemnify those owners for property wantonly destroyed is clear . . . [it would be] an offense against the principles of elemental justice if those innocent victims of the conflict were denied the right to return to their homes while Jewish immigrants flow into Palestine . . . and offer the threat of permanent replacement of the Arab refugees who have been rooted in the land for centuries.[9]

On September 20, Zionist gunmen assassinated Bernadotte in Jerusalem, but the recommendations he had made for the treatment of the refugee problem were incorporated in a General Assembly resolution that called for repatriation of all refugees who wished to return, compensation for those who chose not to return, and indemnities for all private property destroyed by Israeli forces.[10]

It is a true paradox that is real: the state created for the stateless has in effect made stateless the citizens of the state where they sought refuge. The most significant reasons for the upsurge of human rights in modern international law and the Universal Declaration of Human Rights were the events of World War II, the major victims of which were European Jews. It is those same persons who today, in the eyes of many, are guilty of precisely that which they once suffered.

Palestinians had enjoyed the privileges of citizenship and carried Palestinian passports irrespective of their faith. This was specified by articles 5 and 7 of the mandate. British policy since 1922 aimed at maintaining the Palestinian character of that provisionally independent state and reasserted this policy frequently. The Partition Plan of 1947

---

9. United Nations Security Council (S/801), May, 1948, Supp., pp. 103–104.
10. United Nations GAOR (Res. 194), 1948.

was also careful in safeguarding the civil, political, economic, religious, and all human rights and fundamental freedoms of all people concerned.[11]

On December 11, 1948, the U.N. General Assembly adopted resolution 194, of which paragraph 11 stated

> that the refugees wishing to return to their homes and live at peace with their neighbors should be permitted to do so at the earliest practicable date, and that compensation should be paid for the property of those choosing not to return and for loss of or damage to property, which, under principles of International Law or in equity, should be made good by the governments or authorities responsible.

The same resolution established a Conciliation Commission with the purpose of implementing the above quoted paragraph. On May 12, 1949, under the auspices of the U.N. Conciliation Commission, the Lausanne Protocol, in which Israel pledged, among other things, to implement the General Assembly's resolution 194, was signed. Subsequent to the admission of Israel to membership in the United Nations, which was conditioned upon its acceptance of resolution 194, Israel renounced its earlier pledge.

For the next twenty years, the General Assembly in twenty-two resolutions was to reaffirm its resolution 194 only to be consistently disregarded by Israel.

6.

Israeli diversion of the waters of the Jordan River system presents a situation on which the law of nations and the laws of individual states are clear and unequivocal.

In 1939, the Jewish Agency for Palestine asked an American engineer, Walter Lowdermilk, to study Palestine's irrigation problems. The Lowdermilk scheme proposed diversion of the flow of the Jordan River system far beyond the Jordan Valley watershed. Later studies by two other Americans, James B. Hayes and J. V. Savage, consultants to the Jewish Agency, incorporated the Lowdermilk proposal. Its undisguised

---

11. *Parliamentary Papers, 1922,* (London: H.M.S.O., 1922), Cmd. 1700 at 18; *ibid.,* Cmd. 1785; *Parliamentary Papers, 1938–39* (London: H.M.S.O., 1939), Cmd. 6019 at 2 and 3.

purpose was "to take as much as possible of the Jordan's waters right out of the Jordan's own valley, away from the people of it, and run it over the watershed of the basin to irrigate lands far away."[12] In 1956 Israel adopted a ten-year plan which provided for diversion of 700 million cubic meters from the Jordan River system to irrigate agricultural land and meet municipal needs inside her own territory. Since the total flow of the Jordan above Lake Tiberias was only 600 million cubic meters, it seemed obvious that Israel also intended to divert much of the water supplied by the Yarmuk River which enters the Jordan below Tiberias from Jordanian territory.

In 1951 Sir Murdoch Macdonald and Partners, a British firm, suggested to the Kingdom of Jordan an alternative plan for joint utilization of the river waters by all riparian states, including Israel. It differed sharply from the Lowdermilk-Hayes scheme in that it proposed utilization of all the flow of the river system within the Jordan River valley. Macdonald based his program on the general principle, which has an undoubted moral and natural basis, that the waters in a catchment area should not be diverted outside this area unless the requirements of all who use or genuinely intend to use the water within the area have been satisfied.[13]

Miles Bunger, an American associated with the U.S. Technical Cooperation Agency (Point Four) proposed distribution of the Jordan River system's water between Israel and her three Arab neighbors on the basis of need, taking into account particularly the fact that almost all this water originated in Arab countries.[14] The United Nations Relief and Works Agency and the Technical Cooperation Agency approved the Bunger Plan, and work under it began in December, 1953. Abruptly, and without explanation, the United States withdrew its support and offered a new program (generally called the Johnston Plan) which was essentially the original Lowdermilk-Hayes scheme.

But before the Bunger Plan had been approved, Israel, in 1951, had undertaken a project to deepen and straighten the bed of the Jordan at

---

12. M. C. Ionides, "The Disputed Waters of the Jordan," *Middle East Journal,* VII (Spring, 1953), 157; see also James B. Hayes, *T.V.A. on the Jordan* (Washington: Public Affairs Press, 1948).

13. Murdoch Macdonald and Partners, *Report on the Proposed Extension of Irrigation in the Jordan River Valley* (London, 1954).

14. Omar Z. Ghobashy, *The Development of the Jordan* (New York: Arab Information Center, 1961), pp. 13–15.

the south end of Lake Huleh, but desisted when the chief of the U.N. Armistice Commission ruled that this project violated the Syrian-Israeli armistice. On September 2, 1953, in response to a Syrian complaint, the Armistice Commission again ordered Israel to abandon a plan to alter the Jordan River's course to bring it inside Israeli territory. Israel then began to build diversion works on the south shore of Lake Tiberias, with a system of canals, tunnels, and pumping stations to carry the water into the Negev region. In 1964 this system went into operation.

7.

The issue of the use of the flow of streams that touch more than one state has been before European and American courts many times, and the principles governing riparian rights to interstate streams are well established in international law.

A statement on the use of interstate streams was made by the General Conference on Communication and Transit established by the League of Nations,[15] and in 1951 the Economic Commission of Europe compiled a record of international conventions concerned with the use of waterways for purposes other than irrigation. In its 1958 meeting in New York, the International Law Association took up the question of international streams and adopted this principle:

> Except as provided by treaty or other instruments or customs binding upon the parties, each coriparian state is entitled to a reasonable and equitable share in the beneficial use of the waters of the drainage basin. What amounts to a reasonable and equitable share is a question to be determined in the light of all the relevant factors in each particular case.[16]

International jurists appear to agree that the right of national sovereignty does not give any state the right to divert the waters of an international river to the detriment and substantial injury of coriparian

---

15. George Sevette, *Legal Aspects of the Jordan Valley Development* (Geneva, 1953), p. 27.

16. United Nations, Economic and Social Council, *Integrated River Basin Development,* E/3066 (1958), pp. 33–34.

states. Oppenheim, recognized as the leading authority among writers on world law, said:

> The flow of international rivers is not within the arbitrary powers of one of the riparian states, for it is a rule of international law that no state is allowed to alter the natural conditions of the territory of a neighboring state. For this reason, a state is not only forbidden to stop or divert the flow of a river which runs from its own to a neighboring state, but likewise to make such use of the water of the river as either cause danger to the neighboring state or prevents it from making proper use of the flow of the river on its part.[17]

It is not only forbidden that one riparian state divert or otherwise use the flow of an international stream if this act causes injury to coriparian states, but international law also recognizes that every riparian state has specific rights in the waters of a river that flows through or past its territory. Those rights include a right to the volume of water actually used by it for irrigation and a reserved right to use some of the surplus quantity not already used for irrigation by other riparian states and which is lost by the river at its mouth. A similar right exists to the use of surplus water resulting from development plans saving water by prevention of evaporation, drainage, canals, dams, and better storage facilities. On this subject an English authority, H. A. Smith, wrote:

> A riparian state is entitled to as much of the waters of an international river as she was actually using for irrigation prior to any claim by another riparian state.[18]

It follows that any claim put forward by Israel is necessarily subrogated to the uses of the waters of the Jordan River by coriparian Arab states prior to the establishment of the Zionist state. This prior right has been consistently recognized by the United States and is known as the right of prior appropriation.

Existing treaty obligations at the time of the establishment of Israel, which would appear to be binding on Israel in accordance with accepted practices in the matter of state succession, conferred definite

---

17. Oppenheim, *International Law*, 1955, p. 474.
18. *American Supreme Court and International Tribunals* (New York: Oxford University Press, 1920), pp. 79–80.

riparian rights on the Arab states. These are found specifically in the exchange of notes between Great Britain and France dated March 7, 1923, concerning the boundary between Syria and Palestine, which provided that existing Syrian rights in the use of the waters of the Jordan River would be maintained unimpaired. If Israel is a successor state, regardless of the manner and circumstances of its creation, it cannot in law at once claim statehood and reject the legal obligations imposed upon it by a treaty that remained in full force and effect when Israel succeeded to the territory covered by that treaty.

On the basis of all principles of international law, Israel's unilateral diversion of the Jordan River is illegal and unjustifiable.

8.

Israel's most insistent demand in its relations with the U.A.R. has been for the use of the Suez Canal. This demand, supported by the United States and some other governments, has been based on the theory that the Canal is an international waterway open on equal terms to all states.

The Maritime Suez Canal links the Red and Mediterranean Seas across the Isthmus of Suez. It has been and is still governed by the terms of the Constantinople Convention of October 29, 1888.[19] The parties to this convention were France, Germany, the Empire of Austria-Hungary, Spain, Great Britain, Italy, Holland, Russia, and Turkey. When Egypt achieved independence she succeeded to the rights and obligations of Turkey, across whose territory the waterway was constructed, in accordance with international law governing successor states. Article 8 of the Anglo-Egyptian Treaty of 1954 reasserted that "The Maritime Suez Canal . . . is an integral part of Egypt." In addition, Egypt enjoyed certain rights and bore certain obligations specifically set forth in the 1888 convention.

The convention delegated to Egypt execution of the principles and obligations established by the agreement, with these words in article 9: "The Egyptian Government is to take . . . the necessary measures to enforce the execution of said treaty." The language is specific, and Egypt remains the sole judge as to the measures required for implemen-

---

19. M. Cherif Bassiouni, "The Nationalization of the Suez Canal, and the Illicit Act in International Law," *De Paul Law Review,* XIV (Spring, 1965), 258.

tation of the treaty. This cannot be considered a discretionary power to take measures that do not conform to the terms of the convention. Article 14 of the convention stipulated also that obligations imposed by that treaty were not to be limited in time to "the duration of the concessions granted the Universal Company of the Suez Canal"; this article assumes special significance because it clearly distinguishes between the Canal itself and the Universal Maritime Suez Canal Company as the operating agency for the waterway.[20]

Article 14 of the 1888 convention amounted to a clear acknowledgment that Egyptian sovereignty over the Canal and the rights and obligations of the company were two separate matters, in fact and in law.

The Universal Maritime Suez Canal Company was an Egyptian corporation, established under Egyptian law and, like any other private corporation, subject to that law. It was set up to perform a specific, needed public service: construction and operation of a waterway between two seas. It had no independent existence outside the terms of its establishment and no rights or authority beyond those specifically granted to it by the government of Egypt. Its character was no different from that of a public utility corporation in the United States authorized to distribute electric power to communities and individuals within the area prescribed by the terms of its charter and subject to regulation under the laws of the chartering government. That the shares of the company were all owned outside Egypt had no bearing whatever on the character or status of the company. A corporation is in itself a legal entity, whoever may own or control its stock.

The Egyptian decree of July 26, 1956, nationalized the assets of the Canal Company. It did not nationalize the Suez Canal because there was neither need nor reason to assert Egyptian control over what had always been Egypt's own. The right to transmit through the Suez Canal had been spelled out in the convention of 1888, the terms of which Egypt was obliged to carry out. In law the decree of July 26, 1956, altered none of the rights and obligations arising under international law, but merely substituted one operating agency for another. It did, however, have a powerful political impact, and this—a dramatic shift of political power in the whole Middle East region—created the situation that faced the world in the year 1956.

20. *Ibid.*, pp. 265, 266, *et seq.*

9.

Great Britain and France, strongly supported by the United States and less eagerly supported by some other governments, attempted not only to compel Egypt to permit operation of the Canal on their terms but even to undermine Egypt's territorial sovereignty in the Canal Zone.[21] Britain, France, and Israel resorted to war to achieve these aims but abandoned their aggression in the face of overwhelming pressure from the United Nations and world opinion. This conclusion of the 1956 Suez affair settled for all time the question of Egyptian sovereignty over the Canal and the juridical status of the Suez Canal Authority. Unrestricted use of the Suez Canal, however, remains a prime political and economic goal of the state of Israel.

The Treaty of Constantinople guarantees the right of free navigation in the Canal, and it still stands today as the basic document guaranteeing that freedom.[22] Of prime importance in the treaty are articles 1 and 4 which establish the principle of freedom of passage.[23] Article 1 provides:

> The Suez Maritime Canal shall always be free and open, in time of war as in time of peace, to every vessel of commerce or of war, without distinction of flag.
>
> Consequently, the High Contracting Parties agree not in any way to interfere with the free use of the Canal, in time of war as in time of peace.
>
> The Canal shall never be subjected to the exercise of the right of blockade.

The first paragraph of article 4 declares:

> The Maritime Canal remaining open in time of war as a free passage, even to ships of war of belligerents, according to the terms of Article I of the present Treaty, the High Contracting Parties agree

---

21. Anthony Nutting, *No End of a Lesson: The Inside Story of the Suez Crisis* (New York: C. N. Potter, 1967), pp. 52–71.

22. Simcha Dinitz, "The Legal Aspects of the Egyptian Blockade of the Suez Canal," *Georgetown Law Journal*, XLV (1956–1957), p. 175.

23. See also U.S. Department of State, *The Suez Canal Problem* (Washington, D.C.: Government Printing Office, 1956), pp. 16–19.

that no right of war, no act of hostility, nor any act having for its object to obstruct the free navigation of the Canal, shall be committed in the Canal and its ports of access, as well as within a radius of three marine miles from these ports, even though the Ottoman Empire should be one of the belligerent Powers.

Israel was not, of course, in existence when the 1888 convention pledged the right of passage to ships of all nations in peace and war. It has been argued that this right accrued to it as a continuing right available to all states. Authorities have pointed out, however, that this dedication—a stipulation in favor of third parties—is a concept of domestic private law and has no place in international law because it is alien to the techniques and incompatible with the characteristics of this discipline. In 1929 the International Court of Justice ruled specifically that stipulation in favor of third states is not a rule of international law.[24]

It thus appears that Israel acquired no right to the beneficial use of the Suez Canal under the convention of 1888 and that, having never acquired such a right through the implied unanimous consent of all contracting parties by unobstructed habitual transit of the Canal,[25] there is no avenue open to Israel under international law to assert such a right.

On May 4, 1948, Israel declared its independence, and on the same day Egypt, as a member of the Arab bloc, established a general blockade against Israel in the Suez Maritime Canal.

On February 6, 1950, King Farouk I of Egypt issued a decree on the procedure of ship and airplane searches and seizure of contraband goods in connection with the Palestine War. This decree, known as the Embargo Act of February 6, 1950, provided for the continuance of "visit and search" practices. Article 2 of the act provided for customs officials to inspect a suspected ship's manifest and cargo for such contraband as arms, munitions, and war matériel. In article 3 it was stated that "force may be used at all times against any ship attempting to avoid search, where necessary, by firing so as to force the ship to

---

24. International Court of Justice, Case of *The Free Zones of Upper Savoy and District of Cos,* August 19, 1929; see also *Report of Committee on Uses of International Rivers and Canals,* International Law Association Conference, Hamburg, 1960, p. 58.

25. Oppenheim, *International Law,* 1955, pp. 926–27.

stop and submit to search." An amendment to the decree added to the list of contraband "foodstuffs and all other commodities which are likely to strengthen the war potential of the Zionists in Palestine in any way whatever." The Egyptian authorities drew up a "black list" of ships known to be carrying certain materials to Israel and also established a Prize Court at Alexandria to dispose of confiscated goods.

The most frequent argument raised against Egypt's actions of visit, search, and confiscation pursuant to the Embargo Act of 1950, states that such blockade actions are a direct breach of the Treaty of Constantinople which guaranteed free passage and prohibited blockades in articles 1 and 4. This argument can be resolved by an examination of article 10 of that treaty which provides:

> Similarly, the provisions of Articles 4, 5, 7, and 8 shall not interfere with the measures which His Majesty the Sultan and His Highness the Khedive, in the name of His Imperial Majesty, and within the limits of the Firmans granted, might find it necessary to take for securing by their own forces the defense of Egypt and the maintenance of public order.

It is in reliance on this provision of the treaty that Egypt exercised her sovereign right of search for reasons of her own defense. One writer comments:

> For though there is an explicit freedom of use, even in wartime, laid down in the Convention of Constantinople, there is also a provision in Article 10 that neither that liberty nor the other stipulations of the agreements shall hinder measures necessary for the defense of Egypt and the maintenance of public order. In any event, it would be less than realistic to expect a state at war to allow free passage through any portion of its territory to the ships, supplies or nationals of an enemy.[26]

It should also be noted that article 9 of the Treaty of Constantinople declares that "the Egyptian Government is to take the necessary measures to enforce the execution of the Treaty," and article 12 pro-

---

26. P. E. Corbett, *Law and Society in the Relations of States* (New York: Harcourt, Brace, 1951).

vides "that all rights of Turkey [to which Egypt is the successor state] as the territoral power are still reserved."

10.

Taking a historical approach, Egypt's actions are certainly not without precedent. During both world wars Great Britain blockaded the Canal against use by Germany and her allies. The procedure used by Great Britain was first to stop and search the enemy vessel at the entrance to the Canal, and if contraband was found the vessel was directed to proceed through the Canal. The vessel having passed safely through, the enemy halted it and seized the contraband, the effect being a *de facto* blockade.

Another argument advanced against the blockade practices of Egypt in the Suez Maritime Canal, and the Gulf of Aqaba as well, contends that the armistice signed at Rhodes by Egypt and Israel on February 24, 1949, prohibited any further hostilities by the opposing parties and that Egypt's actions pursuant to the Embargo Act of February, 1950, after the armistice had been signed, constitute acts of aggression in violation of the armistice. But paragraph 2 of article 2 of that armistice declares:

> No element of the land, sea or military or para-military forces of either party, including non-regular forces, shall commit any warlike or hostile act against the military or para-military forces of the other party.

As was noted above, under the Embargo Act of 1950 it is provided that visit and search of Israeli and suspect neutral ships be conducted by regular Egyptian customs officials. Strictly interpreting the above article of the armistice, customs officials are neither military nor paramilitary forces.

A further interpretation of the crucial article 2 of the armistice is contained in a statement by the chief of staff of the United Nations Truce Supervision Organization:

> . . . interference with the passage of goods destined for Israel through the Suez Canal is a hostile act, but not necessarily against the General Armistice Agreement, because of the limitations imposed

on the term "hostile act" in the text of Article 2, paragraph 2 of the General Armistice Agreement.[27]

The crux of the argument, and the point which was never resolved, centered about the interpretation to be given the effect of the armistice by the parties.

The Egyptian representative told the United Nations Special Committee of the Mixed Armistice Commission on June 12, 1951, that "We are exercising a right of war. . . . We are still legally at war with Israel. An Armistice does not put an end to a state of war. It does not prohibit a country from exercising certain rights of war."[28]

Oppenheim has stated the effect of armistices as they are traditionally considered:

> Armistices or truces, in the wider sense of the term, are all agreements between belligerent forces for a temporary cessation of hostilities. They are in no wise to be compared to peace . . . because the condition of war remains between the belligerents themselves, and between belligerents and neutrals, on all points beyond the mere cessation of hostilities. In spite of such cessation the right of visit and search over neutral merchantmen therefore remains intact.[29]

In July, 1951, the representative of Israel complained to the Security Council of the United Nations that the armistice signed at Rhodes had terminated the Egyptian-Israeli war, yet Egypt continued to blockade Israeli vessels and neutral vessels destined for Israeli ports. As a result, the Security Council passed a resolution on September 1, 1951, calling upon Egypt to lift its blockade.

Commenting on this action of the Security Council, Colonel Howard S. Levie wrote:

> It is considered more likely that the Security Council's action was based on a desire to bring an end to a situation fraught with potential danger to peace than it was attempting to change a long established rule of international law. By now it has surely become fairly obvious

---

27. Treaty No. 654, between Israel and Egypt, signed at Rhodes, February 24, 1949.
28. L. M. Bloomfield, *Egypt Israel, and the Gulf of Aqaba in International Law* (Toronto: Carswell, 1957), p. 50.
29. L. F. L. Oppenheim, *International Law: Disputes, War and Neutrality*, ed. H. Lauterpacht, 7th ed. (London: Longmans Green, 1952), pp. 546–51.

113

that the Israeli-Arab General Armistice Agreement did not create even a *de facto* termination of the war between those states.[30]

Before the Security Council, the representative of Egypt stated the position of his government on the General Armistice Agreement:

> The fact that the Armistice Agreement is silent on this point [of the right of visit and search], of although it is fairly common practice to include a provision on this subject in armistice agreements, shows, as indeed the Mixed Armistice Commission has confirmed, that the Armistice Agreement of the classical type concluded between Egypt and Israel expressed the joint will of the signatories and left them free to exercise their legitimate right of visit and search.[31]

On October 29, 1956, Israeli forces invaded the Sinai Peninsula, and within a few days occupied Sharm el-Sheikh, thereby gaining control of the Gulf of Aqaba. This invasion by Israel brought an end to the General Armistice Agreement, and in the words of Premier Ben Gurion of Israel to the Israeli Knesset in November, 1956, ". . . the Armistice with Egypt is dead and so are the Armistice lines. No magician can bring back life to those lines." [32]

. After Israeli forces withdrew from the Sinai Peninsula and were replaced by the United Nations Expeditionary Force, the Egyptian government, which had nationalized the Universal Maritime Suez Canal Company, availed itself of the rights of a belligerent and continued to adhere to its interpretation of the Constantinople Convention. On July 18, 1957, however, Egypt accepted the "compulsory" jurisdiction of the International Court of Justice in all matters relating to the interpretation of the Constantinople Convention or freedom of navigation in the Suez Canal. While Egypt is willing to permit the entire question to be settled through the International Court of Justice, Israel has not communicated a corresponding intent.

11.

The Gulf of Aqaba is the eastern arm of two arms of water into which the Sinai Peninsula separates the Red Sea at its northern extremity.

30. Howard S. Levie, "The Nature and Scope of the Armistice Agreement," *American Journal of International Law*, L (October, 1956), 880–906.

31. United Nations, Security Council, *Official Records*, 661st Meeting, March 12, 1954, pp. 9–13.

32. United Arab Republic Information Department, *Navigation in the Suez Canal* (Cairo, 1962), p. 33.

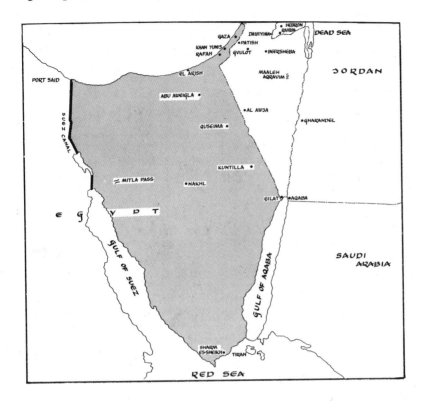

The western arm constitutes the Gulf of Suez. The Gulf of Aqaba is somewhat over one hundred miles in length and varies from three to seventeen miles in width. At the mouth of the Gulf the distance from the Sinai Peninsula headland to the Saudi Arabian Peninsula headland measure nine miles, and since each of these countries claims a territorial sea extending six miles from its coastline, their respective territorial waters overlap. At the entrance to the Gulf are located the islands of Tiran and Sanafir, which are under the control of Saudi Arabia. The only navigable passage into the Gulf is through the strait on the western side of the island of Tiran, and ships passing through this strait pass through the territorial waters of the United Arab Republic.

In 1841 the Ottoman Empire recognized the Port and Gulf of Aqaba as belonging to Egypt, as well as the Sinai Peninsula. Since Egypt obtained its independence in 1922, it has clearly been sovereign of the western shore of the Gulf of Aqaba from Ras Tabah southwards, of the eastern shore of the Gulf from a point two miles south of

115

the port of Aqaba to the Gulf's entrance.[33] Presently, the United Arab Republic occupies the western shore of the Gulf from the town of Tabah to the southernmost part of the Gulf, while Saudi Arabia occupies the area mentioned above. The ten-mile northern shore is occupied to the extent of a four-mile northeastern segment by Jordan, and a five-mile northwestern segment by Israel.

Israel bases her claim to the right of free passage through the Straits of Tiran and into the Gulf of Aqaba on her geographical position as one of the four littoral states bounding the Gulf. This five-mile coastal area now occupied by Israel was not within the temporary borders established for that state by the United Nations Security Council resolution of July 15, 1948. Within two weeks after the signing of the General Armistice Agreement at Rhodes, the Israeli army invaded the Negev desert and proceeded southward to the Gulf af Aqaba, occupying the village of Um Rashrash, today known as the port of Elath. As a result of this action on the part of Israel, the Egyptian government as well as the entire Arab bloc have refused to accept the occupation of this area by Israel as anything else but a belligerent occupation by virtue of military aggression.

Concerning belligerent occupations, Oppenheim states that, "An occupant in no wise acquires sovereignty over such territory through the mere fact of having occupied it."[34] The clearly recognized principle in international law that annexing of a territory occupied by military force can have legal effects only if the state of war ends by the conclusion of a peace treaty has been discussed above. As yet no such treaty has been signed by the United Arab Republic and Israel, and therefore it would appear that Israel remains a belligerent occupant of the area. Considering these facts, the United Arab Republic is justified in blockading the Gulf of Aqaba, inasmuch as the right to free and innocent passage through such waters in suspended to nations which

---

33. See "The Legality of the UAR's Position," *Arab News and Views,* Vol. XII, No. 10 (1967). See also A. E. Hogan, *Pacific Blockade* (Oxford; Clarendon, 1908); and Maron E. Siney, *The Allied Blockade of Germany 1914–1916* (Ann Arbor: University of Michigan Press, 1957). See also authorities cited in G. G. Wilson, *Handbook of International Law,* 3d ed. (St. Paul: West Publishing Co., 1939), pp. 247–48 and 379; and Philip Jessup, *A Modern Law of Nations* (New York: Macmillan, 1950), p. 176; U.S. Department of State, *Bulletin,* Publication No. 46 (Washington, D.C.: Government Printing Office, 1962), pp. 278–79. See also Charles B. Selak, Jr., "A Consideration of the Legal Status of the Gulf of Aqaba," *American Journal of International Law,* LII (October, 1958), 660.

34. Oppenheim, *International Law,* 1955, p. 433.

are at war as well as to nations which carry strategic goods to a belligerent nation and seek passage through the territorial waters of a nation which is a party to the belligerence.

In addition to the argument advanced by the Arab bloc that Israel is a belligerent occupier on the Gulf of Aqaba, the Arab countries, particularly Saudi Arabia, have also proposed that the Gulf of Aqaba itself is a closed sea, or a *mare clausum,* and is governed under the general rules of international law which provide for free and innocent passage in time of peace to all nations who border on the inland sea. The principle applicable in time of war is set out in the preceding paragraph.

Of great importance in the overall discussion of the rights of the littoral states on the Gulf of Aqaba has been this argument between the belligerents, as well as between neutrals in the United Nations, as to the exact nature of the Gulf of Aqaba. Unless the nature of the Gulf itself is determined, the task of applying the international law applicable to the littoral states is extraordinarily difficult.

The Arab position in reference to the nature of the Gulf of Aqaba was made clear in the statement of the representative of Saudi Arabia to the General Assembly on October 2, 1957:

> The Gulf of Aqaba, basically is not an international question. . . . The Gulf of Aqaba is a national inland waterway, subject to absolute Arab sovereignty. The geographical location of the Gulf is conclusive proof of its national character. It is separated from the Red Sea by a chain of islands, the largest being Sanafir and Tiran. The only navigable entrance—which, itself, is within Arab territory—does not exceed 500 metres. Thus, by its configuration, the Gulf is in the nature of a *mare clausum,* which does not belong to the class of international waterways. . . . The Gulf is so narrow that the territorial areas of the littoral States are bound to overlap among themselves, under any kind of measurement, even if we assume that the Gulf comprehends part of the high seas.
>
> In the second place, the Gulf of Aqaba is of the category of historical gulfs that fall outside the sphere of international law. The Gulf is the historical route to the holy places in Mecca. Pilgrims from different Muslim countries have been streaming through the Gulf, year after year, for fourteen centuries. Ever since, the Gulf has been an exclusive Arab route under Arab sovereignty. It is due to this undisputed fact that not a single international authority makes any

117

mention whatsoever of the Gulf as an international waterway open for international navigation.

Israel . . . has no right to any part of the Gulf. Israel's claim ' . . . could only be argued on the United Nations' Plan of Partition or the Armistice lines. On either ground, the claim of Israel falls to the ground. On the plan of partition, Israel cannot claim Eilat because Israel is confined to the lines of the plan. . . . With regards to agreements, . . . under the express provisions of the armistice agreements, the armistice lines are purely "dictated" by "military considerations" and have no political significance.

Thus the area under Israel is nothing but military control without sovereignty whatsoever. Israel has no sovereign status in the Gulf of Aqaba. Israel's position is one of aggression.[35]

12.

In 1958 the United Nations Conference on the Law of the Sea met in Geneva, Switzerland. One of its primary, though undeclared purposes, was to formulate a set of international maritime laws that would be applicable to the Gulf of Aqaba. The end product was the Convention on the Territorial Sea and the Contiguous Zone and the Convention on the High Seas.

The law declared in the convention as it applies to the Gulf of Aqaba so closely parallels the position taken by the United States government shortly after Israel's invasion of the Sinai Peninsula that a brief examination of the events at that time is necessary.

On February 2, 1957, the United Nations passed two resolutions calling on Israel to complete its withdrawal behind the armistice demarcation line without further delay. Israel stated that it was reluctant to do so unless it had a guarantee that in return for withdrawal, the Gulf of Aqaba would remain open to its shipping and that it would be unequivocally recognized as an international waterway.

President Eisenhower stated on February 20, 1957, that

> With reference to the passage into and through the Gulf of Aqaba, we expressed the conviction that the Gulf constitutes international waters and that no nation has the right to prevent free and innocent passage in the Gulf. We announced that the United States was pre-

---

35. United Nations, General Assembly, *Official Records,* 697th Plenary Meeting, October 2, 1957, p. 233.

pared to exercise this right itself and to join with others to secure recognition of this right.[36]

In reliance upon the United States position, the Israeli government announced a full and prompt withdrawal from the Sharm el-Sheikh area and the Gaza Strip, in compliance with the General Assembly resolution of February 2, 1957. Foreign Minister Golda Meir of Israel, in addressing the General Assembly, commented:

My Government has subsequently learned with gratification that the other leading maritime powers are prepared to subscribe to the doctrine set out in the U.S. memorandum of 11 February and have a similar intention to exercise their rights of free and innocent passage in the Gulf and the Straits.[37]

Secretary of State Dulles referred to the Gulf of Aqaba as a "highly complicated question of international law" and went on to say:

In one sense of the word the Straits of Tiran are territorial, because they are less than six miles wide and the generally accepted zone of territorial control is three miles. . . . But it is also a principle of international law that even though waters are territorial, if they give access to a body of water which comprehends international waterways, there is a right of free and innocent passage . . . the United States' view is that the passage should be open unless there is a contrary decision by the International Court of Justice.[38]

In its deliberations on the right to free and innocent passage through Straits, the Geneva Conference on the Law of the Sea was considerably aided by a decision rendered eleven years earlier in the *Corfu Channel Case*. The court stated the law thus:

It is, in the opinion of the Court, generally recognized and in accordance with international custom that states in time of peace have a right to send their warships through straits used for international navigation between two parts of the high seas without the previous

---

36. U.S. Department of State, *Bulletin,* Publication No. 36 (Washington, D.C.: Government Printing Office, 1957), p. 389.

37. United Nations, General Assembly, *Official Records,* 666th Plenary Meeting, March 1, 1957, p. 1275.

38. U.S. Department of State, *Bulletin,* Publication No. 36 (Washington, D.C.: Government Printing Office, 1957), pp. 482–89.

authorization of a coastal state, provided that the passage is innocent.[39]

The rule was somewhat modified to fit the Straits of Tiran, which do not link two parts of the high seas. Article 16, paragraph 4 of the Convention on the Territorial Sea provides:

> There shall be no suspension of innocent passage of foreign ships through Straits which are used for international navigation between one part of the high seas and another part of the high seas or the territorial sea of a foreign state.

Article 14, paragraph 4 declares that:

> Passage is innocent so long as it is not prejudicial to the peace, good order or security of the coastal state.

In summary, even accepting the Geneva Convention's Article concerning the right to free and innocent passage, the United Arab Republic, which still considers itself at war with Israel, could continue to blockade the Gulf of Aqaba insofar as Israeli ships and neutral ships bound for the Israeli port of Elath are not engaged in an innocent passage.

Were Israel to occupy the status of a *de facto* littoral state, the United Arab Republic would still have the right of visit and search since Israeli ships would be forced to pass through territorial waters of the United Arab Republic, and these ships would be flying the flag of a belligerent nation. The result would be the same regardless if the Gulf of Aqaba were considered a closed inland sea or a non-territorial inland sea as Israel suggests. In either case, both the United Arab Republic and Israel are belligerents, and the law of war, and rights thereof, apply to the parties.

13.

In the history of modern world conflicts there is no other instance where the very nature of the conflict can be examined and resolved in

---

39. International Court of Justice, *Corfu Channel Case, Report 28,* 1949.

its entirety in a legal context. This does not imply that a legal determination is possible in the present practice of world affairs, but as almost all the political issues of the Palestine question and the conflict between Israel and some of the Arab states are superimposed on legal claims and moral rationalizations, it is *theoretically* possible to resolve the entirety of the Arab-Israeli conflict on a legal basis. Therefore the Arab states, and the U.A.R. in particular, seek to submit all or some of these legal issues to the International Court of Justice, but Israel consistently refuses.

The lack of compulsory international adjudication of world conflicts provides the perfect escape for any nation which lives in the world community by means of self-serving might, to the detriment of the peace-serving maintenance of world public order. The resolution of world conflicts by the rule of force and not by the rule of law is the most constant threat to world public order. Those who by destiny or by choice are dedicated to the historical pursuit of truth and reject the hysterical search for pragmatic palliatives must reassert their commitment to the quest for world peace through the rule of law.

The United Nations
and the Middle East Conflict
of 1967

In those ominous days of May, 1967, the world again looked help-
lessly on the Middle East, seemingly unable to stem the tide of
events. It was as though some mysterious and irresistible power had
decided to propel that part of the globe yet another time to the brink
of tragedy. As the world's statesmen scurried about seeking to preserve
peace in the region, the crisis grew in intensity, and the din of war
preparations rose in a crescendo. The only glimmer of optimism came
from the prayerful hope that the United Nations would somehow be able
to step in and avert disaster.[1] After all, for what was the United Nations
established—was it not to maintain world peace and security? More
specifically, had not the United Nations, virtually since its inception,
been continuously occupied with the "Palestine Question"? Had it not
maintained an active presence in the Middle East since 1949? Had it not
through the U.N. Emergency Force successfully preserved a more
peaceful Egyptian-Israeli frontier than had ever prevailed before?
Furthermore, had not the United Nations displayed remarkable inge-
nuity in the area of peace keeping in the course of a previous Middle
East crisis?[2]

So much attention had been focused on the United Nations as the

---

1. See, for instance, the *New York Times* editorial for May 22, 1967: "The best
hope, in fact, lies in a continuing role by the United Nations." This sentiment was
shared by U.S. Ambassador to the U.N., Arthur Goldberg, who said: "It is the considered view of the United States . . . that the United Nations has a continuing and
critical role to play in keeping the peace in that area." (*New York Times,* May 19,
1967, p. 14).

2. For the best and most comprehensive treatment of UNEF see Gabriella Rosner,
The United Nations Emergency Force (New York: Columbia University Press, 1963).

only hope for peace in the region that disillusionment was great when it failed to live up to the aspirations set for it. What seemed incomprehensible was that a world organization comprising the overwhelming majority of states in the world community would in the end prove incapable of halting the drift to conflict. Many were incredulous that the complex and magnificent peace-keeping mechanism embodied in UNEF should, in the final analysis, prove so fragile. In an effort to explain this U.N. "failure," some attempted to place the blame at the doorstep of the secretary-general who had ordered the withdrawal of UNEF at the request of the United Arab Republic. Not since the Congo crisis had so much criticism been heaped on a secretary-general.[3] His action was termed "hurried." It "dismayed" many people, including the president of the United States.[4] Others likened UNEF to a "fire brigade which vanishes from the scene as soon as the first smoke and flames appear."[5]

There is every indication that the events in the Middle East in May, 1967, were initially looked upon, particularly in Western countries, as nothing more than another episode in a kind of war of nerves and brinkmanship that had long characterized the region. The tendency was to dismiss developments as designed largely for internal regional consumption with no major likelihood that armed conflict would erupt, especially in view of UNEF's separation of the two potential protagonists.[6] But when UNEF was asked to withdraw, and did, this somewhat complacent attitude suddenly gave way to genuine alarm. World leaders were caught by surprise. In retrospect, all indications are that they had little, if any, contingency planning for such an eventuality. And as they desperately maneuvered for time to find a solution to the increasingly menacing confrontation in the Middle East, their sense of irritation with the United Nations and its chief adminis-

---

3. The debate as to whether the secretary-general should have readily complied with the U.A.R. request for UNEF's withdrawal from its territory still goes on. For the most cogent and tightly reasoned defense of U Thant's action see Louis B. Sohn, *The United Nations in Action* (Mineola, N.Y.: Foundation Press, 1968), pp. 169–93. Theodore Draper, writing in *Commentary,* also found the secretary-general's report of June 27, 1967, on the withdrawal of UNEF "a most convincing formal case," XLIV (August, 1967), p. 43.

4. See the text of President Johnson's May 23, 1967, statement on the Middle East in the *New York Times,* May 24, 1967, p. 16.

5. *Ibid.,* June 20, 1967, p. 17.

6. See, for instance, the assessment made in the *New York Times* editorial for May 24, 1967, p. 40. Also see Hanson Baldwin's analysis in the same edition.

trative officer seemed to grow.[7] It was as though both were responsible, at least in part, for the worsening situation. In short, their disaffection with the United Nations grew in direct proportion to their sense of frustration at their inability to head off an armed conflict.

There is perhaps yet another, though by no means ancillary, explanation for the widespread disenchantment with the U.N. that attended the 1967 Middle East crisis. It derives from an exaggerated view of what the United Nations is capable of doing and an inadequate understanding of its political processes and the forces that shape them.

The United Nations does not represent a supergovernment that functions above everyday international politics and is endowed with an independent will of its own. This point has often been made but is worth repeating because of the remarkable frequency with which the opposite view is betrayed in the discourse of individuals at all levels of public involvement. What is usually overlooked is that the United Nations is only one actor, albeit an important one, among many on the international scene; it affects, and is in turn itself affected by, its environment. Like others, its influence, maneuverability, and capacity for initiative are largely determined by its internal make-up as well as by the pattern of the international system within which it functions. In that respect it is not substantially different from a state whose conduct is governed by such considerations as constitutional and administrative processes; ideological consensus; institutional structure; leadership; and the nature, size, and degree of cohesion of groups within it as well as by the web of relationships that prevail in the universe around it and of which it is a part. And inasmuch as these ingredients are in a constant state of flux, forever shifting and evolving, it is to be expected that the type of role that an actor can and will play is also subject to change.

2.

The Middle East crisis of 1967 found the United Nations in a different condition from what it had been at the time of Suez.[8] In 1956 the

7. The *New York Times* reported that the U.S. Administration wanted "time to cool off the crisis," May 25, 1967, p. 16.

8. For an excellent summary of some of these changes, see Inis L. Claude, Jr., *Swords into Plowshares,* 3d ed. (New York: Random House, 1964), Chapter 9. For greater detail on constitutional interpretation and development, see *Repertory of*

U.N. functioned in a world that during the previous decade had been feeling the full intensity of the Cold War. The period from 1945 to 1955 was one of bipolarity, riddled with such critical milestones as Iran, Greece, the Berlin Blockade, Korea, and Indochina. The two superpowers were pitted against each other in a seemingly perpetual conflict, ever more poised for mortal combat with expanding alliances and continuously increasing arsenals of nuclear weapons. So ominous and intense was the struggle that the world was viewed as essentially divided into two camps. Those relatively few and newly emergent nations of Asia and Africa that sought noninvolvement in either the Soviet or the Western bloc were then looked upon as immoral and "shortsighted." Neutralism was attacked as an obsolete conception— "a pretense that a nation [could] best gain safety for itself by being indifferent to the fate of others."[9]

It was inevitable, of course, that the United Nations' workings would reflect this type of international environment—an environment drastically different from that which the framers of the charter had anticipated. Instead of the United Nations being an instrument of consensus formation among the Big Four, it became a contentious diplomatic arena within which the two major camps wrestled for the attainment of conflicting goals and the legitimization of differing positions. Given the composition and membership of the world organization, the West, the U.S. in particular, virtually always held the upper hand. It seemed almost impossible for the U.N. to adopt or endorse measures that could be deemed pro-Soviet. Thus, the U.S.S.R. opted to incapacitate the United Nations through the frequent exercise of its veto power.[10] It was this paralysis of the Security Council that prompted the United States to push through, over Soviet objections, the Acheson plan which was subsequently adopted by the General Assembly in the form of the Uniting for Peace Resolution of November, 1950. The resolution conferred upon the General Assembly the power to recommend the use of force for the purpose of keeping the

---

Practice of United Nations Organs, 5 vols. (New York: United Nations, 1955), plus supplements.

9. Secretary of State John Foster Dulles in U.S. Department of State, *American Foreign Policy, Current Documents, 1956,* Department of State Publication 6811 (Washington: Government Printing Office, 1959), p. 34.

10. For a review of the record of the use of the veto, see Sydney D. Bailey, "Veto in the Security Council," *International Conciliation,* No. 566 (January, 1968).

peace should the Security Council be stymied by a lack of unanimity among its permanent members. The General Assembly, of course, was free from the Soviet veto, and the United States could effectively muster two-thirds of the votes necessary for the passage of substantive resolutions on matters vital to its interests by the almost assured support of the Latin American and Western European groupings plus the backing of some Asian allies and friends.

When Britain, France, and Israel attacked Egypt in the fall of 1956 the international system, and the role of the United Nations in it, was essentially that described above, although it was rapidly changing. The United Nations, however, proved capable of dealing successfully with the Suez crisis for a variety of reasons, chief among which was the combined opposition of the United States and the Soviet Union to the tripartite invasion. It was a somewhat embarrassing and certainly novel situation for the United States to find itself in agreement with its principal adversary and in opposition to its long-standing allies and friends. What prompted the United States to assume this position was the fear that the attack might generate a series of events which could conceivably result in Soviet entry into the region, thereby precipitating a major confrontation. The U.S. position was due also in part to a certain commitment to the principles of the United Nations Charter which abjure the use of force as an instrument of foreign policy. It must also be recalled that the overwhelming majority of governments expressed their opposition to the British, French, and Israeli action—an action which was generally regarded as illegitimate.[11] Indeed, even in Britain and France substantial segments of public opinion were exceedingly critical of their countries' action. This ground swell of moral indignation lent added weight to the pressures that were being exerted on the three powers to withdraw their troops from Egypt.

Given this near unanimous opposition to the invasion, as reflected in

11. Criticism was perhaps most widespread in Asian and African countries, some of whose leaders tended to view British and French intervention as an attempt on the part of two colonial powers to reassert their previous positions of colonial dominance. For instance, Nehru sent a telegram to Nasser in which he said: "If colonialism succeeds in coming back to Egypt, it will reverse the entire course of history and return to every other country from which it had been forced to go. Therefore . . . colonialism should not be allowed to succeed in Egypt. Otherwise, it will signal a new and long fight for the whole of Asia and Africa." (Gamal Abdul Nasser, "Where Two Worlds Meet," in *A Study of Nehru*, ed. Rafiq Zakaria [Bombay: Times of India, 1959], p. 85).

the various General Assembly resolutions, the U.N. was afforded a singular opportunity to play a meaningful role in the settlement of the conflict. Thanks to the fertile imagination of Canada's Lester Pearson and the resourcefulness of Secretary-General Dag Hammarskjold, a United Nations Emergency Force was hastily assembled and dispatched to Egypt to facilitate the orderly and peaceful withdrawal of the invading armies, and subsequently to perform a task that was later described by Hammarskjold as "preventive diplomacy." This form of diplomacy was later defined by the secretary-general as, "United Nations intervention in an area of conflict outside of, or marginal to, the sphere dominated by Cold War struggles, designed to forestall the competitive intrusion of the rival power blocs into that area."[12] Hammarskjold was convinced that the U.N. was exceedingly limited in its capacity to have any significant bearing on problems that lay within the orbits of the two major power constellations. It could only exercise an influence in those areas which fell outside the central arena of the Cold War but whose conflicts could draw the rivalry of the Great Powers. The function of the United Nations was, as this view had it, the localization of the conflict by intervening in a neutral capacity and filling a vacuum which otherwise might be contested by the two camps.

> Preventive diplomacy, in short, was conceived by Hammarskjold as an international version of the policy of containment, designed not to restrict the expansion of one bloc or the other, but to restrict the expansion of the zone permeated by bloc conflicts; it was put forward as a means for containment of the cold war.[13]

3.

That the United Nations fulfilled Hammarskjold's vision of its role in the Middle East is now a matter of history. For over ten years UNEF patrolled the Egyptian-Israeli border maintaining an unparalleled calm. Indeed, it was so successful that this form of U.N. preventive intervention served as an exemplary model for varying degrees of

---

12. Claude, *Swords into Plowshares,* p. 286. For a more detailed statement, see United Nations, General Assembly, *Introduction to the Annual Report of the Secretary-General on the Work of the Organization, Official Records,* Supplement No. 1A (A/4390/Add:), June 16, 1959.
13. *Ibid.*

future involvements ranging from the somewhat symbolic presence in Jordan in 1958 and in Laos in 1959 to the massive commitment in the Congo in 1960. Nonetheless, strains on this form of intervention were becoming increasingly evident, and the latitude within which the U.N. was permitted to function was progressively narrowed as a result of various transformations in the international system.[14]

The first transformation was in the bipolar power distribution upon which the notion of nonpartisan and neutral U.N. action had been based. This system was rapidly changing in the late fifties to one of diffused bipolarity wherein important members of the two camps were exhibiting a desire to pursue independent destinies often quite at variance with those of their senior partners. A productive role for the United Nations was no longer merely a matter of eliciting the agreement, tacit or otherwise, of the U.S. and U.S.S.R.; the concurrence and compliance of lesser actors became crucial. Second, the rapid decolonization that characterized the second decade of the postwar period meant not only a phenomenal increase in the number of actors on the international level, each with his own peculiar perceptions and aspirations, but also the rise of regional subsystems in Asia and Africa that sought to adjust their relationships from subordination to a status that would be coordinate with the European subsystem. Third, the varying degrees and complexities of interpenetration between system-wide and regional axes of conflict, between global and regional issues, have produced a discordant international system with overtones "that are strongly marked by elements of both congruence and discontinuity."[15]

The impact of these changes upon the role the U.N. could play was perhaps nowhere better illustrated than in the turbulent history of its "neutral" intervention in the Congo. In the course of four years in that

---

14. Nowhere was this more poignantly demonstrated than in the Congo crisis. Adlai Stevenson's remark that "the only way to keep the cold war out of the Congo is to keep the United Nations in the Congo" (United Nations, Security Council, *Official Records*, 16th Year, 934th Meeting, February 15, 1961, p. 9) may have been good rhetoric but was hardly an accurate description of what was then taking place in the strife-torn country. See, among others, Catherine Hoskyns, *The Congo Since Independence: January 1960–December 1961* (London: Oxford University Press, 1965); Ernest Lefever, *Uncertain Mándate* (Baltimore: Johns Hopkins University Press, 1967); Arthur Lee Burns and Nina Heathcote, *Peace-keeping by UN Forces: From Suez to the Congo* (New York: Praeger, 1963).

15. Oran Young, "Political Discontinuities in the International System," *World Politics*, XX (April, 1968) p. 370.

strife-torn country, the U.N. and its secretary-general managed to incur the displeasure of a substantial segment of the Afro-Asian grouping, the disaffection of a number of Western countries, and denunciation from the Soviet bloc. Furthermore, the U.N. became embroiled in a financial crisis that was to shake its constitutional foundation. What the Congo operation demonstrated, perhaps beyond anything else, was the increasing limitations of this form of intervention in a highly discontinuous international system.

In the case of the Middle East crisis of 1967, preventive diplomacy was rendered inapplicable once UNEF was withdrawn. It was no longer possible for the U.N. to interpose itself on the line separating Israeli and Egyptian forces. The secretary-general sought to provide some semblance of effective U.N. presence in the area by the reactivation of the Egyptian-Israeli Mixed Armistice Commission. That effort, however, failed owing to the attitude of the Israeli government which had denounced EIMAC and which for some years had refused to have anything to do with it.[16] The secretary-general, then, was unable to do more than (1) sound the alarm bell and warn the Security Council that the situation in the Middle East had become more menacing than it had been since the fall of 1956 and (2) undertake diplomatic initiatives in an attempt to head off an armed conflict. The fruitfulness of the first course depended on the Great Powers sharing the secretary-general's perception of the situation and being willing to take appropriate measures to prevent the outbreak of hostilities, while that of the second required the receptivity of the governments concerned to the secretary-general's role. For while

> the Secretary-General may act with a view to creating favorable conditions for his initiatives . . . his capacity to do so can hardly be very great so long as governments guard their sovereignty and attempt to act as independently as possible of outside agencies and agents. The firm backing of a deliberative organ is more likely than his own efforts to enhance persuasiveness. Yet even in this situation,

---

16. In the case of the Israeli-Syrian Mixed Armistice Commission (ISMAC), both Israel and Syria had made no use of it since January, 1967. For the text of the secretary-general's report of May 20, 1967, to the Security Council on the situation in the Middle East see the *New York Times*, May 21, 1967, p. 2. For a previous report, given on May 18 to the Assembly, see U.N. Document A/6669.

some modicum of cooperation from the governments involved must be forthcoming if he is not to be halted at his first step.[17]

But the secretary-general was halted, first by the insistence of the Soviet Union that there was in reality no crisis and that the hue and cry were generated by Israel, the Western countries, and their oil monopolies for the purpose of concealing their machinations,[18] and second by the announcement of the government of the U.A.R. that it was reasserting its sovereign rights over the Straits of Tiran and would deny their use to Israeli shipping. This declaration, together with the ominous response it elicited from Israel, made while U Thant was en route to Cairo, automatically changed the substance of the issues involved and in effect superseded the tasks of his original mission. It was no longer a matter of seeking the U.A.R.'s consent to reintroduce United Nations presence on the Egyptian-Israeli border, but of preventing a rapidly deteriorating situation from breaking out into a regional conflagration with the ever-present risk that it might assume wider proportions. However, beyond counseling moderation, there was little that the secretary-general could do. Therefore he quickly returned to New York only to find that the Big Four were far from agreement on what course they and the U.N. should take.[19] All that now remained was the hope that the United States and the Soviet Union would effectively restrain the rapidly mobilizing protagonists in the Middle East from going to war, a hope which proved to be misplaced by the events of June 5. On that day, fighting broke out in the Middle East, and in less than a week Israeli forces occupied the Gaza Strip, Sinai, Jordan's Old City of Jerusalem, Jordanian territory on the West Bank of the Jordan River, and the Golan Heights of Syria.[20]

---

17. Leon Gordenker, *The UN Secretary-General and the Maintenance of Peace* (New York: Columbia University Press, 1967), p. 331; see, in particular, Chapter VIII, "Negotiation and Mediation."

18. See the text of the Soviet Government's statement issued on May 23 in the *New York Times,* May 24, 1967, p. 17.

19. The Soviet representative, Mr. Fedorenko, did not think that a Security Council meeting which had been called at the request of Canada and Denmark for May 24 should have been called; see the *New York Times,* May 25, 1967, p. 16. As an indication of the paucity of ideas, the Security Council had before it a resolution introduced by Canada and Denmark which, aside from giving "full support to the efforts of the Secretary-General," merely requested member states "to refrain from taking any steps which might worsen the situation." No action was taken on that draft.

20. For a summary of the war itself, see Michael Howard and Robert Hunter, *Israel and the Arab World: The Crisis of 1967,* Adelphi Papers, No. 41 (October, 1967).

4.

The United Nations reacted swiftly to the outbreak of hostilities. The Security Council was called into session for the main purpose of bringing an end to the armed conflict. The Council's task, however, depended for its success on two conditions: agreement of the permanent members, and the compliance of the warring powers. Both prerequisites were initially lacking. The Soviet Union insisted that any call for a halt to military activities be coupled with a demand that the opposing forces should withdraw to the positions held prior to the war. In effect, this would have meant the abandonment of all territorial gains made by Israel and a return to the situation wherein Egyptian forces could bar the Gulf of Aqaba to Israeli shipping. The United States, on the other hand, pressed for an unconditional cease-fire. The American view was that a withdrawal of troops to the armistice demarcation lines would merely resurrect the explosive atmosphere that had prevailed before. Instead of replanting the seeds of future conflict, the U.S. argued, a new and fresh start toward a lasting and stable peace ought to be made.[21] On June 6, however, the Soviet Union, spurred by events on the battlefield where Israeli forces were rapidly advancing on all fronts, altered its position and introduced a resolution which was unanimously adopted. It demanded that the belligerents "should as a first step discontinue all military activities." But compliance from all parties was slow in coming, and the Security Council felt compelled to issue additional calls on June 9 and 12 demanding that all hostilities should "cease forthwith'" and condemning "'any and all violations of the cease-fire." These calls were eventually heeded,[22] and the Security Council then went on to adopt a resolution calling upon the government of Israel "'to ensure the safety, welfare and security of the inhabitants of the areas where military operations have taken place and to facilitate the return of those inhabitants who have fled the areas since the outbreak of hostilities." It

---

21. See the statement of President Johnson in the *New York Times,* June 8, 1967, p. 1.

22. At first only Israel and Jordan accepted the cease-fire. However, the Israeli foreign minister took the position that the Jordanian acceptance was "eroded by the absence of acceptance by the United Arab Republic" since "it [was] Egyptian command that now [operated] over the armed forces of Jordan" (*New York Times,* June 8, 1967, p. 18). Egypt accepted the cease-fire on June 8, while Syria waited till June 11.

also recommended to all parties concerned "the scrupulous respect of the humanitarian principles governing the treatment of prisoners of war and the protection of civil persons" in accordance with the Geneva Conventions of 1949. But the Security Council failed to endorse a Soviet draft which condemned "Israel's aggressive activities and continued occupation of part of the territory of the United Arab Republic, Syria, and Jordan" and which asked Israel to remove all her troops from those countries.

Faced with this rebuff, the Soviet Union, on June 13, asked a special emergency session of the General Assembly to convene in order to consider "liquidating the consequences of Israel's aggression against the Arab States and the immediate withdrawal of Israeli troops behind the armistice lines."[23] Despite U.S. objections, the emergency session was held on June 17.[24]

It was quite apparent from the start of the debate that the prospect for a consensus within the confines of the General Assembly was not any greater than it had been in the Security Council. The Soviet and American positions remained as divergent as ever. On the one hand, the Soviet Union wished to focus United Nations attention on what it termed Israeli aggression and mobilize support for a demand for a total and unconditional withdrawal of Israeli forces from Arab lands. The United States, on the other hand, wished to broaden the debate to include the search for a permanent solution to the Arab-Israeli conflict. The former held that withdrawal was a prerequisite to any possible future discussions, while the latter insisted that it should be integrally and inseparably linked to the establishment of a lasting peace. The Arab states, with the support of the Soviet Union, argued that Israel had committed aggression and that the United Nations had to condemn this aggression and erase its consequences. Any negotiation between the Arab states and Israel prior to the withdrawal of the latter's troops

23. *New York Times,* June 14, p. 1. The Soviet request was based on Article 11 of the U.N. Charter which states that the Assembly may "discuss any questions relating to the maintenance of peace and security."

24. See the text of Ambassador Goldberg's letter to Secretary-General U Thant in the *New York Times,* June 16, 1967, p. 4. Goldberg's objection was based on the premise that the Uniting for Peace Resolution of November, 1950, was the only basis on which an emergency session could be held. That resolution allows for such a session upon the failure of the Council to exercise its primary responsibility for the maintenance of peace and security. In the United States' view such a situation had not arisen.

would be tantamount to allowing Israel to dictate the terms of settlement. The Israeli position, championed by the United States and other Western countries, was that were Israeli forces to withdraw prior to some kind of agreement, the Arab states would only revert to their traditional policy of belligerency toward Israel. Before withdrawal could be effected, then, direct negotiations would have to take place between the parties concerned to settle once and for all the long-standing issues of the past.

The chance that either viewpoint would prevail in the Assembly was very much in doubt. In the first place, the majority of members were unwilling to censure Israel for its attack. There was the widespread belief that while Israel had fired the first shot, it had done so out of self-defense. In other words, whereas Israel's action may have been illegal, it was not illegitimate. This view was in the main generated by the recollection of the highly intemperate and inflammatory speeches emanating from various Arab circles on the eve of the war which threatened Israel with political extinction. In a deliberative body whose function had become increasingly one of political legitimization,[25] it was quite obvious from the start that any resolution which carried in it a condemnation of Israel would fail to receive the votes necessary for its adoption. Second, the Assembly had more than doubled its membership since the founding of the United Nations, and the capacity of any power to muster the required two-thirds support on substantive draft resolutions had, as a result, greatly diminished.[26] In this instance either side would have had to obtain the backing of more than eighty delegations, a task which, given the nature of the issues and the deep involvement of the United States as well as the Soviet Union in them, was not likely to meet with success. Third, there was a feeling that even if one viewpoint prevailed over the other, the opposing party would in all likelihood ignore the General Assembly's recommendation.

Nonetheless, each side pressed for the endorsement of its own position. On July 4, the General Assembly acted on two draft resolu-

---

25. Inis L. Claude, Jr., *The Changing United Nations* (New York: Random House, 1967); see, in particular, Chapter 4, "Collective Legitimization as a Political Function of the United Nations."

26. See Hayward R. Alker, Jr., and Bruce M. Russett *World Politics in the General Assembly* (New Haven: Yale University Press, 1965). For an interesting discussion of some of the behind-the-scenes activities of delegations based on the author's own experiences, see Conor Cruise O'Brien, *To Katanga and Back* (New York: Simon and Schuster, 1962), pp. 12–39.

tions, one submitted by Yugoslavia and the other by eighteen Latin American states. The Yugoslav draft called for the immediate withdrawal of Israeli forces from occupied territories and urged "all states to render every assistance to the Secretary-General" in seeing to it that the resolution was implemented. The Latin American draft, which also called for withdrawal, linked such a withdrawal with an end to all forms of belligerency between Israel and its Arab neighbors. It also requested the Security Council to continue "with a sense of urgency the consideration of the situation in the Middle East, cooperating directly with the parties and relying on the presence of the United Nations."[27] Both drafts failed to receive the necessary two-thirds vote. The vote on the Yugoslav draft resolution was 53 to 46, with 20 abstentions, while that on the Latin American draft resolution was 57 to 43, with 20 abstentions.[28]

The vote on the Yugoslav draft resolution produced some interesting alignments. All the Muslim states, from Morocco and Mauritania in the west to Indonesia in the east, voted for it. They were joined by the Communist bloc, including Cuba, and by a number of Asian and African non-Muslim countries. But it also drew support from members with political ties to the United States, namely France, Greece, Japan, and Spain. Significantly, however, it failed to receive the support of a substantial number of African states, ten of which abstained while eight opposed it.[29] This was all the more remarkable considering that many of those states were members of the French Community and thus had been susceptible to the influence of France which favored the Yugoslav draft.

The Latin American draft resolution did not produce any surprises. It drew the support of nearly all of those states which had opposed the Yugoslav resolution and the affirmative votes of some of the African countries that had previously abstained. Conversely, it met with the opposition of those which had favored the Yugoslav draft.

---

27. *New York Times,* July 6, 1967, p. 12, and July 5, 1967, p. 2. It should be noted that the Yugoslav draft did not include a call for the condemnation of Israel. Albania sought to attach an amendment to that effect, but its efforts were defeated by a vote of 32 to 66.

28. *New York Times,* July 5, 1967, p. 2.

29. These were Botswana, Gambia, Ghana, Lesotho, Liberia, Madagascar, Malawi, and Togo. The abstainers were Central African Republic, Chad, Dahomey, Ethiopia, Ivory Coast, Kenya, Niger, Rwanda, Sierra Leone, and Upper Volta.

5.

Deadlocked though the Assembly was on the issues discussed above, it nevertheless adopted a Pakistani resolution expressing the Assembly's deep concern "at the situation prevailing in Jerusalem as a result of the measures taken by Israel to change the status of the City." The resolution declared these measures invalid and called upon Israel to rescind them and "to desist forthwith from taking any action which would alter the status of Jerusalem." It further asked the secretary-general to report to the General Assembly and the Security Council on the implementation of the Assembly's wishes.[30] The resolution was passed by a vote of 99 to 0, with 20 abstentions. Israel did not participate in the balloting, and the United States abstained. All the Latin American states endorsed it, in part because of their belief that the annexation of territory by force of arms was contrary to international legal norms and in part because of the attitude of the Vatican which was then calling for the internationalization of Jerusalem. It is somewhat ironic, however, that the one issue of political substance on which such broad agreement was reached should in the end prove to be the one on which Israel would be most unyielding. Indeed, scarcely more than a week after the resolution's passage the Israeli government declared, for all intents and purposes, its unwillingness to abide by the wishes of the General Assembly.[31] Since then, Israel's attitude has been even more intractable, proclaiming that the question of the future of Jerusalem was not subject to negotiation.

Despite the apparent and very real deadlock that characterized the work of the General Assembly, there did emerge certain areas of agreement from its emergency session. It was generally recognized that Israel should withdraw her forces to the positions held before June 4, that belligerency should be ended, that all states in the Middle East should be able to live in peace, and that all countries ought to respect one another's independence. It was further agreed that the long-deferred refugee problem should be settled and that freedom of naviga-

---

30. Israel did not participate in the vote on the grounds that the issue of Jerusalem was "outside the legal competence of the General Assembly." *New York Times,* July 5, 1967, p. 1.

31. See the text of Foreign Minister Abba Eban's letter to Secretary-General U Thant in the *New York Times,* July 12, 1967, p. 14.

tion through the region's international waterways must be guaranteed. Where the Assembly members sharply differed was on the order of priority for the realization of the above principles and the modalities by which they would be attained. The Arab states believed that withdrawal of Israeli forces was a necessary precondition to any future accommodation that might be reached through U.N. mediation.[32] Israel, on the other hand, insisted on direct negotiations with the Arab states as the only means for settling all outstanding issues, including withdrawal. But there was a latent optimism that a method could be found to reconcile these seemingly divergent positions and that the proper framework for arriving at such a reconciliation was the Security Council. After all, the General Assembly had tried but had failed because of the deep chasm separating the United States and the Soviet Union. Furthermore, given the unwieldy size of the General Assembly, the Middle East crisis, it was felt, had better return to the more manageable, if not always congenial, forum of the Security Council for further action.

After months of negotiations and consultations, often at the highest levels, the Security Council finally adopted, on November 22, 1967, a resolution submitted by Lord Caradon, the British representative.[33] Under the terms of the resolution, the Council (a) emphasized the inadmissibility of the acquisition of territory by war; (b) affirmed that a lasting peace in the Middle East required the withdrawal of Israeli forces from territories occupied in the recent conflict and the termination of all conditions and claims of belligerency with the acknowledgment of sovereignty, territorial integrity, and political independence within secure and recognized boundaries that this entailed; and (c) affirmed the necessity for guaranteeing freedom of navigation through international waterways in the area. The resolution also called for the achievement of a just settlement of the refugee problem and for a

---

32. For an interesting and extensive discussion of the ability of the U.N. and its secretary-general to act in a mediating capacity, see Oran Young, *The Intermediaries: Third Parties in International Crises* (Princeton: Princeton University Press, 1967).

33. For the text of the resolution and a summary of the Council discussion that attended it, see *UN Monthly Chronicle,* Vol. IV, No. 11 (December, 1967) pp. 8–19. It is not my purpose to delve into the numerous complaints and counter-complaints that were presented to the Security Council by Israel and the Arab states. Nor is it my intention to recount the numerous cease-fire violations which persist to this day despite the efforts of the secretary-general, his special representative, and the U.N. observer group on the Egyptian-Israeli line. These are all a matter of record, and they neither add to, nor detract from, the basic issues nor the chances for final settlement.

guarantee of the territorial inviolability and political independence of every state in the region through measures which would include the establishment of demilitarized zones. Furthermore, it requested the secretary-general to designate a special representative to proceed to the Middle East to establish and maintain contacts with the states concerned "in order to promote agreement and assist efforts to achieve a peaceful and accepted settlement in accordance with the provisions and principles in [the] resolution."

On November 23, 1967, one day after the Security Council acted, the secretary-general designated Gunnar Jarring, ambassador from Sweden to the Soviet Union, as the special representative who would proceed to the Middle East. From that time to the present, Ambassador Jarring has been shuttling between Jerusalem, Amman, Cairo, New York, and Cyprus. His first task was to gain acceptance of the resolution from the parties concerned. So far, only Jordan and the U.A.R. have agreed to abide by it. Syria has rejected it outright, while Israel has equivocated. Up to the present no visible signs of progress toward a lasting and just solution can be seen. All that remains is hope. And as John Donne wrote, "Life without hope is like nectar in a sieve, and hope without an object cannot live."

MICHAEL   W.   SULEIMAN

American Mass Media
and the June Conflict

F uture historians studying the events of the summer of 1967 may
well conclude that Israel's greatest achievement was not its military victory but rather its success in communicating its point of view.
Conversely, the Arabs' major defeat was not on the battlefield but in
the competition for men's minds.

As Karl Deutsch put it, "Control of the social institutions of mass
communication, and generally of the storage and transmission of
information, is an obvious major component of power."[1] The campaign to present the Israeli version, and *only* the Israeli version, of
what was happening in the Middle East in the summer of 1967—a
campaign that greatly enhanced Israel's power and bargaining position—was perhaps without comparison in its extent and intensity.

Though no one has yet studied the radio and television coverage of
the June War, a few studies have been made of daily newspapers,
magazines, and books—"instant potboilers" purporting to tell the
latest story of the Arab-Israeli conflict.[2] The American Institute for
Political Communication, a nonpartisan, nonprofit organization interested in "improving the flow of government and political affairs

---

1. Karl W. Deutsch, *The Nerves of Government* (New York: Macmillan, the Free
Press, 1966), p. 203.
2. American Institute for Political Communication, *Domestic Communications Aspects of the Middle East Crisis* (Washington, D.C.: AIPC, 1967); Leslie Farmer, "All
We Know Is What We Read in the Papers," *Middle East Newsletter*, February, 1968,
pp. 1-5; Willard G. Oxtoby, "The War of Words: A Look at the Literature," in
"America and the Middle East," mimeographed (New Haven: New Haven Committee
on the Middle East Crisis, 1968), pp. 31–36; Harry N. Howard, "The Instant Potboilers and the 'Blitzkreig' War," *Issues*, XXI (Autumn 1967), 48–52.

information to the American people," found that of eighteen syndi-
cated columnists with Washington outlets, nine viewed the crisis
"chiefly or primarily from the perspective of American foreign policy,"
six columnists "took a strong, persistent pro-Israeli position," and only
one writer did a column which "set out the difficulties, problems and
needs of the Arabs."[3] Leslie Farmer, Willard G. Oxtoby, and Harry
N. Howard came to similar conclusions in their studies. As Tables 1
and 2 show, my study of the coverage given the June War by American
news magazines corroborates this evidence.

In my analysis, I followed the same procedure employed in a previous study of American news reports during the period of the 1956 Suez
attack.[4] The same magazines—U.S. News and World Report, Newsweek, Time, Life, The Nation, New Republic, and the New York
Times' "The Week in Review"—were used in both studies in order to
detect any change in attitude.[5] The overall results of the May–June,
1967, study are not much different from those of the July–December,
1956, study. However, the extent of support for Israel and the
antagonism toward the Arabs generally, and toward President Nasser
in particular, was significantly greater in 1967. This was true in the
editorials as well as the reporting.

The most striking element continues to be the extreme reluctance on
the part of the American press to criticize Israel—even on the editorial
pages or in feature articles. Very seldom did I come across any
reprimand of Israel or the Israelis without an accompanying justification. Only occasionally is the Arab point of view presented, and even
then it sounds strange and unconvincing to a reader who has been
saturated with the pro-Israeli stance. Sometimes a tactic is employed to
discredit the Arab point of view even while presenting it, for instance,
to let the Communists speak for the Arabs. The New York Times on
June 18 reproduced excerpts from an Izvestia article attacking the
Israelis as aggressors, and Time magazine thus dismissed the looting
and acts of atrocity by Israeli soldiers as a Communist charge. It also

---

3. AIPC, Domestic Communications, p. 2.
4. Michael W. Suleiman, "An Evaluation of Middle East News Coverage in Seven
American Newsmagazines, July–December, 1956," Middle East Forum, XLI (Autumn
1965), 9–30; the methodology is outlined here in some detail.
5. The period of the study extended from May 11, 1967, the date of the Israeli
public statements threatening an "attack" on Syria, to the end of June, 1967.

provided Moshe Dayan's explanation: "An army of regulars and reservists of various ages and psychological drives cannot be perfect."[6]

2.

The attitude of the press toward Nasser is illustrated in Table 3. In contrast to Israeli leaders, including Moshe Dayan, the Egyptian president appeared to be the epitome of all that is hateful and bad. There seems to be a strong tendency to blame one man for all the difficulties of the Middle East. If Nasser is truly *believed* to be the cause of all trouble, then those holding such a view certainly display a good deal of

Table 1

Item Percentage of All Reporting on the Middle East*
May–June, 1967

Name of Magazine	con Nasser	con Syria	con Arab	con France	con U.N.	con U.S.A.	con Israel	con Soviet	pro Nasser
N.Y. Times	30.8	4.0	8.0	4.0	11.5	—	—	—	—
Life	23.1	—	30.8	—	8.0	—	—	8.0	—
U.S. News and World Report	30.2	4.6	21.0	—	2.3	2.3	2.3	9.3	2.3
The Nation	60.0	20.0	—	—	20.0	—	—	40.0	—
New Republic	33.3	—	16.6	16.6	—	16.6	—	16.6	—
Newsweek	44.4	—	7.4	3.7	3.7	—	14.8	14.8	—
Time	10.0	—	50.0	10.0	30.0	—	—	10.0	—
Average percentage	30.2	3.0	17.7	3.0	7.7	1.5	3.8	10.0	0.8

* Except for the column on the extreme right and the bottom row, all figures indicate the percentage (in number of items) of press coverage under each category. If added horizontally, total exceeds 100 percent because the same item can be and often is pro one party and con another.

ignorance concerning the Arab world and the region generally. On the other hand, this attitude might be a deliberate attempt on the part of Nasser's enemies to escape the blame for any of the difficulties involved. One wonders, for instance, whether Israeli leaders have so very few faults or if the American press believed these faults were not "news fit to print."

It is interesting to note that the same magazines that described

6. *Time*, June 30, 1967, p. 27.

Nasser as cautious and not interested in going to war with Israel switched their stand after the war started and began to condemn Nasser as the cause of all trouble.[7] Furthermore, the picture of Nasser as the master strategist playing the East against the West was dropped in favor of a theory that reached conspiratorial proportions in the hands of C. L. Sulzberger of the *New York Times*. According to Mr. Sulzberger, all the troubles in the Middle East were caused by collaboration between the Soviet masters and the Egyptian client, Nasser. It was charged that Nasser merely followed orders and that he stirred up trouble in the Arab-Israeli conflict in order to divert attention from his difficulties in the Yemen war.[8]

pro Syria	pro Arab	pro France	pro U.N.	pro U.S.A.	pro Israel	pro Jordan	Balanced	Neutral	Total Number of Items
—	—	—	11.5	11.5	30.8	—	23.0	8.0	26
—	—	—	—	8.0	38.5	—	—	—	13
—	—	—	—	—	39.5	—	2.3	18.6	43
—	—	—	—	—	—	—	—	20.0	5
—	—	—	—	—	33.3	—	—	—	6
—	—	—	—	—	37.0	3.7	—	11.1	27
—	—	—	—	10.0	50.0	—	—	—	10
—	—	—	2.3	3.8	36.1	0.8	5.4	10.8	130

3.

But disparaging remarks were not restricted to Nasser. Hardly any "good" qualities were attributed to the Arabs generally, whereas the Israelis were portrayed as practically without fault. The old romantic stereotype of an Arab as a wandering desert dweller has given way to that of a "dark, shifty-eyed schemer and coward."[9] It is a stereotype

---

7. See in particular *Time*, June 2, 1967, p. 21; and *Life*, June 9, 1967, p. 4.
8. *New York Times*, June 25, 1967, p. 8E.
9. Marcus Smith, "Reflections in a Mirror," *Middle East Newsletter*, February, 1968, p. 7.

that is reinforced by television and the movies. In contrast, the Israelis are pictured as "young, energetic, fun-loving, hard-working, brave, and deeply suntanned."[10]

Table 4 clearly illustrates the reluctance of the American press to portray the Israelis in a bad light, whereas it enumerates the bad

Table 2

Item Percentage of Editorials on the Middle East*
May–June, 1967

Name of Magazine	con Nasser	con Syria	con Arab	con France	con U.N.	con U.S.A.	con Israel	con Soviet	pro Nasser
N.Y. Times	40	—	20	20	—	—	—	20	—
Life	40	—	40	—	20	—	—	—	—
The Nation	50	25	—	—	—	25	—	50	—
New Republic	20	—	20	20	—	20	—	20	—
Time	—	—	100	—	—	—	—	—	—
Average percentage	35	5	25	10	5	10	—	20	—

* Except for the column on the extreme right and the bottom row, all figures indicate the percentage (in numbers of items) of editorials under each category. If added horizontally, total exceeds 100 percent because the same editorial can be and often is pro one party and con another.

qualities of the Arabs without inhibition. As Leslie Farmer summed it up:

> My intention is not to deny that the Arabs have faults; however, putting all the bad or questionable traits of a people—or person— together and reciting them like an indictment can make them look three hundred percent worse than they are. One could say, with as much truth, "Socrates is ugly, dresses like a disgrace, has a dreadful wife but not the sense to divorce her, and spends most of his time talking."[11]

Table 5 shows that the previous ill-treatment and persecution of the Jews were mentioned but not as frequently as had been anticipated. This element was supplied in advertisements in the *New York Times* in which the public was reminded of "the horror and decimation of the

10. *Ibid.*, p. 6.
11. Farmer, "All We Know Is What We Read in the Papers," p. 5.

European holocaust" from which the people of Israel "are still recovering."[12] The president and the American people were urged to "avoid another Munich" and to act "with other nations if possible—independently if necessary!"[13] Then after the war, Hadassa, the Women's Zionist Organization of America, saluted the "defenders" of Israel.[14]

pro Syria	pro Arab	pro France	pro U.N.	pro U.S.A.	pro Israel	pro Soviet	Balanced	Neutral	Number of Editorials
—	—	—	40	40	20	—	—	20	5
—	—	—	—	20	—	—	—	—	5
—	—	—	—	—	—	—	—	25	4
—	—	—	—	—	40	—	—	—	5
—	—	—	—	—	100	—	—	—	1
—	—	—	10	15	20	—	—	10	20

Israel's alleged interest in peace and security are also emphasized, although it must be added that talk of this nature increased *after* the war in which Israel displayed beyond any doubt that it was in no great danger. The American press began to echo the demands of some Israeli officials that it was not possible to return to the *status quo ante* and that Israel needed to have more "natural" frontiers. This was justified on the basis of "security" and the desire to live "in peace," although it was not immediately obvious to all readers how such an action would make peace more likely between Israel and the Arab countries.

Not only are the Israelis beyond criticism but their achievements, it seems, are beyond compare. One wonders at times how many reporters had visited Palestine before it was taken over by the Israelis in order to speak so authoritatively about how the Israelis "made the desert

---

12. *New York Times,* June 4, 1967, p. 4E.
13. *Ibid.,* p. 7E.
14. *New York Times,* June 11, 1967, p. 5E.

bloom." And the Israelis are, of course, kind and generous to the Arabs whom "fate" entrusted to their care. Such arguments were presented to justify a possible Israeli takeover of any or all land occupied by Israel in the summer of 1967. The arguments sound much like those of colonialists—arguments that were supposedly rejected by the liberals and intellectuals of the West about twenty years ago.[15]

Despite these achievements, the American leaders were constantly being reminded that the United States had a "moral and legal"

Table 3

Characteristics Ascribed to Nasser and to Israeli Leaders*
May–June, 1967

Name of Magazine		NASSER			
	Dictatorial Attitudes	Cause of all Trouble	Associated with Communism	Anti-Western Attitude	Untrust-worthy; Unreliable
N.Y. Times	13	41	39	2	3
Life	3	10	10	1	—
U.S. News and World Report	20	43	26	—	11
The Nation	6	4	4	—	—
New Republic	2	4	4	4	2
Newsweek	8	15	14	6	11
Time	—	3	10	—	3
Total	52	120	107	13	30

* Figures indicate number of times a characteristic is mentioned.

commitment to go to Israel's aid. According to the American Institute for Political Communication:

> The Johnson Administration . . . was beset by a well-organized domestic pressure campaign in behalf of the Israelis in the two weeks immediately prior to the Arab-Israeli conflict. To retain its freedom of diplomatic action and to avoid being pushed into a unilateral

---

15. Paul Giniewski, in arguing for apartheid in South Africa and for the establishment of a separate Bantustan, draws upon the Zionist establishment of the state of Israel for illustration. In a nutshell, his case against assimilation and for apartheid is expressed in a rhetorical question: "Did the Jews not learn that the only political rights, the only nationality which could not be contested, the only flag which could not be imputed a crime were their own, and that instead of being assimilated in foreign nations, instead of being German, English, French, anything but themselves, Hebrew, Palestinian, Israeli?" See his *Two Faces of Apartheid* (Chicago: Henry Regnery, 1961), p. 350.

approach to the Middle East crisis, the Administration was compelled to wage a defensive communications battle.[16]

4.

The amazing fact is that this campaign continued *after* the war. No presidential hopeful, it seems, can escape making a statement on America's "commitment" to Israel. Political commentators continue to

| Playing East vs. West | Inexperienced; Naive | ISRAELI LEADERS | | | |
		"Good" Qualities	Hardworking, Tough, Brave	Pro-West	"Bad" Qualities
—	11	11	5	—	2
—	3	1	—	—	—
—	1	21	10	3	—
—	2	—	—	—	—
—	—	—	3	—	—
—	2	3	6	—	1
—	2	—	17	—	3
—	21	36	41	3	6

extol Israel's great victory while at the same time expressing disbelief that "tiny" Israel can be a threat to the Arab world. The David and Goliath analogy apparently has not lost its appeal. The public is presented a picture of 2.7 million Israelis squared off against estimates of 60–110 million Arabs.[17] Somehow the writer forgets that he had just described those 60–110 million Arabs as inefficient, divided, weak, and nomadic. Furthermore, the *populations* are compared when the relevant facts concern the *military forces*. Troop strengths in 1967 were estimated at 55,000 Jordanians, 70,000 Syrians, 100,000–150,000 Egyptians, and some 10,000 from the other Arab countries. These several armies *at most* total 285,000, against a total of 300,000

---

16. AIPC, *Domestic Communications*, p. 1.
17. *Time*, June 9, 1967.

Israeli reservists and regulars under one command.[18] Given the Israeli army's efficiency, excellent training, and up-to-date weaponry, how any reasonable observer can think of the situation as a David-Goliath match is not clear. Reasonable observers, of course, did not. Hugh Sidey reported in *Life,* a report that was also mentioned by Dan Rather of CBS News, that General Earle Wheeler, then chairman of the Joint

Table 4

Characteristics Ascribed to Arabs and to Israelis*
May–June, 1967

	ARAB CHARACTERISTICS					
Name of Magazine	Nomadic Living	Low Standard of Living	Low Standard of Education	Women: Few Rights	Undemo-cratic Orienta-tion	Dishonest, Unreliable, Inefficient
N.Y. Times	15	1	1	—	3	18
Life	—	—	—	—	2	23
U.S. News and World Report	3	15	—	—	—	15
The Nation	—	—	—	—	—	—
New Republic	—	—	—	—	—	2
Newsweek	2	2	—	—	3	11
Time	5	0	—	—	—	20
Total	25	18	1	—	8	89

* Figures indicate number of times a characteristic is mentioned.

Chiefs of Staff, had provided capability estimates to President Johnson which showed that the Israeli army would gain victory in three or four days.[19] Arthur Goldberg, then U.S. ambassador to the United Nations, and others were skeptical. Wheeler rechecked with CIA director Richard Helms and then came back with the *same* estimate.[20]

Nonetheless, the hue and cry about Israel's "struggle for survival" continues. It might be worthwhile to mention that Palestine was struggling for survival when the Zionists succeeded in establishing the state of Israel. More recently, the U.A.R., Jordan, and Syria have come into that category. Yet James Reston, fully one week after Israel's victory

18. The *New York Times* gave the following estimates of troop strengths: Israel, 250,000; U.A.R., 80,000; Jordan, 55,000; Syria, 70,000 (May 28, 1967, p. 1E). *Time* estimated 71,000 Israeli regulars and 230,000 mobilized reservists (June 9, 1967, p. 38).

19. *Life,* June 23, 1967, p. 32B.

20. Only then, apparently, did the Johnson Administration declare its "neutrality" in the Arab-Israeli conflict.

which he extolled at length, went on to say, "It is not easy to prove that two and a half million Israelis are a dreadful menace to sixty million Arabs!"[21]

Such a stance would seem to create justification for Israel's actions. Thus, news reporters and commentators constantly repeat that the Arabs "threaten" Israel and are intent upon its destruction. Whenever

		ISRAELI CHARACTERISTICS				
Disunited and Contentious	"Good" Qualities	High Standard of Education, Modern	Heroic, Self-Reliant, Hard-working, Efficient	Honest, Self-Confident	Democratic and Western Oriented	"Bad" Qualities
24	5	—	15	6	—	2
14	4	4	24	9	—	—
41	5	4	37	2	1	2
1	—	—	1	—	—	—
3	—	—	7	—	—	—
9	10	5	4	5	3	—
10	12	9	17	4	—	3
102	36	22	105	26	4	7

Israel strikes at its Arab neighbors, mistreats its Arab population, or annexes new territory, such actions are justified, and Israeli arguments are presented as proof of the logic and rightness of the situation. Furthermore, the Arabs were at the time of the June War frequently and almost indiscriminately associated with the Communist camp. Arab demonstrations against what was believed to be American involvement on the side of Israel were given detailed coverage. Perhaps the worst example was a vituperative anti-Nasser, anti-Egyptian, three-page attack by Thomas Thompson, *Life*'s Paris Bureau chief, entitled "Cairo Diary of U.S. Humiliation."[22]

21. *New York Times,* June 18, 1967, p. 14E.
22. *Life,* June 23, 1967, pp. 70–74; Smith, "Reflections in a Mirror," p. 7, reports how his friends and acquaintances would not believe that he was returning to Lebanon to teach after a summer visit to the U.S. Their image of the Arab was apparently shaped by articles such as Thompson's.

What of the Arab refugees? Here, the American press accepted the Israeli version of how the Arab leaders allegedly asked the Palestinians to leave their homes until the battle was over, whereas the Zionists supposedly asked them to stay.[23] No effort was ever made to check the veracity of these statements. Some mention of the plight of the Arab refugees at least was made, although the most that any commentator suggested was a token repatriation on the part of Israel

Table 5

Attributes Characterizing Israel and the Arab States*
May–June, 1967

Name of Magazine	Previous Ill-treatment of Jews	Israel's Desire for Peace and Security	Israel's Achieve-ments	Israel strong but small underdog	Arabs intent upon Israel's destruction	Justifying Israel's Actions
N.Y. Times	—	24	30	11	18	58
Life	6	10	23	4	24	28
U.S. News and World Report	1	6	4	34	26	19
The Nation	—	3	—	1	7	5
New Republic	—	—	1	1	2	3
Newsweek	4	8	2	—	5	7
Time	12	20	11	3	30	30
Total	23	71	71	54	112	150

* Figures indicate number of times an attribute is mentioned.
† Not reported

(which had ignored repeated U.N. resolutions requesting repatriation or compensation for the refugees). One writer added that all of the refugees could be resettled in "underpopulated Iran and Syria."[24]

5.

It has already been pointed out that the party which succeeds in persuading others of its own version of the conflict has won a major victory. One element which helped Israel in this regard was that most of the "news" came from Israeli or pro-Israeli sources.

Table 6 does not convey a correct picture of the situation *unless* one adds the "U.S.A. or No-Source" indicated column to the "Israel" column. This is not unjustifiable since most of the material with "No

23. *Life*, June 23, 1967, p. 4.
24. *Ibid.*

Source" indicated came from Israeli sources or sources sympathetic to Israel. *Time* and *Life* provided a listing of their correspondents covering the events in the Middle East. *Time* had one reporter in Beirut who also followed developments in Jordan and Syria, one reporter in the U.A.R., and three in Israel.[25] *Life* had sixteen men in the area, and the locations of nine of these correspondents were indicated. Of the nine, five were in Israel, two in the U.A.R., one in Jordan, and one

Arabs "mistreat" Israel	Mention of Arab Refugees	Arab's desire for Peace and Security	Arab's Achieve- ments	Israel "mistreats" Arabs	Justifying Arab's Actions	Arabs connected with Soviets	Arabs anti- West
47	19	—	—	4	4	18	—
46	11	—	—	6	3	16	—
29	1	2	—	8	†	91	28
9	5	—	—	1	—	10	—
4	3	—	—	1	†	5	1
22	13	1	—	7	†	10	9
47	14	—	—	31	8	13	14
204	66	3	—	58	15	163	52

with the American Sixth Fleet in the Mediterranean.[26] If it is assumed that these are not atypical figures (except for *The Nation* and *New Republic* which are not news magazines), then it appears that about 60 percent of the reporting originated in Israel.

The scarcity of reports from the Arab countries involved in the conflict or of accounts portraying the Arab side was attributed in some quarters to restrictions, harassment, and censorship by the Arabs.[27] But these should not have proved insurmountable odds to enterprising correspondents who are supposed to search for a different point of view or an original story. Besides, it was admitted that the Israelis also applied censorship and travel restrictions.[28] Furthermore, definite

25. *Time,* June 9, 1967, p. 27.
26. *Life,* June 23, 1967, p. 3.
27. *Newsweek,* June 19, 1967, p. 82; *Life,* June 23, 1967, p. 3.
28. *Newsweek,* June 19, 1967, p. 82.

Table 6

Item Percentage of Origin of Material on Middle East*
May–June, 1967

Name of Magazine	U.A.R.	Jordan	Syria	Lebanon
N.Y. Times	3.9	—	—	—
Life	15.4	7.7	—	—
U.S. News and World Report	2.3	2.3	—	11.6
The Nation	—	—	—	—
New Republic	—	—	—	16.6
Time	20.0	10.0	—	—
Average percentage	5.8	2.9	—	5.8

* Except for the column on the extreme right and the bottom row, all figures indicate the percentage (in number of items) of press coverage originating from or written about the particular country or area. If added horizontally, total exceeds 100 percent because some reports supposedly originated in more than one country.

attempts were made to present anti-Zionist or pro-Arab positions, but such attempts were resisted by the news media.[29] What was demonstrated was a reluctance to present the other side of the coin rather than a difficulty in obtaining information. A salutary exception was the *Christian Science Monitor* which gave fair coverage to both sides. The television networks also deserve praise for their extended coverage of the United Nations Security Council debates.

6.

It is instructive to follow the developments of the June, 1967, Arab-Israeli conflict as the American press reported them. In the process, I will point out the sins of omission and commission as well as the major themes that emerged from this and other studies of the press during this period.

Prior to the beginning of the hostilities, the press argued that Nasser had regained some lost prestige in the Arab world and that he was *not* interested in a war with Israel, especially since he realized that neither the U.A.R. alone nor the Arab states together were capable of defeating the Israelis. Furthermore, the press "laid emphasis on employing the United Nations to resolve the crisis."[30]

After the start of the war, however, Nasser was branded as the

29. AIPC, *Domestic Communications*, p. 3; Oxtoby, "War of Words," p. 34.
30. AIPC, *Domestic Communications*, p. 2.

Europe	U.S.A. *or* No Source	U.N.	Israel	Total Number of Items
—	90.2	—	3.9	26
—	77.0	7.7	46.1	13
16.3	41.8	—	16.3	43
—	100.0	—	—	5
—	50.0	16.6	16.6	6
10.0	80.0	30.0	40.0	10
7.8	66.0	4.9	18.4	103

aggressor and the cause of all trouble in the Middle East. The issue of who actually attacked whom was muddled. Whether or not there was an intentional attempt to obscure the issue may be judged by the following examples. Hugh Sidey, in his June 16 column in *Life,* first reported that a CIA monitoring operation told the U.S. government that "the U.A.R. has launched an attack on Israel" and that later checks confirmed the report. Later in the same article, he writes, "Then secret sources noted that a number of Arab airfields appeared to be inoperative and the pattern of attack began to emerge. The Israelis, *whether first to strike or not,* were moving hard and fast against the U.A.R. Air Force."[31] Another classic example of a most indirect and slanted reporting is Theodore H. White's version of how Israel decided to mount a surprise attack:

> Thus, finally, on Sunday afternoon [June 4, 1967] the Israeli cabinet faced a decision: to wait for diplomatic help, delay which might mean death; or let the army decide time, dimension and method of response to Egyptian attack. Eighteen men met that afternoon and voted yes.[32]

The United Nations suffered in prestige and consequently in effectiveness when a good deal of criticism was directed against Secretary-

---

31. *Life,* June 16, 1967, p. 24B (italics added).
32. *Ibid.,* June 23, 1967, pp. 24B, 24C.

General U Thant for withdrawing UNEF from the Egyptian-Israeli border at the request of President Nasser. However, it occurred to no reporter or commentator to suggest that—if these troops could indeed keep the peace which Israel allegedly was interested in preserving— UNEF be stationed on the Israeli side of the border. Not only was the suggestion not made, but few bothered to mention that Israel had refused since 1956 to station such troops within its borders and that it turned down U Thant's request to move them to the Israeli side after Nasser asked for the "removal of several UNEF posts along the Sinai Line."[33]

The double standard which is displayed in the attitude of some Westerners to the Arabs and the Israelis is illustrated further by the campaign, launched after Israel's victory, to discount the United Nations as an agency capable of helping to resolve the conflict.[34] At the same time, Israel's very existence was upheld by the argument that it had been created by the United Nations.[35] The *New York Times* provided another example of the double standard which was employed. It begins by arguing that "when World War II ended, a Jewish state was ready to be born." While admitting that "in the process, nearly a million Palestinian Arabs were dispossessed," the *Times* reprimands the Palestinians and the Arabs generally for "their refusal to come to terms" with Israel. Then it goes on to justify Israel's actions: "Once President Nasser proclaimed the closing of the Strait of Tiran leading into the Gulf of Aqaba war became a certainty, since the Israelis felt their survival was jeopardized."[36] The reader cannot escape the conclusion that to the *Times* editor the survival of the Palestinians was not important, whereas that of the Israelis was.

The press employed various tactics to discredit the Arabs or their point of view while helping the Israeli cause. The *New York Times* in late May, for instance, headlined "Egypt's Stand: Nasser's Dangerous Gamble" and "Israel's Stand: A Life and Death Matter."[37] *Life* had a

---

33. Charles W. Yost, "The Arab-Israeli War: How It Began," *Foreign Affairs*, XLVI (January, 1968), p. 313; Mr. Yost's article is one of the best studies written on the crisis and how it developed.

34. See in particular Nadav Safran and Stanley Hoffmann, "The Middle East Crisis: Guidelines for Policy," *The Nation*, June 26, 1967, pp. 806–8.

35. *Time*, June 23, 1967, pp. 24–25.

36. *New York Times*, June 11, 1967, p. 12E.

37. *Ibid.*, May 28, 1967, p. 1E.

picture of a wounded Arab soldier tended by an Israeli medic.[38] In a background article in the same issue it was mentioned that 90,000 Jews were in Palestine by World War I, but it was not pointed out that this constituted only 10 percent of the population. The reader is told that by 1947 the Jewish population soared to 600,000—again not mentioning that the Arabs constituted two-thirds of the total population. While mentioning that the U.N. mediator Count Folke Bernadotte was assassinated by terrorists, the fact that the terrorists happened to be Zionists was conveniently ignored.

Perhaps one of the saddest aspects of American press reporting of the latest Middle East war was the presentation of the issue as an Arab-Jewish, or Muslim-Jewish, conflict.[39] Unfortunately, examples abound. C. L. Sulzberger wrote, "France understandably wants to regain a favored place in the Arab world and the easiest way, alas, is by euchring out the English-speakers and ceasing to coddle the Jews."[40] *Time* magazine wrote that Mohammed El-Kony, U.A.R. ambassador to the U.N., "scrapped a 20-page diatribe against the Jews" and gave U Thant a note accepting a cease-fire.[41]

One wonders again if this muddling of the issue is intentional. The conflict is not between Arab and Jew but rather between Arabs, particularly those of Palestine, and the Zionist-Israelis. It is rather ironic that when Arab *secular* nationalism began to emerge late in the nineteenth century, a Jewish nationalism based on *religion* and race also began to gather momentum. The result was the state of Israel. As I. F. Stone, himself an American Jew, put it, " 'It's hard to be a Jew' was the title of Sholom Aleichem's most famous story. Now we see that it's hard to be a goy in Tel Aviv, especially an Arab goy."[42]

The last point that should be mentioned is the dehumanization of the Arab in the American press. This is accomplished by repeatedly reinforcing the stereotype, especially when presenting the "bad" qualities. Marcus Smith observes that "the Arabs are now a prejudice object in the United States."[43] Crude and cruel jokes at the expense of

---

38. *Life,* June 16, 1967, p. 38A.
39. Senator Gore also presented the issue in religious terms; see Howard, "Instant Potboilers," p. 50.
40. *New York Times,* June 18, 1967, p. 14E.
41. *Time,* June 16, 1967, pp. 16–17.
42. I. F. Stone, "Holy War," *New York Review of Books,* August 3, 1967.
43. Smith, "Reflections in a Mirror," p. 6.

the Arabs appeared in various magazines after the June War. Cartoons, especially those of Bill Mauldin, practically constitute a hate campaign against the Arabs. The various comedy shows on television, especially the "Rowan and Martin Laugh-In," carried the anti-Arab theme further. All this is happening at a time when efforts toward understanding and accommodation among the various racial, ethnic, and religious groups in and outside the United States are gaining momentum.

"The quality of the information we have on other peoples determines the images of them we have in our heads."[44] This survey of American press treatment of Arabs and Israelis shows a definite slighting of the Arabs and their cause. A more responsible press would perform its appointed role in a democracy and help bring about better understanding between Arabs and Americans.

---

44. Louis M. Lyons, in his introduction to Wilton Wynn's *Nasser of Egypt: The Search for Dignity* (Clinton, Massachusetts: The Colonial Press, 1959), p. viii.

United States Policy
toward the June Conflict

The question of what forces acted to ignite the 1967 June War remains shrouded in confusion, arguments, and rebuttals. Many observers, however, view the progression of events leading to the June War as a result not only of the strategies and diplomacy—or failure of diplomacy—of the states involved, but also as a manifestation of external pressures on these states. The Arab-Israeli conflict is thought by some to have been exacerbated by Soviet and American ambitions to maintain or extend their influence over the resources of the Middle East and over the minds of its people. Others regard the June War and its aftermath as an extension of East-West Cold War strategy, and point to the considered efforts of the Zionists to involve the United States at this level through their consistent attempts to identify the Arabs as Soviet protégés. While interpretations of the intent and effect of pressures exerted at the international level vary, it is clear that the United States in particular has economic and policy interests in the Middle East and that American international relations reflect domestic politics which are strongly influenced by an articulate and powerful Zionist bloc.

The immediate *casus belli* in 1967 appears to have been the closing of the Straits of Tiran to Israeli shipping, although even here the issue is not clear. Rabbi Elmer Berger, one of the several observers who views the conflict at the level of international politics, however, argues that the real target of the 1967 conflict was not the Gulf of Aqaba or the Straits of Tiran, nor was the real issue Israeli sovereignty; according to him, "both the British and the United States wanted Egyptian

155

forces out of Yemen."[1] It is not hard to imagine that the United States and Britain might have found the influence, stamina, and success of President Nasser in southern Arabia more than annoying. Isaac Deutscher, who sees the Palestine problem as an element of the Soviet-American competition, blamed the war on America's "imperialist" desire to get rid of Nasser, as well as on Israeli militarism. Had Nasser fallen from power, "Egypt might have become another Ghana or Indonesia."[2] In his opinion, Israel acted with the knowledge of Western sympathy toward its goal and was "absolutely sure of American and to some extent British, moral, political and economic support."[3]

To focus our attention in this essay on the United States with regard to the 1967 Arab-Israeli conflict is not to deny that there were enormous forces acting within the Middle East to impel the states involved to armed conflict. Certainly on the Arab side there was a genuine fear of Israeli expansion, and as a result of the constant provocations along a long frontier both sides bristled with hostility. The consistent Israeli attempt to expand by establishing "demilitarized zones" did not help matters. The refugees, in a wretched condition, and Israel's refusal to repatriate them despite frequent United Nations resolutions, were factors and a constant reminder to the host states. The refugee camps became hothouses for extremist tendencies and fertile grounds for demagoguery.

The Israelis have systematically pursued an expansionist policy, and Israeli leaders are fond of stating their militant belief that the Arabs "understand only the language of force." Deutscher suggests that Israel's security rests on the doctrine of "periodic warfare which every few years must reduce the Arab States to impotence."[4] A specific concern for Israel in 1966 and 1967 was, of course, its desire to topple the highly verbose left-wing Ba'th regime in Syria. Since the advent to power of this regime in February, 1966, it has pursued a bellicose

---

1. Rabbi Elmer Berger, "Problems of American Policy Makers" (Lecture given at Southern Massachusetts Technological Institute, November 15, 1967), p. 10.
2. Isaac Deutscher, "On the Arab-Israeli War," *Arab Journal,* V (Summer 1968), 36, reprinted from the *New Left Review,* July-August, 1967, pp. 30–45.
3. *Ibid.,* p. 32. On July 14, 1966, while Israeli airplanes were attacking Syrian workers seeking to divert the Hasbani River, Mr. Joseph J. Sisco, U.S. assistant secretary of state for intergovernmental affairs, was lunching at the Israeli Foreign Office.
4. *Ibid.,* p. 31.

policy in its declamations and vituperative utterances against Israel. When President Nasser prudently cautioned the Arabs about their lack of preparedness for a confrontation with Israel, Damascus retorted that Nasser was "soft" and that he was "hiding behind the United Nations troops in Sinai." Along with the provocative utterances and threats went a flurry of what Western mass media refers to as "sabotage" activity. Syria not only encouraged the Palestinian Liberation Movement, Al-Fateh, but it made its territory a base for resistance activities and helped in the training of volunteers.

A discussion of the "causes" of the 1967 conflict, however, cannot do much more at this point in history than indicate the complexity of the question. Motives that seem clear at first sight are soon beclouded with uncertainty and confusion. It does, however, seem apparent that the outbreak of hostilities in June of 1967 was part of a long-range Israeli plan. The Israeli air-attack on Syrian territory on July 14, 1966, was the first in a series of escalating "reprisals." This was followed by the seemingly senseless attack on the village of Al-Sammū', Jordan, on November 13, 1966. On April 7, 1967, the Israeli air force carried its "'reprisal'" as far as Damascus itself. Such activity was calculated to inflame tempers and force the Arabs to some sort of retaliation that Israel could use as an excuse for a full-fledged invasion.

2.

In retrospect, it is also clear that United States policies before and following the conflict are contradictory, and that the United States commitment to preserve the *status quo* in the area worked only to the advantage of Israel and in support of Israel's intention to maintain and consolidate its claims to territories occupied by force.

The United States commitment, as expressed by President Johnson on May 23, 1967, is most pertinent to the issue at hand.[5] Responding to the Arab blockade of the Straits of Tiran and to the worsening situation in the Middle East, Mr. Johnson reiterated what he called United States long-standing policy in the area. He began by stating that the world community has an interest in maintaining "peace and stabil-

---

5. For full text as well as other useful documents on U.S. policy, see Committee on Foreign Relations, United States Senate, *A Select Chronology and Background Documents Relating to the Middle East* (Washington, D.C.: Government Printing Office, 1967).

ity in the Near East." The President went on to clarify the United States position with regard to the closing of the Straits of Tiran to Israeli shipping, stating that the United States considered the blockade illegal and that "the right of free, innocent passage of the international waterway is a vital interest of the entire world community."

The Arabs, on the other hand, asserted their rights over the entire Gulf of Aqaba which at least for the past 1,300 years has been regarded as an inland Arab territorial water. They maintained that Israel's presence on the Gulf was in the first place illegal since Israel occupied Om Rashrash two weeks *after* it had concluded the armistice agreement with Egypt on February 24, 1949. Even if one were to consider the creation of the state of Israel by the United Nations as a legal act, the 1947 Partition Plan did not include any coastline on the Gulf of Aqaba for the Zionist state.[6] Furthermore, the most recent definition of innocent passage set forth at the United Nations Conference on the Law of the Sea held at Geneva in 1958 states in article 16, section 4: "Passage is innocent so long as it is not prejudicial to the peace, good order or security of the coastal state."[7] Certainly the actions of Israel and its aggressive "reprisal" raids on Jordan and Syria in 1966 and 1967 were not of an "innocent" nature. Mr. Roger Fisher, professor of international law at Harvard, asserted that Israeli raids in April of 1967 were carried out as an exercise of the "belligerent right of retaliation" and did provide a "fair basis for the U.A.R. to assert the right to exercise comparable . . . belligerent rights—namely to close the Strait of Tiran."[8] Was the U.A.R. to wait for Israel to bring in strategic cargo and other supplies with which to conduct further attacks on Arab territories? It has been the practice of all nations to blockade others in time of war or when a state of war exists. The British blockaded Napoleon and closed the Suez to enemy ships in the First and Second World Wars. The United States blockade of Cuba was commenced on the high seas, and the United States has continued to refuse passage through the Panama Canal to Mainland Chinese shipping.

6. See Anthony S. Reynar, "The Straits of Tiran and the Sovereignty of the Sea," *Middle East Journal,* XXI (Summer 1967), 404.
7. Charles B. Selak, Jr., "A Consideration of the Legal Status of the Gulf of Aqaba," *American Journal of International Law,* LII (October, 1958), 686.
8. *New York Times,* June 11, 1967.

In his statement of May 23, 1967, President Johnson made the following statement:

> I wish to say what three American Presidents have said before me—that the United States is firmly committed to the support of the political independence and territorial integrity of all nations of that area. The United States strongly opposes aggression by anyone. . . . This has been the policy of the United States led by four Presidents—President Truman, President Eisenhower, President John F. Kennedy and myself—as well as the policy of both our political parties.[9]

Mr. Arthur Goldberg, speaking for the United States at the United Nations Security Council on May 24, 1967, repeated the President's pledge and added, "'United States opposition to the use of aggression and violence of any kinds, on any side of this situation, over the years, is a matter of record." On May 29, 1967, again at the Security Council, Mr. Goldberg reiterated the United States policy of preserving the *status quo* adding, "Ours is not an attitude of partisanship."[10] (Only a week earlier, on May 22, 1967, President Nasser commented in a speech, "The peace talk is heard only when Israel is in danger. But when Arab rights and the rights of the Palestinian people are lost, no one speaks about peace, rights or anything."[11]) At the United Nations and elsewhere American policy makers kept insisting that the 1949 armistice lines between the Arabs and Israel must not be breached. The U.A.R. clearly agreed, and on May 31, 1967, submitted a proposal to the Security Council to revive the Egyptian-Israeli Mixed Armistice Commission which Israel had been boycotting. Even Syria was asking for moderation and was seeking ". . . the good offices of the Madrid Government in conveying to the United States the hope that Israel would be dissuaded from embarking on any military action."[12] On June 2, 1967, as on previous and later occasions, Nasser said, "We have no intention of attacking Israel."[13] This pledge

---

9. Committee on Foreign Relations, *A Select Chronology*, p. 138.

10. *Ibid.*, p. 147.

11. *Ibid.*, p. 134.

12. *New York Times*, May 31, 1967; also quoted in "How the War Began: Part II," *Middle East Newsletter*, October, 1967, p. 4.

13. Charles W. Yost, "The Arab-Israeli War: How It Began," *Foreign Affairs*, XLVI (January, 1968), 317.

was also given to Secretary-General U Thant, to the Soviet Union, and to the United States at its request. It is doubtful whether the United States asked for similar assurances from Israel.

The events following Israel's attack on her neighbors on June 5, 1967, gave further evidence of the extent of American commitment to Israel's designs for conquest and expansion. The blitzkrieg was quick and devastating; the battle ended in the first three-hour aerial attack on the U.A.R.'s air force. But the six days that followed saw the Israeli octopus stretch its military tentacles and gather in whatever Arab territory it could before the United Nations agreed on a cease-fire formula. The activities of Arthur Goldberg, the American ambassador to the United Nations, his delaying tactics to give Israel maximum time to finish its business, were a disgrace to the concept of "even-handedness"—a principle proclaimed by the same man only a few days before. The Syrian ambassador was so astonished that he wondered aloud whether Mr. Goldberg worked for the United States or for Israel.

On the first day of the fighting, the United States, perhaps already aware of the destruction of the Egyptian air force, declared itself "neutral." Though Israel had evidently won the battle, the United States stand was then changed from "neutral" to "non-belligerent." At the United Nations, from the moment the Security Council met to demand a cease-fire, the American delegation would not permit passage of a resolution condemning Israeli aggression. Such has been the position of the United States despite the fact that territories of three members of the United Nations are occupied by force. The United States insisted, as it still insists, that one party cannot be singled out for condemnation. Furthermore, the United States delegation would not allow the passage of a resolution calling for cease-fire and a simultaneous withdrawal of troops. From the beginning of the war a shift in the American delegation's stand was felt, a shift which became very clear in the weeks and months that followed the cease-fire of June 9, 1967.

3.

Less than a week after the cease-fire was effected, White House "sources" said that President Johnson's May 23, 1967, pledge to support the "territorial integrity of all nations" in the Middle East was "flexible" enough to permit Israel to acquire territory. The White House sources justified this by stating that Israel needed "buffer zones" to "protect" herself from her neighbors.[14] Israel's speedy defeat of all her neighbors combined apparently caused no one in the White House to wonder who really needed protection.

At about the same time, on June 13, 1967, Mr. Goldberg began speaking at the United Nations of settlement of all outstanding issues between Israel and the Arabs and of the hope of achieving a "lasting peace" in the area; but he spoke disparagingly of efforts to pass a resolution asking Israel to withdraw to the pre-June, 1967, armistice lines. Only a few days before, a return to the pre-June *status quo* had been the major goal of the United States delegation. Now the American delegation said such a return was a "prescription for renewed hostilities. . . . what the Near East needs today are new steps toward peace, not just a cease-fire . . . not just withdrawal. . . . Real peace must be our aim." Mr. Goldberg repeatedly spoke of a resolution of *all* "outstanding questions" and urged a "new foundation for peace."[15] That this statement was contradictory to President Johnson's pledge of May 23, 1967, did not seem to concern the American delegate. Mr. Johnson's pledge had been to support the territorial integrity of the states in the area without any stipulations or conditions, and it spoke simply of preserving the *status quo,* that is, retaining the 1949 armistice lines. But by mid-June Mr. Goldberg was proposing in effect the liquidation of the entire Palestine question. He was stating that unless the Arabs were to agree to Israel's demands, then Israel must retain whatever territory it had conquered. Otherwise, Mr. Goldberg's logic said, a return to the *status quo* is a "prescription for war." The American delegate was asking the Arabs to negotiate while vast areas of their land were occupied. That the acceptance of negotiations by the Arabs under the prevailing conditions would mean a settlement under duress was not important to the American delegate, not did this consideration in any way alter the stand taken by the United States. On the surface it may have seemed that no change in the U.S. position had taken place, for the United States, along with almost everyone else, had always asked for a peaceful settlement. But the change, while

---

14. *Knoxville News Sentinel,* June 13, 1968.
15. U.S. Department of State, *United States Policy in the Near East Crisis,* publication 8269 (Washington, D.C.: Government Printing Office, 1967), pp. 12–14.

seemingly a shift in emphasis rather than an about-face, was very real.

Defeated in attempts at the United Nations Security Council to achieve the passage of a resolution condemning Israel and calling on her to withdraw, the Soviet Union decided to call a meeting of the General Assembly to consider the Uniting for Peace Resolution. In the larger body containing many African and Asian nations, it was hoped there would be more sympathy for the Arabs and solidarity with their cause. Soviet Premier Aleksei Kosygin was to address the opening session. In its resolutions and plans the Soviet Union called for withdrawal, guaranteed maritime rights, an end to rights of belligerency, and a condemnation of the aggressor. The day following the announcement of the Soviet plan, June 19, 1967, President Johnson, in a State Department speech, presented America's outline for a settlement of the Middle East crisis.

The president's new policy set down five principles for a settlement.

> The first . . . is, that every nation in that area has a fundamental right to live . . . another basic requirement . . . a human requirement [is] justice for the refugees. . . . A third . . . that maritime rights must be respected. . . . Fourth, this last conflict has demonstrated the danger of the Middle Eastern arms race . . . I should like to propose that the United Nations immediately call upon all of its members to report all shipments of all military arms in the area. . . . Fifth, the crisis underlines the importance of respect for political independence and territorial integrity of all the states of the area . . . we reaffirm [this principle] again today.

The shift in emphasis from the president's May 23 statement became apparent when he refrained from calling upon Israel to withdraw pending a peace settlement. Furthermore, in a curious reference to Jerusalem, occupied by Israel, the President said, ". . . there just must be adequate recognition of the special interest of three great religions in the holy places." What this reference meant at the time was a puzzle; it became clear less than a fortnight later when Israel formally annexed the Jordanian sector of Jerusalem and promptly promised that it would adequately recognize "the special interest of three great religions in the holy places." The statement deserves further scrutiny. The United States was among twenty who abstained at the

162

General Assembly from voting to declare invalid Israel's "administrative unity" of Jerusalem. Israeli contempt for the international body was displayed by her refusal to vote, declaring the issue "outside the legal competence of the General Assembly." In an interview with *Newsweek* of July 3, 1967, Mrs. Golda Meir, former Israeli Foreign Minister, said, "If a resolution is passed not to our liking, so what?" On June 29, Avraham Harman, the Israeli ambassador, told Mr. Eugene V. Rostow that the annexation was merely an extension of "municipal services."

A closer look at the June 19 policy statement reveals a few more startling factors. Absent was any reference to a condemnation of the aggressor. Also absent was any reference to a return to the *status quo* before June, that is, to the 1949 armistice lines as had been the American stand until June 5, 1967, only fourteen days earlier! No less startling, the United States went formally on record denouncing the *status quo ante bellum* and calling for a "new" start based, as Abba Eban put it, on the "new reality of the situation." Mr. Arthur Goldberg stated on June 20 in the General Assembly that he wanted "permanent peace." "I repeat," he said, *"permanent peace."*[16] The Soviet Union also failed in the General Assembly, as in the Security Council, to pass even a simple resolution of condemnation: its entire political and diplomatic effort at the United Nations ended in failure. Subsequently, Kosygin and Johnson met at Glassboro. After two meetings, on June 23 and June 25, the two leaders emerged "arm in arm and with broad smiles." The "broad smiles," the "spirit of Glassboro," the hasty Russian "retreat" from their support of the Arabs during the fighting, and the frantic use of the "hot line" at the behest of the Soviet Union, suggested to some that there might be collusion between the two Great Powers.[17] The cry of "deal" was heard. On June 24, 1967, all technical aid to the United Arab Republic was halted.

4.

Throughout 1967 and 1968, the United States maintained the posture revealed in the president's June 19 statement. The slogan that a

---

16. U.S. Department of State, *United States Policy in the Near East Crisis*, p. 21.

17. On the use of the "hot line," see a fascinating article by Lester Velli, "The Week the Hot Line Burned," *Readers' Digest*, August, 1968, pp. 37–44; see also Deutscher, "On the Arab-Israeli War," p. 37.

restoration of the 1949 armistice lines would be a "prescription for war" was boldly advanced by the United States. The American position, which firmly supports Israeli demands and aspirations, has been completely oblivious to Arab protestations that Israel's rigid and inflexible terms cannot be swallowed.

At their Khartoum summit conference, the Arab leaders agreed to seek a peaceful settlement, a political rather than a military settlement, based on substantive help from the United Nations or some other third party. Three important Arab conditions were non-recognition, withdrawal before negotiation, and indirect negotiations. The Arab stand was prompted by the fear that recognition or negotiation before withdrawal would enable Israel to gain legal status prior to withdrawal. The Arabs pointed out that in 1949 they entered negotiations for the armistice agreement in the hope that the 1947 Partition Plan and subsequent United Nations resolutions on the refugees would form the basis for that agreement. Once Israel had gained *de facto* status as a result of negotiations and the ensuing armistice agreement, it refused the Partition Plan as a basis and stated there was a "new reality." Abba Eban in 1967 and 1968 declared that the June War had "shattered beyond repair" the 1949 armistice agreements. The Arabs could not dislodge Israel from the "new reality" after 1949, nor can they now. Israel's consolidation of her grip on the occupied territories makes the Arabs apprehensive of direct negotiation and legal recognition.

Although the United States agreed to a November 22, 1967, United Nations resolution—a resolution actually based on President Johnson's June 19, 1967, policy statement—which resulted in the appointment of Dr. Gunnar Jarring as a peace mediator, it has refrained from applying any form of pressure on Israel to cooperate seriously with the peace mediator. Israel commented on this resolution, which called for indirect negotiations, by saying, "we can live with it." The Israelis were pleased with the appointment of Jarring. On the day the resolution was passed one "source" said, "If he attempts to bring the parties together . . . that will be fine with us. But if he tries to serve as a party arbitrator, going from one capital to another . . . he'll get nowhere."[18] The Arabs have accepted the resolution as it stands from the beginning; Israel refused and still refuses to adhere publicly to its

18. *New York Times*, November 23, 1967.

provisions. Israel insists on retaining the occupied territories pending direct negotiations.

On October 7, 1967, King Hussein of Jordan, cognizant of the new situation with regard to the Palestine question, offered to end the state of belligerency with Israel. Three days later Israeli spokesmen described King Hussein's peace plan as "subterfuge."[19] About a month later the King again offered peace to Israel: "Our offer would mean that we recognize the right of all to live in peace and security."[20] The following day King Hussein reiterated his offer and added that his views and those of President Nasser on the peace offer were "very close." Israel once more refused the offer.[21] Dr. Mohammed H. al-Zayyat, official spokesman for the United Arab Republic, then stated that his government guaranteed "the right of Israel to exist." Again Israel rejected the peace offer.

One year later King Hussein was "urgently seeking" a peaceful settlement and hoping, obviously against hope, that his Western orientation would evoke United States pressure on Israel. From November, 1967, to September, 1968, the king diligently maintained his "Western orientation" and turned down generous Soviet offers of aid. The Jordanian minister of information, perhaps overly optimistic, observed on September 24, 1968, "Is it not remarkable that this monarch . . . has stuck to his friendship with the United States?" Indeed, the Arab intention to safeguard their neutrality, as in the case of Syria, the U.A.R., Iraq, and Algeria, or to maintain friendship with the United States, as in the case of Jordan and Saudi Arabia, is nothing short of miraculous. American reaction to the plight of Jordan has been watched very carefully by friends and enemies alike. In a lucid article outlining the Arab view of United States support for Israeli Zionist aims, Drew Middleton concludes by quoting a Western diplomat:

> Sometime some President of the United States will have to review the entire American policy for the area, specifically considering whether the cost to the United States of support for Israel is worth the economic and political losses in the Arab world.[22]

---

19. *Ibid.,* October 9, 1967.
20. *Ibid.,* November 6, 1967.
21. *Ibid.,* November 8, 1967.
22. *Ibid.,* July 17, 1968.

165

On September 25, 1968, a Soviet plan for peace in the Middle East was brought to light. The U.S.S.R. plan, accepted by the Arabs, called for an end to belligerency; withdrawal to pre-June, 1967, frontiers; a reinvigorated United Nations presence in the area; and a four-power guarantee of peace by the Soviet Union, the United States, France, and Britain. Maritime rights, refugees, and the status of Jerusalem were to be negotiated and agreed upon at a later stage. On the next day Abba Eban rejected the proposal.[23] Mr. Eban stated that the plan did not meet with Israel's basic demands and pointed out that the several points of the Soviet proposal had been rejected by "the majority of governments" (that is, the United States) "last year." In the meantime, Israel's stand received total American support. On September 10, 1968, President Johnson, speaking before B'nai B'rith, reiterated America's policy of support to Israel. Likewise, Israel could not but be strengthened by the effusions of support from Hubert Humphrey and Richard Nixon, candidates for the presidency of the United States. Nixon's enthusiastic support of Israel was so strong that even the *New York Times* blushed and issued an editorial questioning its wisdom.[24]

Israel's stand today is very similar to the position it took after the 1949 armistice agreements were concluded. The Arab attitude toward a peaceful settlement has changed significantly, but Israel still refuses to reach an acceptable compromise. The United States is the only country with enough influence to induce Israel to come to terms. Unfortunately, domestic politics in America have dictated the U.S. reaction to the Arab-Israeli conflict, and no American leader, whatever his stature or party affiliation, has had the political courage to suggest that a re-examination of American policies might be in order.

Israel's influence on American politics stems from a variety of factors that should be mentioned. First is the concentration of the "Jewish vote" in the five key states of New York, Pennsylvania, Ohio, Illinois, and California.[25] No candidate aspiring to the White House can ignore the electoral votes of these states. The "Jewish vote" is large enough in these states to swing the majority one way or the other. The financial contributions of firms and of wealthy pro-Israeli Ameri-

---

23. *Ibid.,* September 26 and 27, 1968.
24. *Ibid.,* September 10, 1968.
25. On the "Jewish vote," see R. R. Nolte in *The United States and the Middle East,* ed. Georgiana G. Stevens (Englewood Cliffs, N.J.: Prentice-Hall, 1964), p. 156.

can Jews to the campaigns of the political parties are equally important. Another element is the Jewish influence in, if not near-control of,
American mass media. Related to this cultural and political influence
through the mass media is the influence of Jewish intellectuals and
their presence in large numbers at many colleges and universities in
America. This influence in the theatre, the film industry, radio and
television, newspapers, publishing houses, literary and scientific journals, and in the colleges and universities, is reinforced by a built-in
sympathy on the part of the guilt-ridden Christian conscience. The
Arabs cannot match the formidable combination of voting power,
wealth, and intellectual-cultural influence of this group in the United
States.

5.

Since the war, Israel, with obvious American support, has refused to
withdraw from the occupied territories. Tiran is now "christened"
Yotvat, Sharm el-Sheikh is called Mifratz Shlome, and Om Rashrash
has been given the Biblical name Elath. The West Bank is called Judea
and Samaria, the Gulf of Aqaba has been renamed the Gulf of King
Solomon, and the Golan Heights is now the Hagolan. Israeli families
are establishing settlements in the occupied territories—an action
which the American news media regard as illustrative of the Israeli
"pioneering spirit."

In the face of this clear Israeli intention to retain all the occupied
territories, the Arabs seem to have no choice but to refuse to negotiate.
Were they to negotiate, they would automatically relinquish their rights
as belligerents and would have little to bargain with. The Arabs deny
that the present occupation lines are the only framework for negotiations. The present armistice lines were occupied and maintained
illegally by Israel, thus presenting the Arabs with another *fait accompli,* another "new reality." So far Israeli strategy has played on
Arab emotional reactions and their outraged sense of justice. Israel,
the strategist, ". . . thrives on the anger of her opponent. It makes her
appear objective and rational. It puts her opponent into the camp of
scandalized defenders of obsolete prejudices."[26]

---

26. Anatol Rapoport, *Strategy and Conscience* (New York: Harper & Row, 1964),
p. xix.

167

How long can Israel play the game? It is neither in the best interests of Israel or the United States to push the Arabs to extremism. It might be disastrous for both. The United States policy, a one-sided policy for the advancement of Zionist aspirations, must mature and change.[27] The United States must come to the realization that a settlement under duress is not peace but dictation. President Wilson once said, "A peace forced upon the loser, a victor's terms imposed upon the vanquished, would be accepted in humiliation, under duress, a bitter memory upon which terms of peace would rest . . . as upon quicksand." The Six Days have passed. Will the Seventh—the Day of Rest—come honorably? Will the United States help bring it about?

---

27. See R. R. Nolte's remarks on this point in the *New York Times,* September 24, 1967.

The American Left
and the June Conflict

The six fateful days of June, 1967, in which Israel struck a devastating blow against the military forces of the U.A.R., Syria, and Jordan, caught the world unaware. Although tension had been building up in the area, ostensibly as the result of the closure of the Straits of Tiran, U.A.R. Vice-President Mohieddin's announced plans to visit the U.S. for consultations on the crisis suggested that a diplomatic settlement of the tension was being pursued.[1] The U.S. conveyed its assurances to Israel via its commitment to the territorial integrity of all states in the Middle East, and the hot line between Moscow and Washington produced mutual promises that both powers—the U.S. and Russia—would constrain their respective allies in the area.[2]

Having decided that the moment was opportune to eliminate a potential Egyptian military threat and acquire new territory, Israel understood the American position to be one of neutrality and subsequent diplomatic inactivity, with the implication, however, that should Israel's fortunes at any time be failing, American intervention was

1. I have used the word "ostensibly" because the bulk of the reportage on the war and the events which led up to it failed to point out that on April 7, 1967, there had been a major Israeli air attack on Syria, and on May 15, 1967, twenty days before the 1967 June War, Prime Minister Eshkol stated in an Independence Day interview that Israel was ready to make a lightning military strike against Syria, powerful enough to change the heart of the government in Damascus and quick enough to prevent any other countries from rallying to Syria's support; see *Jewish Chronicle*, May 19, 1967.

2. Nasser's complaint after the war that the U.S. had been guilty of "diplomatic deception" referred to this Soviet–U.S. agreement. On May 26, 1967, at 2:30 A.M., the Soviet ambassador in Cairo woke up Nasser to warn him that the Egyptian army must not be the first to open fire; see Isaac Deutscher, "On the Arab-Israeli War," *New Left Review*, July–August, 1967, p. 34.

assured. The powerful Sixth Fleet was alerted, and no countervailing Soviet force in the Mediterranean menaced American strategic deployment.[3]

The reaction of the American public to Israel's stunning victory was one of astonishment at the proportions of the Arab rout. The American mass media closely followed the victorious Israeli giant killer who had, only a few days earlier, been a small beleaguered nation menaced by hostile and pugnacious neighbors sated with Russian military hardware. The astonishment at, and identification with, the Israeli feat which emanated from American mass media indicated that the defeat of the Arabs was not viewed solely as an Israeli victory but as a victory for Israel's supporters and benefactors in the West as well. Some sources unabashedly stated that Israel had done the meritorious job of bailing out U.S. interests in the area.[4] After all, who had threatened U.S. interests in the Middle East more than Syria and the U.A.R., aided and abetted by the Soviet bloc? With the success experienced by the West in Indonesia, Ghana, and the Dominican Republic, the elimination of the nationalist Arab governments in Damascus and Cairo would offset the reverses of the nasty little war in Southeast Asia. The American public generally, although not verbalizing it in terms of American economic or strategic interests, sensed that its side had won a victory.

One segment of the American public, revolutionary Marxists and New Left radicals, understanding the dynamics of the Arab-Israeli conflict, roundly condemned the Zionist imperialist war of June, 1967. In fact, among the American political left of the last two decades, only the revolutionary Marxists have been consistently anti-Zionist; social

---

3. The *Wall Street Journal* of June 6, 1967, assured its anxious readers: its headline read, " 'Neutral' to a Point—U.S. Hinges its Policy on Hopes that Israel Will Win, and Quickly: Washington Fears It Will Be Forced to Intervene Alone if Arabs Get Upper Hand." Washington was prepared for the first contingency. The *Washington Observer* of July 15 revealed that "The President . . . ordered alerts to the 82nd Airborne Division and to the 101st Airborne. . . . Divisional officers were summoned to secret briefings at Ft. Bragg, N.C., and assigned their missions and targets in the Arab world which included protection for American oil installations." According to a report in the *Brooklyn Jewish Press* of September 15, 1967, the U.S. ambassador to the U.N., Arthur Goldberg, disappeared at the time Syria had agreed to a cease-fire in order to buy time for Israel to gain as much Syrian territory as possible before any cease-fire went into effect.
4. House Minority Leader Gerald Ford stated that the U.S. should lend Israel a destroyer to replace the one sunk by Egypt because "Israel had done a pretty good job of bailing out U.S. interests in the area" (*Detroit News*, October 30, 1967).

democrats and socialists generally have been, with varying degrees of intensity, pro-Israeli and apologists for Zionist policy.[5] The recent exception to this pattern has been the New Left radicals, since the New Left, for good reasons, approaches the issue as a question of support for the Third World against imperialism and its tools. The impact of the June War and the changed stance of the American Left was indicated in a letter to the *National Guardian,* an independent radical newsweekly, defending an editorial stand (which had condemned Israel and supported the Arabs) against a charge of anti-Semitism. "For eighteen years," the reader said, "the *Guardian* had been keeping me in the dark about what was happening in Israel by feeding me a steady diet of cozy stories of the brave people of Israel tending their 'socialist' farms with the submachine gun strapped to their backs." It was not until the trouble in June, 1967, he continued, that he became aware of the real nature of Zionism—specifically that the Israelis had acquired their "homeland" by stealing it from the Arabs and that they carried the submachine guns to forestall Arab repossession of it.[6]

The American peace movement was badly shaken by the Israeli blitzkrieg. Hawks on Vietnam had a field day with doves who had called for American intervention on the side of Israel. The question of Israeli aggression was raised at the administrative committee meeting of the Spring Mobilization to End the War in Vietnam, in June, 1967. A revolutionary socialist organization, Youth Against War and Facism, attempted to put the question as a special priority item on the meeting's agenda. Representatives on the administrative committee of

---

5. For example, Irving Howe in his journal *Dissent,* the American edition of *Encounter,* has frequently expressed pro-Zionist sentiments. Stanley Plastrik in the March-April, 1968, issue of that journal had a "few questions" to ask about matters which have "brought growing concern to friends of Israel." They were, exclusively: "Has the Israeli leadership become expansionist? Have they become indifferent to the fate of the Arab refugees? And, are the Israeli proposals narrow and nationalistic, lacking in conciliatory content?" On the other hand, M. S. Aroni, editor of *The Minority of One,* a highly regarded left-wing monthly, revealed himself as a Zionist in radical garb. He labored in the most tortured fashion to demonstrate that the Arabs were really Nazis and anyone who did not support Israel was, *ipso facto,* a Nazi; see Aroni, "Special Issue: Rights and Wrongs in the Arab-Israeli Conflict," *The Minority of One,* IV (September, 1967). The pictures and research for this issue very likely came from the Israeli government.

6. Dan Mahoney, *National Guardian,* September 16, 1967. The *National Guardian* has until recently been in control of old-line leftists who refrained from criticizing Israel for fear of alienating Jewish radicals in the U.S. the *National Guardian's* position on the June War reflected the "radicalization" of the American Left.

SANE, Trade Unionists for Peace, and others—with an eye to the Jewish section of the American peace movement—opposed the move to have the Middle East question placed on the agenda on the grounds that it was "divisive" and "antidemocratic." It was agreed, as a compromise measure, that it be placed on the agenda for the next meeting.[7]

Immediately after the Israeli aggression in June, the Ad Hoc Committee on the Middle East was organized in New York City; among its sponsors were a number of radicals and antiwar activists including black attorney Conrad Lynn, poet A. B. Spellman, and Free University organizer Allen Krebs. The committee issued a call to the antiwar movement not to oppose only *one* case of U.S. aggression. Its advertisement in the *National Guardian,* announcing a demonstration in front of the Israeli mission to the U.N., called attention to the fact that Moshe Dayan received his training in the use of napalm from U.S. generals in Vietnam a few months before the war and that Eshkol had told *U.S. News and World Report* after his visit to Washington in April that, "When we asked for more arms we were told . . . don't spend your money. We are here. The Sixth Fleet is here."[8]

2.

Alarmed at the reaction of the American Left to the Israeli blitzkrieg against the Arabs, Zionist sympathizers and Zionists posing as radicals, arrived at the conclusion that "Israel Is Not Vietnam." In the July, 1967, issue of *Ramparts,* a popular New Left magazine which was generally sympathetic to the Arab case, Michael Walzer and Martin Peretz labored to answer the questions, "How can unilateral American military action be demanded in the Middle East and opposed in Vietnam, and why should the national liberation of the Arabs be resisted and that of the Vietnamese not be resisted?" They set out by indicating that at first they did not take the questions seriously because they "came only from the right" and from "sources close to the White House." They then assured us that, "if we were quicker to rush to Israel's defense than we might have been on behalf of another country, that was, *of course,* because of our loyalties, emotional and moral"

---

7. *Workers World,* June 24, 1967, p. 2.
8. *National Guardian,* June 11, 1967, p. 9; and *ibid.,* July 8, 1967, p. 5.

(emphasis theirs). The authors were "surprised" to find that many people on the left agreed that "the cases of Vietnam and Israel were similar." This, they promptly labeled similar to the "mad consistency" of cold warriors. They were distressed that Israel was regarded by many on the left as a "bastion of imperialism on guard against the rise of the Third World" and were "delighted" to see such views "disowned" in a statement of support for Israel by Jean-Paul Sartre and other French leftist intellectuals. The incidence of such erroneous views concerning Israel made it "imperative" for Walzer and Peretz to "outline key arguments against them," those being: (a) The Jewish (*sic*) colonization of Palestine differs from other colonizations in Africa and Asia in that the immigrants were committed to do their own work through socialist groups and not exploit the Arab population; (b) Israel is not a European colony because the majority of its Jewish population comes from North Africa and the Middle East; (c) the creation of the Jewish state (*sic*) was not sponsored by so-called imperialist powers or supported by their economic interests in the Middle East, but rather was achieved despite the fierce opposition of both; (d) Nasser is not a socialist; (e) the Arab threat to Israel's existence and the failure of the Third World and Communist countries to recognize that threat is disgusting.[9]

This tendentious reasoning did not, for the most part, occupy subsequent issues of *Ramparts*. The managing editor of *Ramparts*, Robert Scheer, who spent six weeks in the Middle East investigating the effects of the June War, wrote two thoughtful, if not cogent, articles which appeared in the magazine in November, 1967, and January, 1968.[10] These two articles could not be considered as being sympathetic to the Arabs, but they did attempt to explicate in detailed fashion some of the forces at play in the conflict.

The second article, entitled "Oil and the Arabs," presented a bird's-eye view of the conflict in terms of East-West rivalry and a critique of the Arab failure to effectuate a thoroughgoing social revolution in the U.A.R. and Syria. It condemned the progressive Arab failure to eliminate the feudal elements in Arab society and gain control of Arab

---

9. Michael Walzer and Martin Peretz, "Israel Is Not Vietnam," *Ramparts*, July, 1967, pp. 11–13.

10. "Oil and the Arabs," *Ramparts*, January, 1968, pp. 37–42; "The Story of Two Wars," *Ramparts*, November, 1967, pp. 85–98.

oil. Scheer counsels the Arabs that "Arab identification of Israel with Western imperialism confused and misdirected the Arab Revolution" because it thwarted the "essential task of challenging the West for control of Arab resources." Further, Scheer contends, it is Great Power meddling that continues the conflict, and the "issues which currently divide Arab from Jew are not as basic to their well-being as the interests they share." The denial by each side of the other's legitimate right to nationhood is "the subject of deserved ridicule." Thus, he concludes, "a solution of the Mideast crisis demands a revolt on both sides against short-sighted nationalism and against the incursions of the Great Powers into the Mideast." "It means above all," Scheer divines from his own argument, "a confrontation of Arab nationalism with the Western governments which control this area, rather than with Israel." "Israel," he concedes, "must support the Arabs in this effort." The burden for engendering such Israeli support, however, Scheer places on Arab progressives who must "come to accept Israel as a partner in the effort to free the Mideast from Western domination."

The folly of such sophistry, given the Arab experience with Zionism and the continuous struggle that has taken place between the progressive and reactionary elements in the Arab world, is clear. Scheer, desirous of being equitable, further asserts that the confrontation between Israel and the Arabs is a conflict between two nationalisms which must be equally regarded with socialist disdain. Scheer does not consider that Arab nationalism, whatever its negative aspects, is a concomitant to the struggle against imperialism, with practical criteria for nationhood, *in its own territory,* of which Palestine is approximately the heartland.

In his first article, entitled "The Story of Two Wars," Scheer opens the same line of argument with a statement made by Fidel Castro in an interview with K. S. Karol in September, 1967: "True Revolutionaries never threaten a whole country with extermination. We have spoken out clearly against Israel's policy, but we don't deny her right to exist." Omitted were Fidel's pointed remarks in the same context referring to Israel's aggression, "carried out under the protection of Yankee imperialism." Scheer says, in this connection, that Arabs who "claim to be progressives or socialists have been incapable of separating the needs of an Arab social revolution—of which the Western world is the serious opponent—from a frantic Arab nationalism preoccupied with Israel's existence." That Israel came into existence through and with

174

the cooperation of Western colonial domination; that all Israeli governments have staked Israel's existence on a Western orientation; that Israel's economy has depended on the influx of Zionist and American capital; that Israel participated with two of the most notorious imperialist powers, Britain and France, in the tripartite aggression against Egypt in 1956; that Israel opposed the Algerian struggle for independence and, in close collaboration with the Western imperial powers and feudal Arab rulers, has opposed Arab unity; and that she presently occupies and will retain Arab lands as the result of the 1967 June War make Israel a ready ally for the Arabs. The Arabs need only accept her. This type of reasoning, used by several left-liberals, must be characterized as nonsense.

Notwithstanding Scheer's interpretations, his presentation of the Arab-Israeli problem was generally honest. The *New York Times,* however, reported that the March issue of *Ramparts* was being held up by lack of finances. In this connection, the *Times* reported:

> It was learned, however, that two of the magazine's major financial backers had pulled out their financial support of the brash and slick publication over its stand on the Arab-Israel war and the black power movement in the United States.
>
> These supporters were said to have become disenchanted with what they believed to be the magazine's pro-Arab position on the Middle East and its continued support of militant black power advocates.
>
> The backers who pulled out were Prof. Martin Peretz of Harvard University, and his wife, and Richard Russell, a Hartford, Connecticut, businessman.[11]

Mr. Peretz was to proffer his psycho-political analysis of the American Left and Israel in the November, 1967, issue of *Commentary,* although he was still a member of *Ramparts* board of directors. He described the Left's condemnation of the Zionist imperialist war, "however hyperbolic and egregious its verbal and tactical excesses," as being explained or justified by the Left in reference to its minority status. This state of affairs is attributable, he assures us, to the "radical ideologues at the top," while the "rank and file" feel both "existential and rational ties to the people of Israel." Of the Student Non-Violent

---

11. *New York Times,* March 13, 1968, p. 49.

Coordinating Committee's stand on the Arab-Israeli question, Peretz says, "SNCC's hapless forays into international affairs were at once cause and effect of its failure as an indigenous radical movement." The reaction of the American Left to the Arab-Israeli war resulted, Peretz continues, out of "a certain naïveté about the purity and virtue of the revolutionary world" which has characterized much left and antiwar sentiment in America. A consequence of this naïveté was that the response of many radicals was "confused by the fraternal greetings from Ho Chi Minh to Nasser," and "a converse confusion was created by Marshal Ky's statement of support for Israel." He then advises readers of *Commentary* that

> Those of us in the radical community then, for whom Israel's rights are on the same moral plane as the rights of the Vietnamese, have drawn a kind of moral cut-off line on this issue; other radicals cannot deny or reasonably plead against it in the name of unity. For certain anti-Israel positions cast a shadow over the intellectual probity and political responsibility of men and movements which had commanded serious attention and strong loyalties as a result of their early and forthright stand against the war in Viet Nam.[12]

3.

The vanguard of black liberation in the United States, the Student Non-Violent Coordinating Committee, created a furor when it published its June-July, 1967, issue of the *SNCC Newsletter*. Starting with that issue, the *Newsletter* was to contain a news and analysis feature on what was happening around the world and how it related to the black struggle in the U.S. The note of the editor indicated that "since we know that the white American press seldom, if ever, gives the true story about world events in which America is involved," SNCC was taking this opportunity to present documented facts on the Palestine problem. "These facts," the editor went on, "not only affect the lives of our brothers in the Middle East, Africa and Asia, but also pertain to our struggle here."[13]

What followed, under the heading "The Palestine Problem: Test Your Knowledge," were thirty-two facts concerning the origin and

12. "The American Left and Israel," *Commentary*, November, 1967, pp. 27–34.
13. "Third World Round-Up," pp. 4–5.

nature of the Palestine problem. Three illustrations accompanied these facts, including two showing massacres of Arabs in Gaza in 1956 and a third depicting a hand with the Star of David and dollar sign on it pulling nooses around the necks of Nasser and Mohammed Ali (Cassius Clay). A black arm labeled "Third World" was cutting the nooses with a sword labeled "Liberation Movement."

In taking its stand against imperialism and colonialism in the Middle East, SNCC, like many other radical groups in the U.S., was influenced by the work of the late Frantz Fanon, a black psychiatrist-author who fought with the Algerian rebels against France, and also by the experiences and work of the late Malcolm X, whose visit to the Middle East had a profound influence on his development. In the uproar caused by the *SNCC Newsletter* and the subsequent attacks upon SNCC as being "anti-Semitic, anti-Israeli, and pro-Communist" there was no attempt to refute the facts which SNCC had published.[14] Ralph Featherstone, SNCC's program director, stated unequivocally that SNCC is drawn to the Arab cause because it is working toward a "third world alliance of oppressed people all over the world—Africa, Asia and Latin America—and considers that the Arabs have been oppressed continually by Israelis and by Europeans as well in such Arab countries as Algeria."[15] In the September-October, 1967, issue of the *Newsletter* an article by Junebug Jabo Jones, was accompanied by two photographs of Arabs who had been burned by Israeli napalm. Jones spelled it out clearly:

> The reactions in the mass media to SNCC's statement on the Mid-East crisis proves and bears further witness to (1) deep rooted racism in America (the nerve of blacks, of all people, to meddle into international affairs), (2) Zionist attempts to suppress the facts in the U.S. communications media, and (3) a real fear of black people learning the truth surrounding such international issues. Of the groups that have condemned us, none have offered to disprove the facts we presented. Their defense is only that it follows a "pro-Arab, Soviet" line. Red baiting is upon us again. It is unfortunate that so

14. Kathleen Teltsch, "SNCC Criticized for Israel Stand," *New York Times,* August 16, 1967.

15. Gene Roberts, "SNCC Charges Israel Atrocities," *New York Times,* August 15, 1967, pp. 1, 15.

many Jewish liberals have allowed their political perceptions to dissolve under the power of emotion. . . .

SNCC has placed itself squarely on the side of oppressed people and liberation movements of people to rid themselves of this oppression. Perhaps we have taken the liberal Jewish community or certain segments of it as far as it can go. If so, this is tragic, not for us but for the liberal Jewish community. For the world is in a revolutionary ferment; oppressed people in Africa, Southeast Asia, the Middle East, Latin America and Afro-America are rising up to overthrow the white oppressors of the West. Our message to conscious people everywhere is "Don't get caught on the wrong side of the revolution."[16]

The New Politics Convention, held in Chicago from August 31 to September 4, 1967, brought 3,500 delegates and observers—the largest New Left assemblage since the New Left became a discernible political force in America. This convention placed the Arab-Israeli question squarely in the New Left lap.[17] The black caucus in the convention, made up of 400 representatives of the Southern Christian Leadership Conference, the Congress of Racial Equality, SNCC, the Mississippi Freedom Democratic Party, and various other groups, and led by black nationalist elements in the caucus, presented the white New Leftists with a thirteen-point resolution which, in return for black participation in the convention, the whites were asked to endorse.

Ten of the thirteen points were easily acceptable: give blacks half the representation on each committee; change the slogan "peace and freedom" to "freedom and peace"; self-determination for "black people"; support of the African, Asian, and Latin American revolution; and so on. But three points met with white opposition. One demanded support of *all* resolutions from the Black Power Conference held in Newark; another called for "white civilizing committees in all white communities to civilize and humanize the savage and beastlike character that runs rampant throughout America"; the third, and most seriously opposed, was the resolution condemning the "imperialist Zionist war," with the added phrase that the condemnation did not mean anti-Semitism. This raised the hackles of Jewish liberals and

---

16. "The Mid-East and the Liberal Reaction," *SNCC Newsletter*, September-October, 1967, p. 5.
17. Sid Lens, "The New Politics Convention: Confusion and Promise," *New Politics*, VI (Winter 1967), pp. 9–10.

socialists at the convention, some of whom stomped out in disgust. Martin Peretz was furious. It was significant that when Robert Scheer, author of the two *Ramparts* articles discussed above, rose to make an amendment calling on Israel to return to prewar borders and the Arab states to recognize Israel, the convention voted to deny him the floor. The black caucus resolution passed overwhelmingly because a new radicalism was abroad that refused to compromise the struggle against imperialism in order to mollify the Jewish section of the American Left.

4.

I. F. Stone, editor of *I. F. Stone's Weekly* and a venerable figure in the American Left, reviewed the collection of articles put together by Jean-Paul Sartre, *Le Conflit Israelo-Arabe*.[18] This review, written by a highly regarded member of the American Left, was perhaps one of the most lucid and reasonable presentations of the problem. While Stone does not, in the review, set forth a panacea for the Palestine problem, in his newsletters he takes a position calling for accommodation by both sides.[19] He is disturbed by Israel's use of napalm and its treatment of Arab refugees but is generally relieved that the problems of victory for Israel are less than those of defeat, although he warns of the dangers to Israel of an all-too-easy lapse into a posture of militarism and chauvinism toward the Arabs. He argues that Israel must begin, even unilaterally, to make greater efforts at reconciliation with the Arabs. To move in that direction, the Israelis have to come to understand that the roots of Arab hostility to Israel lie in real, not in imagined, wrongs committed against them. Generally speaking, Stone favors an Arab-Israeli confederation between a Palestinian Arab and Jewish state.

The polemical onslaught against Stone brought on by his audacity in suggesting that Arabs have some legitimate grievances which Zionists have refused to recognize reached a peak in the form of three separate articles in *Midstream,* a Zionist journal sponsored by the Theodor Herzl Foundation. These led to articles in two successive issues of

---

18. I. F. Stone, "Holy War," *New York Review of Books,* August 3, 1967, pp. 6–14.

19. *I. F. Stone's Weekly,* July 3, 1967, pp. 2, 4; *ibid.,* June 19, 1967, pp. 1–2.

Commentary.[20] Martin Peretz could not constrain himself from launching a full-scale attack on Stone's sincerity, and in a *Commentary* article he offers his gratuitous statement that "apparently, however, there is wide distress at Mr. Stone's inability to weigh the divergent claims of Arab and Israeli fairly."[21]

The March-April, 1968, issue of *Spartacist,* billed as an "Organ of Revolutionary Marxism," characterized Israel not as a puppet of imperialism but as a weak ally which acts in conjunction with imperialism for its own interest. In an article entitled "Turn the Guns the Other Way," *Spartacist* takes the position that the Arabs must first liberate themselves before they liberate Palestine. Israel's imperialist alignment impedes the Arab social revolution because it facilitates the uniting of the Arab masses with their domestic class enemies, especially the Nasser-Ba'th type. It states that

> it should be clear to Marxists that the proletariat has no interest in the victory or defeat of either side in the June, 1967, war because the continuing hostilities have enabled the bourgeoisie of Israel and the Arab countries to deflect the struggle between classes during a period when domestic problems created internal crises.[22]

Thus, *Spartacist,* like *Ramparts,* takes the position that the Arab-Israeli conflict is one between two rival and equally reprehensible nationalisms which serve, in the first instance, the native bourgeoisie, and, ultimately, the interests of imperialism and that the solution to the Palestine problem lies in revolutionary class unity across national lines.

Paul Sweezy and Leo Huberman in the October, 1967, edition of *Monthly Review* set forth two left-wing responses.[23] Sweezy argues

20. Such attempts to discredit non-Zionist Jewish views on the Arab-Israeli problem constitute part of the Zionist effort to obliterate any distinction between Judaism and Zionism. Of course, Zionists were unable to label anti-Israeli sentiment by Jews as being anti-Semitic.

21. "The American Left and Israel."

22. *Sparticist,* March-April, 1968, pp. 4–7.

23. Sweezy, "Israel and Imperialism," pp. 1–8; Huberman, "Israel Is Not the Main Enemy," pp. 8–10. This insistence on presenting "two views" on the subject of the Arab-Israeli conflict was manifested in a number of left-wing publications. One leftist in Detroit handled his mixed emotions by donating money after the June War both to Israel and to Arab refugees from the war. The Detroit Chapter of the National Lawyer's Guild, a bar association of radical lawyers, was able to pass a Zionist-inspired resolution condemning Russia for supplying arms to the Arabs.

that Israel and the imperialist powers, each for its own reasons, see their interests as essentially parallel and are committed to the maintenance of a weak and divided Arab world. To concentrate the struggle on support of a nationalistic political and propaganda line against Israel is to soft-pedal the class struggle in the Arab countries. He concludes that Israel appears as the catalyst for Arab revolution because Arab revolutionaries have recognized the bankruptcy in their own governments by their inability to wage conventional warfare against Israel, thus necessitating the move to a people's war as the main form of struggle in the future. Huberman, on the other hand, adopting *Spartacist* internationalism, calls for the joining of Arab and Israeli revolutionaries to rid themselves of the exploiters in both camps.

The series of articles dealing with the Arab-Israeli conflict which appeared in 1967 in successive issues of *New Politics* merits close examination—particularly Hal Draper's discussion with Elliott Green and Bernard Rosen.[24] Draper details the four stages of the destruction of the Palestinian nation as being (1) the beginning of the Zionist movement up to World War I during which there was a trickle of European Jews to Palestine; (2) the promulgation of the Balfour Declaration to the rise of the Nazis' anti-Jewish drive; (3) the rise of the Nazis' anti-Jewish drive to 1947 during which large-scale Jewish colonization of Palestine took place; and (4) the expulsion of the Palestinian people in 1948.

In the analysis, despite his thoroughgoing historical review, Draper sees the problem primarily as a clash of chauvinisms, although he carefully points out that Zionism set out to destroy the nation inhabiting Palestine and, moreover, did so. His analysis points to the basic aim of "de-Zionization" of Israel, which would be made politically concrete in a program for a genuine binational state. A binational state would mean abandoning the "Jewish state" concept for that of the state as the home of two peoples. Draper states, moreover, that since war is determined by the politics *of which it is the continuation*

---

24. Draper, "The Origins of the Middle East Crisis," *New Politics*, VI (Winter 1967), pp. 13–22; Draper, Green, and Rosen, "The Middle East Crisis," *New Politics*, VI (Spring 1967), pp. 73–90. Apparently the fires have not yet died down. In the following issue of *New Politics* a veritable assault by three writers was launched against Draper's articles charging him with "exorcism" and a "caricature of discussion" for advancing such seditious anti-Zionist views.

(emphasis Draper's), the politics of the Israeli-Franco-British aggression in 1956 against Egypt and those of the Israeli attack against the Arabs in 1967 were the politics of imperialism.

5.

As indicated above, unequivocal support for the Arab position came primarily from groups with a revolutionary socialist program and from the independent radical Left. Included among these groups were the Trotskyite Socialists Workers Party and Young Socialist Alliance, the Workers World Party, Youth Against War and Facism, the Organization of Black Students, the Student Non-Violent Coordinating Committee, People Against Racism, the *National Guardian,* and Citizens for New Politics.

The *National Guardian,* which has the largest weekly circulation of any New Left publication in the U.S., made its stance clear in an editorial which was written on the day Israel launched its attack on the Arabs:

> Two underlying conflicts assure the continuation of sharp tensions and almost certainly, unless changes are made, war in the Middle East. U.S. dominated oil imperialism vs. Arab aspirations and struggle for national self-determination and control over their own economy and future; Israel's effort to carve out a national homeland in a territory until recently populated by a majority of Arabs, more than a million of whom still live in refugee camps on its borders.
>
> The tragic nexus between these two conflicts is the alliance of the Israeli government with imperialism against the Arabs, contributing to Israel's isolation from her neighbors and their continued enmity.[25]

The *Guardian* editorial called for the de-Zionization of Israel and its political and economic integration into the Middle East. "The Arab refugees must be rehabilitated on the land or in jobs, in Israel or elsewhere, as they desire." All of this "requires a 180-degree shift in the present pro-imperialist policies of Israel."

Irving Beinin, in the next issue of the *Guardian,* elaborated the options Israel had vis-à-vis twenty years of Arab hostility toward her:

---

25. "Viewpoint," June 10, 1967, p. 1.

Two choices were available to Israel. One was to seek an agreement with the Arabs, no matter how difficult, and to elaborate national policies toward this end. The other response, the one which prevailed, was escalation of nationalist anti-Arab sentiment, glorification of the Jewish military and reliance on might to establish Jewish hegemony.

The first course would have demanded a shift to the left in Israeli politics, and a closer relationship of Jewish national aspirations and those of the surrounding Arab nations. . . .

The second alternative—war—implies a shift to the right. It is not accidental that the Labor government in a country where the socialist parties have an electoral majority, added three rightist cabinet members in the recent crisis: Moshe Dayan of the aggressively nationalist Rafi party, Menahem Begin, former Irgun terrorist leader and now head of the ultra-right Herut Party, and the conservative, Joseph Saphir.[26]

The Ad Hoc Committee on the Middle East published a pamphlet, "The War in the Middle East, June, 1967: What Were the Forces Behind It." This analysis, quoting from the U.S. press, concerned itself with the use of Israel by the U.S. as a powerful gendarme in the Middle East to protect Western interests in the area. "The object of the June attack was the overthrow of Cairo and Damascus, the restoration of the Royalist regime in Yemen, and the protection of the pro-West Hussein." The pamphlet detailed the events leading up to the Israeli aggression stating: "The 'integrity' of Israel, of the Strait of Tiran, is no more the reason for the war than a PT boat in Tonkin [Gulf] was for the bombing of North Viet Nam or the 'interests of U.S. nationals' for the invasion of the Dominican Republic." The pamphlet went on to describe the origins, growth, and methods of Zionism and how it had become the ally of Western oil interests in the Arab world.

The connection between the Arab nationalist drive to secure the Arab oil wealth for the development of all the Arabs and the use of Arab animosity toward Zionist Israel to dampen the antifeudal struggle within the Arab world was made by a number of left-wing analyses, although the meaning to be drawn from the relationship differed. Generally, the view was that Israel had become the spearhead in the Middle East against the drive for Arab unity and popular control of oil

---

26. "The Mideast War Solves No Problems," June 17, 1967, p. 8.

resources. This position, taken by the *Workers World,* gave little credit
to those arguments of Scheer and *Spartacist* which held that Israel was
driven by Arab enmity toward her to become the instrument of
imperialism, and thus Israel only served Western interests as an unwilling partner in an Israeli-American alliance. Such views by Scheer and
Spartacist, granting little freedom of choice for the development of
Israeli policy in relationship to the global anti-imperialist struggle,
were categorically rejected. The "Workers World Party Statement on
the Mideast" spelled this out:

> There isn't one single reliable prop for imperialism among the
> Arab states—aside from the most reactionary and decadent mon-
> archies, whom the slightest revolutionary wind would blow down
> . . . thus the U.S. is reduced to backing Israel, contradictory and
> embarrassing though it may be for the oil companies, because of the
> lack of any reliable puppet.[27]

The Workers World statement outlined a five-point solution: (1)
the U.S. should get out of the Middle East; (2) the Palestinian Arabs
should be returned to their homeland on a *status quo ante* basis; (3)
the Israelis should renounce all ties to imperialism and seek an alliance
with the Arabs against it; (4) there should be no interference in the
internal affairs of the Arab and Jewish nations by an outside power;
and (5) the oil in the Mideast should belong to the peoples of the
Mideast.

One of the strongest and most consistent anti-imperialist positions in
the American Left was taken by the Trotskyite Socialist Workers Party
and its youth organization, the Young Socialist Alliance. Its organ, the
Militant, along with *Workers World* of the Workers World Party and
the independent radical weekly, the *National Guardian,* gave the
widest and most complete coverage of the June War, its background,
and aftermath, of all left-wing newspapers in the U.S. The Young
Socialist Alliance actively set up forums on the Middle East, organized
and participated in demonstrations against Israel, attended and reported on Arab-student conferences in the U.S., and generally sought
to learn the facts in the Arab-Israeli conflict. The YSA published the
booklet, *Zionism and the Arab Revolution: The Myth of Progressive*

---

27. *Workers World,* June 9, 1967, pp. 1–2.

184

Israel. Written by Peter Buch, a former active member of Hashomer Hatzair, a socialist-Zionist youth organization, it was premised on the thesis that "the current struggles in the Middle East can only be understood in the broader context of the worldwide struggle between the underdeveloped countries and the advanced imperialist powers, particularly the United States." Buch's thesis is that the progressive Israeli argument is untrue because Israel has an artificially transplanted, heavily financed, European-type capitalism that causes it to act as guardian of imperialist interests in the Middle East. The pamphlet also contains an "Israeli Socialist Appeal" by an Israeli Marxist organization, and an article entitled "Politics in Israel" by the same organization.

The Socialist Workers Party position on the conflict was set forth in an editorial after the war:

> . . . despite its victory, Israel remains but a pawn in the hands of the imperialist powers that brought it into being—most specifically, the United States. Israel's financial stability and military supplies are derived not from any independent productive resources but from the aid given by the U.S. and, to a lesser extent, Great Britain.[28]

6.

The two biggest problems that the American Left faced in dealing with the Arab-Israeli conflict were, first, Zionist harping on the idea that the Arabs intended to "annihilate" Israel and, second, the fact that no Arab country, even the so-called progressive Arab regimes, had experienced a social transformation or was committed to a social transformation on the Cuban or Chinese model.

With regard to the first difficulty, the bulk of radical writing, while it did not fall into the trap of sanctifying Israeli sovereignty against all considerations, did distinguish between the Jewish *nation*—meaning the Jewish people—and a Jewish *state*. That is, when the left-wing call for Arab recognition of the Israelis was made, it was the call for a

---

28. "Enduring Mideast Peace," *The Militant,* June 19, 1967, p. 3. The June 12, 1967, statement issued by the United Secretariat of the Fourth International and published in *The Militant* stated that "the task of the international workers movement is to form a bloc with the Arab peoples in their revolutionary struggle against the State of Israel and its imperialist masters in this difficult stage of their fight for freedom."

recognition of the existence of a Jewish *state*. Given the position of the Left regarding South Africa or Rhodesia, under certain conditions the surrendering of Israeli sovereignty—or failing this, the liberation of Palestine—could be one of the bases upon which a sound peace in the Middle East might be established. If the litmus test of justice was to be predicated only on Israel's right to exist, or any state's right, as was the implication of Zionist complaints against Arab threats, then leftists were faced with a fairly clear choice. Given certain facts about the creation of Israel and, more important, Israel's role in the anticolonial and anti-imperialist struggle of the Arabs, the question became, does Israel have a right to exist? Those who supported the idea of the return of Arab refugees, the de-Zionization of Israel, or the creation of a bi-national state—that is, majority of American leftists and radicals —did so on the basis that Jewish *statehood* was not, in the context of the historical, political, and social considerations involved, compatible with socialist ideals, or, more abstractly, the litmus test of justice. Yet, chauvinist or ultra-nationalist statements made by some Arabs, and zealously catalogued and circulated by the Zionists, would naturally strike the sensibilities of individuals with humanist inclination. But those of the American Left who supported the Arabs acknowledged that the acceptance or recognition of Israel as it is would represent an unconditional capitulation to a colonial and imperialist *fait accompli* which no progressive Arab movement could accept without condemning itself by playing a reactionary role.

In dealing with the second difficulty, leftists were faced with a problem that, superficially, at least, could not be challenged. Bourgeois nationalist military regimes, reformist in nature, had largely characterized the "progressive" forces in the area in the post-colonial period. While those regimes have made some changes, the changes were neither fundamental nor thoroughgoing. The continued prevalence of parasitic traditional and class elements had effectively and rapidly dissipated the energies of transformation into revolutionary rhetoric, as witnessed by the performance of the progressive Arab states in the June War. A lack of will to attack those institutions that continue to contribute to Arab underdevelopment, the leftists argued, was to be found in methodology and the ideological basis, or lack of it, for that methodology. The recurrent failure to galvanize the Arab masses, to create discipline and organization, and to engender a consciousness among the Arab peasantry had, they continued, been the hallmark of

186

progressive Arab regimes. Moreover, the continued failure to eliminate opportunism and the vested interests inherited from the colonial division of the Arab world, coupled with the failure to secure Arab oil wealth for Arab economic development, attested to the short distance traversed since political independence. This sentiment was expressed, with varying degrees of intensity, in numerous radical discussions. For Zionists posing as radicals it was one more argument they would use against the Arabs. For some it caused ambivalence. For radicals who supported the Arabs in the war it was a point of criticism but was not to temper their support. But the fact that so many of those who unequivocally supported the Arab struggle concerned themselves with this problem indicates its importance.

For those who condemned the imperialist Zionist war this was an issue apart from the rights and wrongs of the Arab-Israeli conflict. If the Arab-Israeli conflict is merely a confrontation between two nationalisms, two chauvinisms, as some left writers have suggested, then those writers must be charged with political simplism. Two eminent socialist scholars dealt with this problem. Maxime Rodinson wrote:

> A consistent socialist cannot place himself at an equal distance between two nationalisms and form his opinions on the basis of his feelings about the "mentality" of those involved in the conflict, about the methods used and the past sufferings on one side or the other. There are many powerful factors which *tend* to make nationalism on the Arab side adopt *global* socialist structures, on the one hand, and on the other, to take part in the struggle against the hegemony of imperialist capitalism.[29]

Isaac Deutscher made the same point:

> The nationalism of the people in semi-colonial or colonial countries, fighting for their independence, must not be put on the same moral-political level as the nationalism of advanced western capitalist countries. The former has its historic justification and progressive character which the latter does not have.[30]

---

29. "The Israeli-Arab War and the Future Socialism," *International Socialist Journal,* August, 1967, p. 513.
30. Deutscher, "On the Arab-Israeli War," p. 37.

European Jewish nationalism, and thus, Israel, clearly belongs to the latter category, while Arab nationalism belongs to the former. Thus, the question of "Who is more progressive?" in the context of the Arab-Israeli conflict is irrelevant. It must be given the same weight as the argument that the Israelis have made the deserts bloom. Such sophistical arguments are designed to confuse the fundamental issue of what interest was, and is, being served by Israel.

The American Left agreed that the war must not be taken outside of the international context and viewed as an isolated phenomenon. In the 1960s American imperialism and the forces associated with it, and supported by it, have engaged in a tremendous political, ideological, economic, and military offensive over a vast area of Asia and Africa, while the forces opposed to American imperialism, the socialist camp and Third World anti-imperialist nationalists, have suffered regression. The Soviet Union, bent on coexistence, has, for numerous reasons, shrunk from mounting any real challenge to these Western victories.

The overthrow of Nkrumah in Ghana, the bloody triumph of the reactionary Indonesian military, and the right-wing coup in Greece have all been serious setbacks for the anti-imperialist struggle and victories for reaction. The Arab-Israeli war in its global context belongs to this chain of events. Cairo and Damascus, two centers of anti-imperialist sentiment and potent forces in the Third World, have been, while not eliminated, effectively silenced. The Arab nationalist threat to Western oil interests on the Arabian Peninsula has been checked by securing the Egyptian withdrawal from Yemen, and the Arabian Gulf has, for the time being, remained untainted by the winds of revolution. The psychological victory scored by the U.S. was stunning, and Arab progressives were demoralized to learn that twenty years of political independence has not made a substantial difference in their ability to guard that independence.

Active American political involvement in the Middle East has been of recent vintage. France and Britain, the two colonial powers most concerned with the region, retained strong interests in the area, including the importance of Mideast oil to their economies. Having lost their far-flung colonies, however, their power and importance were of diminishing significance against American and Soviet dominance. As late as the Suez war of 1956, the U.S. could still adopt an "anti-colonialist" stance because she was concerned with eliminating the old colonial powers, and so long as this was the case the principle of "self-

188

determination" was a viable part of American foreign policy. But the vacuum created by the withdrawal of the colonial powers meant that native nationalist or revolutionary forces could emerge, adopting socialist or quasi-socialist structures internally and an anti-imperialist position internationally. These nationalist or revolutionary forces threatened certain U.S. interests and the maintenance of the international *status quo*.

The first active military intervention by the U.S. in the Middle East occurred in 1958 when U.S. marines landed in Lebanon and the British landed in Jordan to forestall the tide of revolution created by the overthrow of the pro-Western Iraqi monarchy. This was accompanied by the promulgation of the Eisenhower Doctrine placing nationalist Arabs on notice that the U.S. considered her strategic and economic interests in the area of such "vital importance" that she would not tolerate any disruption of her allies in the Arab world.

The U.S. has, in the Middle East as in other areas of the world, relied on the states governed by elements, however unpopular, whose interests would compel identification and alignment with the West. In the Middle East, this has been Iran—the alignment of which was secured by the CIA planned and executed overthrow of the Iranian nationalist Mossadegh—Libya, Kuwait, Saudi Arabia, Jordan, and Lebanon, and the mainstay, Israel. Efforts were continuously made by America, feeling itself menaced by nationalist anti-imperialism, to secure more tractable governments in the U.A.R. and Syria. Israel, whose creation and continued existence was guaranteed by the West, was bent on developing a European capitalist economy in the Mideast with strong ties in the Western Jewish community reinforcing that trend. Vis-à-vis the surrounding Arab countries, Israel, like the U.S., was interested in maintaining Arab disunity and weakness. Having inherited colonial divisions and borders and local vested interests opposed to unity among the Arab states, the Arab people saw Israel as one more of colonialism's devices. Since her creation Israel has proved the validity of this view as she has remained an alien outpost in the geographical center of what is otherwise a culturally, linguistically, and, in terms of its colonial past, politically homogeneous area.

The vast superiority of an organized Israeli society possessing the magic wand of technology has effectively thwarted the anti-imperialist struggle, *on the level of conventional warfare,* in the Mideast, but it has also radicalized the Arab people to the extent that the possibility of

189

fundamental changes in Arab society and an attack on the forces of Arab underdevelopment have become very real. Thus, Israel, rather than being a convenient sponge for Arab grievances against their own governments, as suggested by *Ramparts,* may well be the *catalyst* for Arab revolution.

Selected
Bibliography

Abdulla, Ahmed. *The Middle East Crisis: Causes and Consequences: A Study in Retrospect.* Karachi: Tanzeem Publications, 1967.

Abu-Lughod, Ibrahim. "The Arab-Israeli Confrontation: Some Thoughts on the Future." *Arab Journal,* V (1968), 13–23.

"Anatomy of a Crisis." *New Outlook,* X (March–April, 1967), pp. 21–25.

Angeloglou, Christopher, and Haynes, Brian. *The Holy War of Israel.* Paris: R. Laffont, 1967.

Anner, Ze'ev, and Alkone, Yoseph, eds. *The War 1967.* Tel Aviv, 1967.

Associated Press. *Lightning Out of Israel: The Six-Day War in the Middle East.* New York: The Associated Press, 1967.

Avnery, Uri. *Israel Without Zionists.* New York: Macmillan, 1968, pp. 110–12.

Ayagu, Odeyo. "Africa's Dilemma in the Arab-Israeli Conflict." *Pan African Journal,* Vol. I, No. 2 (1968).

Badeau, John. "The Arabs, 1967." *Atlantic,* December, 1967, pp. 102–10.

Bar-On, Mordechai, ed. *Israel Defense Forces: The Six-Day War.* Philadelphia: Chilton, 1968.

Bashan, Raphael. *The Victory: The Six-Day War of 1967.* Edited by O. Zmora. Chicago: Quadrangle, 1968.

Bell, J. Bowyer. *The Long War: Israel and the Arabs Since 1946.* Englewood Cliffs, N.J.: Prentice-Hall, 1969.

Belyayev, I.; Kolesnichenko, T.; and Primakov, Y. *The "Dove" Has Been Released.* Washington: Joint Publication Research Service, 1968.

Benson, Alex, ed. *The 48-Hour War: The Arab-Israeli Conflict.* New York, 1967.

Besancon, Julien. *Bazak, le guerre d'Israel.* Paris: Editions du Seuil 1967.

Blaxland, Gregory. *Egypt and Sinai: Eternal Battle Ground.* New York: Funk and Wagnalls, 1968.

Bondy, Ruth; Zmora, Ohad; and Bashan, Raphael, eds. *Mission Survival.* New York: Sabra Books, 1968.

Brown, Neville, et al. *Has Israel Really Won?* London: Fabian Society, 1967.

Bucher, Henry H. "A Symposium: The Significance of the June 1967 Israeli-Arab War." *Issues,* Winter, 1967–68, pp. 11–36.

Byford-Jones, W. *The Lightning War: The Israeli-Arab Conflict.* Indianapolis: Bobbs-Merrill, 1968.

Carta. *Israel and the Arab States: The Arab Deployment for Attack, 4 June 1967.* Jerusalem, 1967.

Cattan, Henry. *Palestine, the Arabs and Israel.* London: Longmans Green, 1969.

Chace, James, ed. *Conflict in the Middle East.* New York: H. W. Wilson Co., 1968.

Chesnoff, Richard; Klein, Edward; and Littell, Robert. *If Israel Lost The War.* New York: Coward-McCann, 1969.

Churchill, Randolph S., and Churchill, Winston S. *The Six-Day War.* Boston: Houghton Mifflin Co., 1967.

Curtis, David, and Crane, Stephen G. *Dayan.* New York: Citadel Press, 1967.

Dawn, C. Ernest. "The Egyptian Remilitarization of Sinai." *Journal of Contemporary History,* III (1968), 201–24.

Dayan, David. *Strike First!* Translated by Dov Ben-Abba. New York: Pitman, 1968.

Dayan, Yael. *Israel Journal: June 1967.* New York: McGraw-Hill, 1967.
———. *A Soldier's Diary: Sinai, 1967.* London: Weidenfeld & Nicholson, 1967.

Deutscher, Isaac. "On the Arab-Israeli War." *Arab Journal,* V (Summer, 1968), 36. Reprinted from *New Left Review,* July–August, 1967, pp. 30–45.

Dodd, Peter, and Barakat, Halim. *River Without Bridges: A Study of the Exodus of the 1967 Palestinian Arab Refugees.* Beirut: Institute for Palestine Studies, 1968.

Donovan, Robert J. *Six Days in June (June 5–10, 1967): Israel's Fight for Survival.* New York: New American Library, 1967.

Douglas-Home, Charles. *The Arabs and Israel.* London: Bodley Head, 1968.

Draper, Theodore. *Israel and World Politics: Roots of the Third Arab-Israeli War.* New York: Viking, 1968.
———. "The Origins of the Middle East Crisis." *New Politics,* VI (Winter, 1967), 13–22.

Draper, Theodore; Green, Elliott; and Rosen, Bernard. "The Middle East Crisis." *New Politics,* VI (Spring, 1967), 73–90.

Eayrs, James, and Spencer, Robert, eds. *Middle Eastern Reverberations.* Special issue of *International Journal,* XXIII (Winter, 1967–68).

192

Ered, E., et al. *Israel at War*. New York: Valentine, 1967.

Forward, Robert, et al. "The Arab-Israeli War and International Law." *Harvard International Law Journal*, IX (1968), 232–76.

Fuldheim, Dorothy. *Where Were The Arabs?* Cleveland: World Publishing Co., 1967.

Gervasi, Frank. *The Case for Israel*. New York: Viking, 1967.

Glubb, Sir John Bagot. *The Middle East Crisis: A Personal Interpretation*. London: Hodder and Stoughton, 1967.

Gruber, Ruth. *Israel on the Seventh Day*. New York: Hill and Wang, 1968.

Hadawi, Sami. *The Arab-Israeli Conflict (Cause and Effect)*. Beirut: Institute for Palestine Studies, 1967.

———. *Bitter Harvest: Palestine Between 1914–1967*. New York: New World Press, 1967.

———. *Palestine in Focus*. Beirut: Institute for Palestine Studies, 1968.

Halderman, John W., ed. *The Middle East Crisis: Test of International Law*. Special issue of *Law and Contemporary Problems*, XXXIII (Winter, 1968).

Henriques, R. D. *A Hundred Hours to Suez*. New York: Pyramid, 1967.

Higgins, Rosalyn. *United Nations Peacekeeping, 1946–1967: Documents and Commentary*. The Middle East, Vol. I. New York: Oxford, 1969.

Horton, Alan W. "The Arab-Israeli Conflict of June 1967: Part I: Some Immediate Issues." AUFS Reports Service: Northeast Africa Series, Vol. XIII, No. 2. New York: American Universities Field Staff, 1967.

Howard, Michael, and Hunter, Robert. *Israel and the Arab World: The Crisis of 1967*. Adelphi Papers, No. 41. London: Institute for Strategic Studies, October, 1967.

"The Israeli-Arab War and the Future Socialism." *International Socialist Journal*, August, 1967, p. 513.

Katz, Samuel. *Days of Fire*. New York: Doubleday, 1968.

Keesing's Research Report. *The Arab-Israeli Conflict: The 1967 Campaign*. New York: Scribner, 1968.

Kerr, Malcolm H. *The Arab Cold War, 1958–1964: A Study of Ideology in Politics*. 2d ed. London: Chatham, 1967.

———. *The Middle East Conflict*. Headline Series, No. 191. New York: Foreign Policy Association, 1968.

Khadduri, Majdia, ed. *The Arab-Israeli Impasse: Expressions of Moderate Viewpoints on the Arab-Israeli Conflict by Well-Known Western Writers*. Washington: Robert D. Luce, 1969.

Khouri, Fred J. *The Arab-Israeli Dilemma*. Syracuse, N.Y.: Syracuse University Press, 1968.

Kimche, David, and Bawley, Dan. *The Sandstorm: The Arab-Israeli War of June, 1967: Prelude and Aftermath*. New York: Stein and Day, 1968.

Kimche, Jon. *The Unromantics*. London: Weidenfeld & Nicholson, 1968.

Kishon, Ephraim, and Dosh, K. *So Sorry We Won*. New York: Bloch, 1968.

Kosut, Hal, ed. *Israel and the Arabs: The June 1967 War.* New York: Facts on File, Interim History, 1968.

Lall, Arthur. *The UN and the Middle-East Crisis, 1967.* New York: Columbia University Press, 1968.

Landau, Eli. *Jerusalem the Eternal: The Paratroopers Battle for the City of David.* New York: Bloch, 1968.

Landau, Jacob M. *The Arabs in Israel, a Political Study.* New York: Oxford University Press, 1969.

Laqueur, Walter Z. *The Road to Jerusalem: The Origins of the Arab-Israeli Conflict, 1967.* New York: Macmillan, 1968.

Lens, Sid. "The New Politics Convention: Confusion and Promise." *New Politics,* VI (Winter, 1967), 9–10.

Love, Kenneth. *Suez: The Twice-Fought War.* New York: McGraw-Hill, 1969.

MacLeish, Roderick. *The Sun Stood Still.* London: Macdonald, 1967.

Marshall, S. L. A. *Swift Sword: The Historical Record of Israel's Victory, June, 1967.* New York: American Heritage, 1967.

Mezerik, A. G. *Arab-Israeli Conflict.* New York: International Review Service, 1967.

Nissenson, Hugh. *Notes from the Frontier.* New York: Dial Press, 1968.

Nutting, Anthony. *No End of a Lesson: The Inside Story of the Suez Crisis.* New York: C. N. Potter, 1967.

O'Brien, William V. "International Law and the Outbreak of War in the Middle East." *Orbis,* II (1967), 692–723.

"Oil and Arabs." *Ramparts,* January, 1968, pp. 37–42.

Palestine War 1967. New York: New World Press, 1967.

Peretz, Martin. "The American Left and Israel." *Commentary,* November, 1967, pp. 27–34.

Reich, Bernard. *Background of the June War.* McLean, Virginia: Research Analysis Corp., 1968.

Resistance of the West Bank Arabs to Israeli Occupation. New York: New World Press, 1967.

Reynar, Anthony S. "The Straits of Tiran and the Sovereignty of the Sea." *Middle East Journal,* XXI (1967), 404.

Rodinson, Maxime. *Israel and the Arabs.* Translated by Michael Perl. London: Penguin, 1968.

Safran, Nadav. *From War to War: The Arab-Israeli Confrontation, 1948–1967.* New York: Pegasus, 1969.

Safran, Nadav, and Hoffman, Stanley. "The Middle East Crisis: Guidelines for Policy." *The Nation,* June 26, 1967, pp. 806–8.

Sharabi, Hisham B. *Palestine and Israel: The Lethal Dilemma.* New York: Pegasus, 1969.

Skousen, Willard C. *Fantastic Victory: Israel's Rendezvous with Victory.* Salt Lake City: Bookcraft, 1967.

Smith, Marcus. "Reflections in a Mirror." *The Middle East Newsletter,* February, 1968.

Stevenson, W. *Strike Zion!* New York: Bantam, 1967.

Stock, Ernest. *Israel on the Road to Sinai, 1949–1956, with a Sequel on the Six-Day War, 1967.* Ithaca, N.Y.: Cornell University Press, 1967. 1967.

Stone, I. F. *I. F. Stone's Weekly,* July 3, 1967, pp. 2–4; June 19, 1967, pp. 1–2.

————. "Holy War." *New York Review of Books,* August 3, 1967.

"The Story of Two Wars." *Ramparts,* November, 1967, pp. 85–98.

Sykes, Christopher. *Crossroads to Israel.* London: Collins, 1965.

Teveth, Shabtai. *The Tanks of Tammuz.* New York: Viking, 1969.

Thomas, Hugh. *Suez.* New York: Harper & Row, 1967.

Tuchman, B. W. "Israel's Swift Sword." *Atlantic,* September, 1967, pp. 56–62.

Vance, Vick, and Laver, Pierre. *Hussein of Jordan: My War with Israel.* New York: William Morrow, 1969.

Velie, Lester. *Countdown in the Holy Land.* New York: Funk and Wagnalls, 1969.

Walzer, Michael, and Peretz, Martin. "Israel Is Not Vietnam." *Ramparts,* July, 1967, pp. 11–13.

Werstein, Irving. *All the Furious Battles: The Saga of Israel's Army.* New York: Meredith Press, 1969.

Yasuf, K. F. *Arab-Israeli War of June 1967.* Lahore: Al-Bayan, 1967.

Yost, Charles. "The Arab-Israeli War: How It Began." *Foreign Affairs,* XLVI (1968), 304–20.

Yosut, Hal. *Israel and the Arabs: The June 1967 War.* New York: Facts on File. Interim History, 1968.

Young, Peter. *The Israel Campaign 1967.* London: Kimber, 1967.

Index

197

Index

Jerusalem, 10–48, 96; Arabic names for, 14; captured, 11, 46; Jewish population of, 17, 31, 32; as Muslim holy city, 14–15, 22, 23–24; partition of, 42–43; synagogue in, 18–21, 25–26, 31, 44–47; U.S. policy toward, 162–63; Zionist battalions in, 35, 37
Jerusalem Tract, 19
Jew, image of, 5
Jewish Agency, 93, 94, 103
Jewish Encyclopedia, 38
"Jewish vote," 166–67
Johnson, Lyndon B., 84–86, 157, 158, 159, 161, 162–63
Jones, Junebug Jabo, 177–78
Jordan, 52, 61, 90, 116, 146–47, 189
Jordan River, 60, 78; diversion of, 26, 103–7. *See also* Riparian rights; June 1967 War, 130; Arab mistakes in, 63; cost of, 57; Israeli strategy in, 45; role of U.N. secretary-general in, 129–30

Kaabah, 17
Kāmil al-Husaini, 36
Kellog-Briand Pact (1929), 100
Khartoum summit conference, 164
Kimche, Jon, 79–80 n
Koestler, Arthur, 59
Koran. *See* Qur'ān
Kosygin, Aleksei, 162–63
Kuwait, 189

Lausanne Protocol (1949), 81, 103
Lausanne, Treaty of (1924), 92
League of Nations, Covenant of, 100
Lebanon, 61, 189
Lefort, Jacques, 5–6
Libya, 189
Life, 139–52
Litani River, 60
Löfgren, Eliel, 41
Lowdermilk, Walter, 103

Macdonald, Sir Murdoch, 104
MacMahon Agreement (1951), 92
al-Madrash al Ashrafiyyah, 26
Maghāribah Gate, 29, 41
Maghāribah Mosque, 13, 22–23
Al-Mahdi, 15
Mahmud II, 27
Malcolm X, 177
Mamluk sultans, 26, 27
Al-Ma'mūn, 15
Al-Mansūr, 15
Mecca, 11, 12, 14, 15, 17, 18
Medina, 14, 15, 17
Meir, Golda, 119, 163

Mixed Armistice Commissions, 52, 81, 129, 129 n, 159
Mohieddin, Zakaria, 55, 169
Mossadegh, Mohammed, 189
Mount of Olives, 11, 43
Muhammad, 11–12, 14
Muhammad 'Ali, 29, 30
al-Muqaddasi, 17, 19
al-Mu'tasim, 15

Nasir-i-Khusrau, 17–18
Nasser, Gamal Abdul, 54–55; leadership of, 51, 75, 156; and U.S. press, 140–41, 144–45
The Nation, 139–51
National Guardian, 171, 171 n, 182–83, 184
Nehru, Jawaharlal, 126 n
New Politics, 181, 181 n
New Politics Convention, 178–79
New Republic, 139–51
Newsweek, 139–51
New York Times, 139–52, 166
Nimr, Dr. Faris, 35
Nixon, Richard M., 166
North Africa, 61, 74
Nuclear weapons, 62

Oil, 183–84, 188
Omar, Mosque of, 14
Oppenheim, L. F. L., 106, 113, 116
Organization of Black Students, 182
Ottoman Empire, 115
Ottoman sultans, 26–28

Palestine, 28, 43; British mandate in, 37–38, 44, 92–97; Jewish immigration to, 41, 93, 94–95; Jewish population of, 34, 93; partition of, 42–43. *See also* Partition Plan of 1947
Palestine Liberation Organization, 79
Palestine Mixed Armistice Commission, 52
Palestinian Arabs, 61, 102–3; and resistance to Zionism, 69, 72–73, 75, 78, 88. *See also* Refugees
Partition Plan of 1947, 78, 88, 92–93, 96–97, 102–3, 158, 164; legality of, 99–100
Pasha, Jamal, 34–35
Pearson, Lester, 127
Peretz, Martin, 7–8, 172–73, 175–76
Perez, Shimon, 80–82
Popular Liberation Front, 79
Press, U.S., 138–54; origins of reports in, 148–50; reporting of 1967 June War, 150–53

199

Index

Universal Maritime Suez Canal Company, 108, 114
U.S.S.R., 125, 126, 162, 166

Vietnam war, 84–87, 170

Wailing Place. *See* Wailing Wall
Wailing Wall: 1967 capture of, 45–46; history of, 18, 21, 22, 24, 28; Jewish worship at, 28, 29–33, 35–42. *See also* al-Ḥaram
Walzer, Michael, 7–8, 172–73
Weizmann, Chaim, 35–36
Westmoreland, General William, 86
Wheeler, General Earle, 146
Wilhelm II, 43
Workers World, 184

Workers World Party, 182, 184
World War II, 102
World Zionist Organization, 92, 93

Yarmuk River, 104
Yemen, 89, 155–56, 183, 188
Yost, Charles, 54–55, 57
Young Socialist Alliance, 182, 184
Youth Against War and Fascism, 171, 182

al-Zayyat, Dr. Mohammed H., 165
Zionism, 88, 92–97, 183; diplomatic strategy of, 64–65; origins of, 31–32; propaganda of, 38–39
Zionist Commission, 35, 37
Zionist Congress, 16th, 40

201